THE C.S. LEWIS ENCYCLOPEDIA

A Complete Guide to His
Life, Thought, and Writings

COLIN DURIEZ

CROSSWAY BOOKS • WHEATON, ILLINOIS
A DIVISION OF GOOD NEWS PUBLISHERS

The C. S. Lewis Encyclopedia

First U. S. edition published 2000 by
Crossway Books
a division of Good News Publishers
1300 Crescent Street
Wheaton, Illinois 60187

By arrangement with Send the Light, Ltd., an imprint of Paternoster Publishing, Carlisle, Cumbria, England.

First British edition published 1990 by Monarch Publications, Ltd.

Cover design: David LaPlaca

Cover photo: © 2000 Arthur Strong

Printed in the United States of America

Library of Congress Cataloging-in-Publication Data
Duriez, Colin.
[C.S. Lewis handbook]
The C.S. Lewis encyclopedia : a complete guide to his life, thought, and writings / Colin Duriez.
p. cm.
Originally published: Grand Rapids, Mich. : Baker Book House, © 1990.
Includes bibliographical references.
ISBN 1-58134-136-9 (alk. paper)
1. Lewis, C.S. (Clive Staples), 1898-1963—Encyclopedias. 2. Christian literature, English—Encyclopedias. 3. Fantasy fiction, English—Encyclopedias. 4. Authors, English—20th century—Biography—Encyclopedias. I. Title.
PR6023.E926 Z6429 2000
823'.912—dc21 99-048055
CIP

15 14 13 12 11 10 09 08 07 06 05 04 03 02 01 00
15 14 13 12 11 10 9 8 7 6 5 4 3 2 1

To

My father,

Charles Duriez

CONTENTS

PREFACE

C. S. Lewis is probably the greatest popularizer of the Christian faith in recent times, and certainly one of the most widely read believers in the history of the church. His The Chronicles of Narnia are consistently among the best-selling children's books, firmly established as classics along with *Alice in Wonderland*, *The Hobbit*, and *The Wind in the Willows*.

Yet how well is C. S. Lewis known? I suspect that many of his readers have only read one kind of his wide range of writings—his science fiction perhaps, or his children's stories, or his popular theology (especially *The Screwtape Letters* and *Mere Christianity*), or his literary criticism. Some will undoubtedly have discovered his work through seeing the film *Shadowlands*.

The C. S. Lewis Encyclopedia has been written to encourage an exploration and discovery (or rediscovery!) of the "Christian world of C. S. Lewis," a phrase used as a title of a book by Clyde S. Kilby—a book that is very much the inspiration for this guide. When I was a young student, Clyde Kilby's book introduced me to a world that has been a permanent part of my life ever since, strengthening my faith and opening both my mind and imagination.

The rich variety of C. S. Lewis's writings is part of an integrated whole. He was able to combine reasoning and imagination in a unified and bright vision of reality and of the God who made a gift of the reality we inhabit.

I see C. S. Lewis as a modern John Bunyan, even though the roots of the two men are very different. Both were concerned to capture the minds and imaginations of ordinary people and take them into a richer world of thought and experience—indeed, into a world unimaginable in its depths and splendor. Both sensed the possibilities of ordinary humanity. Both employed folk traditions of fairy tale and myth as a vehicle for theological meanings, recognizing the natural symmetry between story and theology. Both in their way defended the method of allegory and symbolism, and both had deep insight into the psychology of human experience.

An Oxford student was on his way to meet C. S. Lewis for his first tutorial. Outside he met Lewis's great friend, J. R. R. Tolkien, who was able to direct him to Lewis's rooms. He added, "C. S. Lewis—you will never get to the bottom of him!"

C. S. Lewis is an enigmatic figure. Different people seek to understand him in their own image, and this includes Christians in a variety of denominations. In the Sir Richard Attenborough version of *Shadowlands*, for instance, Lewis is a retiring bachelor don, quarantined from children and women, who is brought out into the real world by his love for the abrasive dying American, Joy Davidman Gresham. After her death by cancer he grieves in a temporary agnosticism. To his close friends in the Inklings, however, Lewis was the jovial life and soul of the party, pipe puffing, swilling his theology down with the best bitter or cider, and delighting in a good joke or pun. For an enormous number of evangelicals, Lewis has been the defender of the faith, and for very many he was the media evangelist who led them to Christ, particularly through the published BBC radio talks, *Mere Christianity.* Such has been the impact of Lewis that he is an honorary American Evangelical. In countries with large Roman Catholic communities, such as Spain or Poland, Lewis's writings are also warmly received, with a number of postgraduates pursuing dissertations on his work.

For people who met Lewis but weren't in his close circle of friends, he was reserved and distant, though he did mellow somewhat in later years. They couldn't get close to him. Many people found him formidable, some bullying in argument. A small number of his tutees responded to his intellectual challenges and became his friends, such as George Sayer, John Wain, and Harry Blamires. Many found him hard work, including the later British poet laureate Sir John Betjeman, who found it hard to forgive him, though in later years they were reconciled.

Much of this reserve, of course, was the typical product of his background, the shaping of his early-century, upper-middle-class environment in Ulster. Also, he was fundamentally shy, having a rich inner life that he guarded and shared mainly in his writings. Psychologically, much might be explained by the death of his mother in childhood, poignantly reflected in his Narnian Chronicle *The Magician's Nephew.* This inner life, of course, we can all enjoy now. Lewis also felt himself part of an older world—what he called The Old West—seeing himself as a relic, a dinosaur. His roots and orientation were premodernist. He was in fact fervently antimodernist, surrounding himself with those who shared his antipathy. As usual with Lewis, there was no sitting on the fence. His view of the modern West is either true or the biggest conspiracy theory imaginable.

The nourishment we receive from Lewis bypasses our normal criteria for judging what grouping a particular Christian belongs to. We have to step into a larger world to appreciate and to be enriched by his writing, reasoning, and imagination. As adult readers and perhaps pupils ourselves of Lewis, we have to do an equivalent of stepping through a magical wardrobe. Just as reading the Narnian Chronicle

The Voyage of the "Dawn Treader" can prepare a child for a surprised recognition of Homer's *The Odyssey* in later years, reading Lewis as an adult can be a bridge into the wonderfully articulate mind and imagination of the premodernist world, dominated first by paganism and then by Christianity. The fact that our culture is now, in Lewis's words, "post-Christian" is more pertinent, if he is correct, than the fact that it is increasingly postmodernist.

My own debt to Lewis is enormous. I cannot see myself on familiar terms with him. I should have found him formidable had I met him. I can't imagine calling him "Jack" (the name used by his friends). Yet his vision of reality has become an integral part of the way I think, feel, perceive, and imagine. Allow me a brief personal note.

My attraction to Christian faith as a child very much centered around biblical narratives. Like G. K. Chesterton, I've always "felt life first as a story." Until my teens there were very few books in my home. My younger brother and I were voracious readers. Where we lived in a depressed mining area, there was no bookshop that I remember. The only source of books was a secondhand book stand in the nearby market, at which I used up most of my meager pocket money, and the local library. My brother and I systematically worked our way through the children's section of the library, particularly relishing its fiction. When we found an author we liked, we read everything by him or her we could find.

The point of this tale is that neither of us found a Narnian Chronicle. I didn't encounter Lewis until I had moved to the English Midlands and started my last two years of high school. In a religious knowledge class we read and discussed his *Mere Christianity*. I was immediately deeply attracted by Lewis's arguments and analogies. At that same time a friend told me about some books that he felt sure I would enjoy. He proceeded to outline the plots of Lewis's science-fiction trilogy.

I was hooked. Following the pattern I had learned, I read eagerly everything I could lay my hands on by Lewis, delighting in his autobiography *Surprised by Joy,* his constantly stimulating apologetic *Miracles* (which gave my mind growing pains), and of course the Narnian Chronicles—beginning in the canonical order of *The Lion, the Witch and the Wardrobe* first. Through Lewis I very soon discovered his friends J. R. R. Tolkien and Charles Williams, reading everything of theirs I could find.

At this same period (over three or four years) I had the chance to study for some months under Francis Schaeffer, the great evangelical apologist, at the L'Abri community in Switzerland. There I found it enormously stimulating and spiritually enriching to integrate his teaching, and that of similar people, with Lewis's vision of reality. As part of that study there was the opportunity to give a paper. I chose, with fear and trembling, to argue that fantasy and the imagination can give valid knowledge, employing many of the ideas of Lewis and Tolkien. I expected to be slaughtered by the very rational Francis Schaeffer. To my great surprise he warmly and publicly endorsed the direction I had taken (even though, looking back, I see many flaws in that paper). This was an enormous encouragement to me to continue to seek to integrate the exciting biblical teaching exemplified by Schaeffer and others like him with the imaginative vision and Christian humanism of Lewis. I returned to the United Kingdom to continue my university education, and my writing and study on C. S. Lewis and his friends soon commenced. Of course I am not alone in my debt to Lewis, as I've discovered in many countries.

To allow my readers to follow through themes and subjects that capture their interest, I have used asterisks within the articles in this book to show other references. If a significant cross-reference is not included, I give it at the article's end. Where appropriate I have added further reading. There are a number of general articles, providing mind-maps to aid exploration and discovery. At the end of the book is a list of C. S. Lewis's works (most of which are described within the *Encyclopedia*). There is also a simple reference guide at the end that groups together many of the related articles. A modest book like this dares only claim the range of an encyclopedia because its subject was truly encyclopedic in Lewis's constantly fascinating interests, friendships, reading, concerns, and writings—facets of him I have tried to capture.

The A to Z character of this book helps it to avoid the trap of becoming specialist, perpetrating the common separation of the different aspects of C. S. Lewis's thinking and imagination. My hope is that this book extends Lewis's own aims in the breadth of his writings. At the same time I have tried to do justice to the subtlety and profundity of Lewis's thought by avoiding oversimplifying and by suggesting links to the deeper intellectual and literary currents of his day. Behind all the exploration that my guide hopes to encourage is the quest for an answer to the puzzle of Lewis's continuing and growing relevance to the world that is opening up to us at the beginning of a new millennium, a world with place both for wild hope and a distressing sense of the dangers that face our increasingly global society.

A passage in one of his letters encourages me to think that C. S. Lewis may not have been totally out of sympathy with my book. I hope that the enjoyment that went into its writing will mark its reading.

> To enjoy a book . . . I find I have to treat it as a sort of hobby and set about it seriously. I begin by making a map on one of the end leafs; then I put in a genealogical tree or two; then I put a running headline at the top of each page; finally I index at the end all the passages I have for some reason underlined. I often wonder—considering how people enjoy themselves developing photos or making scrapbooks—why so few people make a hobby of their reading in this way. Many an otherwise dull book which I had to read have I enjoyed in this way, with a fine-nibbed pen in my hand: one is making something all the time and a book so read acquires the charm of a toy without losing that of a book (C. S. Lewis, 1932).

It is ten years since the appearance of *The C. S. Lewis Handbook,* upon which this book is based. A multitude of books have appeared on Lewis, and many conferences on him have taken place, not only in the United States and the United Kingdom, but also in many other parts of the world. It has been my privilege to participate in some of these and related conferences in Wheaton, Illinois; Turku, Finland; Oxford; Cambridge; Belfast, Northern Ireland; Granada, Spain; and Warsaw, Poland. I was the grateful recipient of the 1994 Clyde S. Kilby Research Grant from the Marion E. Wade Center, for research on the Inklings, from which this book has benefited. Even with the excellent *C. S. Lewis: A Companion and Guide* (Walter Hooper) and also the *C. S. Lewis Reader's Encyclopedia* (edited by Jeffrey D. Schultz and John G. West), there is still need for a guidebook aimed at the general reader who has read some of Lewis's work and wishes to explore further without too much specialized knowledge being presupposed.

Parts of this book are greatly altered versions of material that has appeared as articles elsewhere or has been given as lectures. Feedback that I have received from readers of those articles, from reviews of and letters received from readers of the original book, and from those attending the lectures was a great help in preparing the new edition. One of the greatest gifts Lewis has bequeathed to a troubled world is to bring people together.

Particularly, I simply don't know where to start in thanking people near and far who have played a part in making this book by their encouragement, examples of courage, or perspectives on Lewis, the man and his work, but they include, in no order: David and Trisha Porter; Elizabeth Fraser; Dr. Andrew Walker; Marjorie Mead and her ever-helpful colleagues at the Wade Collection; Leland and Mary Ryken; George and Phyllis Dunseth, Liz Smith, Richard Koelling, and others at St. Luke's; Pip Land; Garry Friessen and his friends; Mirek Pieszka, Anna Nawrot, Renata Giedrojc, Rysiek Derdziñski, and other friendly Poles; Heidi Jaakkola; Suzie Kirby; Dr. Stan Mattson; Graham Hedges; Marta Garcia de la Puerta, Margarita "Maggie" Carretero González, and Encarnación "Encarni" Hidalgo Tenorio; Maria Kuteeva; John Marsh; Walter Hooper; the hospitable staff of Scargill House, North Yorkshire; Christopher and Paulette Catherwood; Dr. Paul Cavill; David Mills; Gavin McGrath; John and Rosalind Gillespie; Sue Gowans; Dr. Bruce Edwards; Chris Sinkinson; Tony Gray; Professor Stephen Williams; and many friends in The Tolkien Society and The Arts Centre Group. My thanks also to Walter Hooper and to Douglas Gresham for reading through the manuscript (though, of course, any errors are my own). Thanks also to Lila Bishop, my much appreciated editor at Crossway Books.

COLIN DURIEZ,
DECEMBER 1999

A

Abolition of Man, The (1943) In a letter Lewis ruefully commented that *The Abolition of Man* "is almost my favorite among my books but in general has been almost totally ignored by the public" (in *Letters to an American Lady**). Since Lewis wrote that in 1955, appreciation of the relevance of the book has increased steadily.

This powerful essay defends the objectivity of values such as goodness and beauty over against the modern view that these qualities are merely in the mind of the beholder. Lewis gave a fictional expression to his case in his science-fiction story *That Hideous Strength.** Lewis argues that "until quite modern times all teachers and even all men believed the universe to be such that certain emotional reactions on our part could be either congruous or incongruous to it—believed, in fact, that objects did not merely receive, but could *merit,* our approval or disapproval, our reverence or our contempt."

If values are objective, argued Lewis, one person may be right and another wrong. If one says that a waterfall is beautiful, and another says that it is not, only one of them is right. A similar situation exists over the goodness or badness of an action. Judging goodness or badness is not simply a matter of opinion. Lewis argued indeed that there is a universal acknowledgment of good and bad over matters such as theft, murder, rape, and adultery—a sense of what Lewis called the Tao.* "The human mind has no more power of inventing a new value than of imagining a new primary color, or, indeed, of creating a new sun and a new sky for it to move in."

The abandonment of the Tao that is characteristic of modern thought spells disaster for the human race. Specifically human values such as freedom and dignity become meaningless; the human being is merely part of nature.* Nature, including humanity, is to be conquered by the technical appliance of science. Technology, with no limits upon it, becomes totalitarian—it is now technocracy. As technocracy advances, the control of the human race falls into fewer and fewer hands. An elite plans the future generations, and the present generation is cut off from the past. Such an elite is the most demonic example conceivable of what Lewis called the "inner ring."*

Lewis sums up the urgency of the point he makes in *The Abolition of Man* elsewhere:

> At the outset the universe appears packed with will, intelligence, life and positive qualities; every tree is a nymph and every planet a god. Man himself is akin to the gods. The advance of knowledge gradually empties this rich and genial universe: first of its gods, then of its colors, smells, sounds and tastes, finally of solidity itself as solidity was originally imagined. As these items are taken from the world, they are transferred to the subjective side of the account: classified as our sensations, thoughts, images or emotions. The Subject becomes gorged, inflated, at the expense of the object. But the matter does not end there. The same method which has emptied the world now proceeds to empty ourselves. The masters of the method soon announce that we were just as mistaken (and mistaken in much the same way) when we attributed "souls," or "selves" or "minds" to human organisms, as when we attributed Dryads to the trees. . . . We, who have personified all other things, turn out to be ourselves personifications. . . . And thus we arrive at a result uncommonly like zero ("The Empty Universe" in *Present Concerns*, 1986).

The book is a contemporary defense of natural law. Lewis attempts to rehabilitate the approach to virtue of the premodernist Old West,* the common presupposition of the Greco-Roman and Judeo-Christian traditions. Lewis also tries to demonstrate that an objective morality is essential to our humanity. His view of humanity "with chests" is graphically portrayed in the Mappa Mundi* included in *The Pilgrim's Regress.**

Adonis In Greek mythology, a beautiful youth loved by the love goddess Aphrodite, mother of Cupid* or Eros. He was killed while boar-hunting but was allowed to return from the underworld for six months every year to rejoin her. The anemone sprang from his blood. Adonis was worshiped as a god of vegetation and was known as Tammuz in Babylonia, Assyria, and Phoenicia. He seems also to have been identified with Osiris, the Egyptian god of the underworld.

Lewis's interest in Adonis was, apart from his respect for pre-Christian paganism,* that this myth embodied the idea of death and rebirth explored in *Miracles*.* See also: MYTH BECAME FACT.

***Aeneid, The,* Virgil** This classical epic poem was considered by Lewis one of the books that most influenced his vocational attitude and philosophy of life (see: READING OF C. S. LEWIS). Written between 29-19 B.C., the poem embodies Roman imperial values in its Trojan hero Aeneas. He is destined to found a new city in Italy. After the fall of Troy, the home-seeking Aeneas roams the Mediterranean with his companions. Landing in North Africa, he falls in love with Dido, Queen of Carthage. He later abandons her and establishes the Trojans in Latium, where the king offers him his daughter Lavinia in marriage. Turnus, a rival suitor, opposes him until slain in single-handed combat. The poem builds upon a rich tradition, including Homer's *Odyssey* and *Iliad*.

Aesthetica A southern region of the world in *The Pilgrim's Regress,** charted on the Mappa Mundi.* In it lies the city of Thrill.

Affection See: *THE FOUR LOVES.*

"After Ten Years" An unfinished fiction published in *The Dark Tower and Other Stories.** Lewis abandoned it after the death of Joy Davidman Lewis.* It concerns Menelaus (called "Yellowhead" in the story) and his wife, Helen of Troy, after the Trojan War. The intended novel appears to reflect themes of love deepened by Lewis's friendship with Charles Williams, particularly the impact of Williams's *Descent into Hell* (1937). The story would have carried on the exploration of paganism most realized in Lewis's *Till We Have Faces.** Menelaus, it appears, would have had to choose between true love or an idealized image of Helen, as Scudamour has to choose between two Camillas in the flawed but powerful fragment "The Dark Tower."

Agape See: *THE FOUR LOVES.*

Ahoshta In the Narnian* Chronicle *The Horse and His Boy,** he was an elderly Tarkaan and Grand Vizier. He was due to marry Aravis* in an arranged marriage.

Alambil In The Chronicles of Narnia,* one of the Narnian stars, whose name means "Lady of Peace." When in conjunction with the star Tarva, it spells good fortune for Narnia. See also: NARNIA—GEOGRAPHY.

Alcasan, Francois In *That Hideous Strength,** a distinguished radiologist, an Arab by descent, who cut short an otherwise brilliant career in France by poisoning his wife. His severed head was rescued by the N.I.C.E.* after his execution on the guillotine and kept alive perched on a metal bracket in a laboratory at Belbury.* He is (in Lewis's grim joke) the Head of the Institute, embodying its belief that the human body is now an unclean irrelevance in mankind's evolutionary development, and revealing that physical immortality is a possibility. It is, in fact, uncertain that Alcasan himself has survived, because the macrobes, the bent eldila,* speak though his head, needing human agents for their devilish activities. He parallels the dehumanization of the Un-man* of Perelandra, illustrating Lewis's belief in the gradual abolition of humanity in modern scientific society. See also: *THE ABOLITION OF MAN.*

Alcasan's bearded head wore colored glasses, making it impossible to see his tormented eyes. His skin was rather yellow, and he had a hooked nose. The top part of the skull had been removed, allowing the brain to swell out and expand. From his collar protruded tubes and bulbs necessary to keep the head alive. The mouth had to be artificially moistened, and air was pumped through in puffs to allow its labored speech.

Mark Studdock* is introduced to the Head as sign of his deeper initiation into the N.I.C.E. Dr. Dimble* speculates that the Head's consciousness is one of agony and hatred.

Aldwinckle, Estelle "Stella" (1907-1990) While reading theology at Oxford, South-African-born Stella Aldwinckle came under the influence of Lewis's friend Austin Farrer.* In 1941 she became a member of the Oxford Pastorate, devoted to serving Oxford undergraduates. Later that year she founded the Oxford University Socratic Club,* choosing Lewis as its first president.

Alexander, Samuel (1859-1938) A realist philosopher born in Australia, he was Professor of Philosophy at Manchester University, England, 1893-1924. He sought to develop a comprehensive system of ontological metaphysics, leading to a theory of emergent evolution. He proposed that the space-time matrix gestated matter; matter nurtured life; life evolved mind; and finally God emerged from mind. His books include his Gifford Lectures published as *Space, Time and Deity* in 1920. He later worked on aesthetic theory and wrote *Beauty and Other Forms of Value* (1933).

Alexander's distinction between enjoyment and contemplation was pivotal to Lewis's thinking, especially about the dialectic of desire, or joy.* This distinction was, relatedly, basic to Lewis's idea of transposition.* In *Surprised by Joy* he confessed: "All my waiting and watching for Joy, all my vain hopes to find some mental content on which I could, so to speak, lay my finger and say, 'This is it,' had been a futile attempt to contemplate the enjoyed." There are parallels between this distinction and Michael Polanyi's notion of tacit indwelling, where one focuses away from particulars towards a higher whole (see Polanyi, *Personal Knowledge*, 1958). See: IDEALISM, C. S. LEWIS AND.

Alimash In the Narnian* Chronicle *The Horse and His Boy*,* a captain of the chariots in Calormen and the cousin of Aravis.*

All My Road Before Me: The Diary of C. S. Lewis 1922-1927 (1991) Edited and abridged by Walter Hooper, these handwritten diaries record some of the days in Lewis's life between 1922 and 1929. The title is a quotation from *Dymer*,* a poem that Lewis was writing at this time. The choice of events and contents has in mind Mrs. Janie Moore,* with whom Lewis shared a home and to whom he read most of the entries as they were written. Therefore, as Owen Barfield* discovered upon reading them, there is sadly no record of the "Great War"* of ideas between himself and Lewis. The diaries vividly render the daily domestic life that Lewis shared, as well as walks, weather, books, writing, and uncertainties over employment.

Allegory An extended metaphor, or sustained personification. In literature, a figurative narrative or description that conveys a hidden meaning, often moral. Key examples in English Literature are John Bunyan's *The Pilgrim's Progress* and Edmund Spenser's *Faerie Queene*. Tolkien's short story *Leaf by Niggle** is an allegory, as is Lewis's *The Pilgrim's Regress.** The biblical parables have allegorical elements—allegory is a type of instruction. Lewis gives his own definition in a letter written December 29, 1958: "a composition . . . in which immaterial realities are represented by feigned physical objects."

When Tolkien's *The Lord of the Rings** first appeared, some interpreted the One Ring* as meaning the atomic bomb. In his foreword to a new edition, he corrected this impression: "I much prefer history, true or feigned, with its varied applicability to the thought and experience of readers. I think that many confuse 'applicability' with 'allegory'; but the one resides in the freedom of the reader, and the other in the purposed domination of the author." Contrasting myth* and allegory, Lewis similarly wrote: "A myth is a story out of which ever varying meanings will grow," whereas allegory suggests one meaning (letter, September 22, 1956).

Lewis discusses allegorical interpretations of the Psalms in his *Reflections on the Psalms** (chapter 12). Allegorical interpretation of the Bible was common in the Middle Ages when allegory was popular.

Lewis's fondness for allegory was part of his eclecticism. He was at home in the vast range of the premodern imagination, from the ancient Greeks through the entire medieval and Renaissance periods. See also: FANTASY; ASLAN; *THE ALLEGORY OF LOVE.*

Allegory of Love, The (1936) Subtitled *A Study in Mediaeval Tradition*, this book is among the outstanding works of literary criticism of the century. "To mediaeval studies in this country Lewis's logical and philosophical cast of mind gave a wholly new dimension," commented Professor J. A. W. Bennett. This interest in ideas is shown in his concern with the philosophical and semantic development of the terms *Phusis, Natura*, and *Kind*. Lewis traced these concepts from the beginnings of allegory* through Chaucer and Spenser, turning to them again near the end of his life in his book *Studies in Words.**

Lewis began work on *The Allegory of Love* in 1928, and so it spanned the period of his conversion to theism and then to Christianity. He also wrote *The Pilgrim's Regress,** influenced both by his discoveries about the allegorical tradition and his conversion. Material he gathered while writing the study eventually led to his Oxford Prolegomena Lectures, and ultimately to a key book on the history of ideas, *The Discarded Image.** In a letter written in 1934, as *The Allegory of Love* neared completion, he suggested that the secret to understanding the Middle Ages, including its concern with allegory and courtly love, was to get to know thoroughly Dante's *The Divine Comedy*, *The Romance of the Rose*, the classics, and the Bible (including the apocrypha). The Middle Ages provide the key and the background to both Lewis's thought and fiction.

While in search of a publisher he summarized the book to Oxford University Press, who accepted it for publication: "The book as a whole has two themes: (1) The birth of allegory and its growth from what it is in Prudentius to what it is in Spenser. (2) The birth of the romantic conception of love and the long struggle between its earlier form (the romance of adultery) and its later form (the romance of marriage)."

Something of the intellectual excitement of the book can be conveyed by a small selection of statements from it: "We shall understand our present, and perhaps even our future, the better if we can succeed, by an effort of the historical imagination, in reconstructing that long-lost state of mind for which the allegorical love poem was a natural mode of expression" (p. 1). "'Love,' in our sense of the word, is as absent from the literature of the Dark Ages as from that of classical antiquity" (p. 9). "Allegory, besides being many other things, is the subjectivism of an objective age" (p. 30). "We have to inquire how something always latent in human speech [allegory] becomes, in addition, explicit in the structure of whole poems; and how poems of that kind come to enjoy an unusual popularity in the Middle Ages" (p. 44). "The allegorist leaves the given—his own passions—to talk of that which is confessedly less real, which is a fiction. The symbolist leaves the given to find that which is more real" (p. 45). "Symbolism is a mode of thought, but allegory is a mode of expression" (p. 48). "Men's gaze was turned inward. . . . The development of allegory [was] to supply the subjective element in literature, to paint the inner world" (p. 113).

The Allegory of Love demonstrates Lewis's characteristic interest in the Christianization of paganism* (in this case, romantic love), an interest deeply shared by Tolkien. Harry Blamires points out that Lewis "revived the genre of historical criticism by his work on medieval and Renaissance literature in *The Allegory of Love* (1936) and *English Literature in the Sixteenth Century* (1954)." His revival of this genre is perhaps even more significant than these works themselves. Notably, while Lewis's conclusions in the books are by no means always accepted, the books as historical scholarship are universally admired.

Andrew, Uncle Andrew Ketterley, the Edwardian uncle of Digory Kirke* in the Narnian* Chronicle *The Magician's Nephew*.* He is the uncle to which the title refers, an amateur magician, who forces Digory and his friend Polly Plummer* into the Wood Between the Worlds by means of magic rings. He is tall, very thin, with a long, clean-shaven face and a sharply pointed nose, extremely bright eyes, and a great tousled mop of gray hair.

Angels As an orthodox Christian, Lewis believed in the literal existence of angels. He considered them real beings in the actual universe (letter, December 29, 1958). They appear historically, for example, in the Gospels at the annunciation of Christ. In parts of *The Discarded Image** Lewis summarizes medieval beliefs about angels.

For Lewis angels are beings who are supernatural in relation to the nature we perceive through our five senses (*Miracles,** Appendix A). For imaginative force and freshness, Lewis avoids the term *angel.* In his *The Space Trilogy* (for which he acknowledged that the book of Ezekiel was an important source for angels), he employs the terms *Oyarsa* and *eldila.*

It is interesting that Lewis does not have an intermediary role for angelic beings. God directly and personally communicates (as in Aslan, the creator-lion of Narnia) as well as using messengers and angelic interpreters. His most important imaginative use of angels is in his science-fiction trilogy, where he draws upon a medieval imaginative picture of reality, admirably documented elsewhere in his *The Discarded Image.**

Lewis's most well-known depiction of angels is in *The Screwtape Letters,** which concerns the machinations of fallen angels, or demons, in trying to ensure the damnation of a young man, who is entrusted to the bungling demon Wormwood.*

Famous forerunners of Lewis on angels include John Milton (*Paradise Lost*), William Blake (many works), and Dante (*The Divine Comedy*). They also include the unjustly neglected John Macgowan and his *Dialogues of the Devil.* Angels accompany Mr. Weston (representing God) in T. F. Powys's *Mr. Weston's Good Wine* (1927). Angels appear prominently, though disguised, in the events of the three Ages of Middle-earth depicted in Tolkien's *The Silmarillion*, *The Hobbit,* and *The Lord of the Rings.*

Annie, Aunt Anne Sargent Hamilton (1866-1930) was married to Gussie, the brother of Lewis's mother, Flora Lewis.* Both Jack and his brother, Warren Lewis,* were very fond of her, especially after the loss of their own mother.

Anradin In *The Horse and His Boy,** a Tarkaan of Calormen, and master of Bree,* the stolen talking horse of Narnia.* He treated Bree badly and tried to buy Shasta.*

Anscombe, G. E. M. (1919-) Between 1970 and 1986 Elizabeth Anscombe was Professor of Philosophy at Cambridge University. A Roman Catholic, she was a member of the Oxford Socratic Club.* She is a translator and editor of works of the eminent philosopher Ludwig Wittgenstein (1889-1951), under whom she studied while a research student at Cambridge. After the war she took on a research fellowship at Somerville College, Oxford, and was a fellow there from 1964 to 1970.

Elizabeth Anscombe's debate with Lewis at the Socratic Club, where she challenged one of his central arguments propounded in his book *Miracles,** has entered the Lewis mythology (a number of elements of which have been perpetrated by Lewis's biographer A. N. Wilson). According to this mythology, which has a surprisingly wide acceptance, Lewis was so discouraged by the encounter that he abandoned theoretical Christian apologetics and turned to the writing of fantasy for children—that is, The Chronicles of Narnia.* This is simply not true. The writing of the Chronicles is part of a development in Lewis's popular imaginative apologetics that began with *Out of the Silent Planet.**

Elizabeth Anscombe's critique was powerful and was intended to be constructive. She felt that Lewis responded to it in an honest and serious way, evidenced by the fact that he substantially revised the third chapter of *Miracles* (appearing in the new paperback edition of 1960). The issues debated concern some of the deepest issues of human thinking.

The philosopher Basil Mitchell recalls that in the 1960s, the Anscombe-Lewis debate was rerun, with Elizabeth Anscombe again participating and the philosopher John Lucas presenting Lewis's case. In Basil Mitchell's view, John Lucas was able to sustain Lewis's side of the argument. Lewis's thesis, he concluded, was a robust philosophical one (interview with Basil Mitchell, in *A Christian for All Christians*, Hodder, 1990). See also: NATURALISM AND SUPERNATURALISM.

FURTHER READING

Elizabeth Anscombe, *An introduction to Wittgenstein's* Tractatus (1959); *Collected Philosophical Papers: Ethics, Religion and Politics* (1981); *Collected Philosophical Papers: Metaphysics and the Philosophy of Mind* (1981)—containing her original paper challenging Lewis.

Cora Diamond and Jenny Teichman, eds., *Intention and Intentionality: Essays in Honour of G. E. M. Anscombe.*

Ansit, Lady In *Till We Have Faces,** Bardia,* the captain of the king's guard in Glome,* marries her for love, and she bears him many children. After Bardia's death, Ansit tells Queen Orual,* who was also in love with Bardia, how much her possessiveness stole him from his wife and family.

Anthroposophia A region of the world in *The Pilgrim's Regress,** situated to the south of the main road, referring to the ideas of anthroposophy.* See: MAPPA MUNDI.

Anthroposophy A modern "spiritual science" founded by Rudolf Steiner (1861-1925) and followed and promoted by Owen Barfield.*

It contains Eastern and Western philosophical elements. Both Steiner and Barfield considered this gnostic movement compatible with Christianity, even though it is far from orthodox. Anthroposophists recognize that the being they call Christ is to be acknowledged as the center of life on earth. His claim was no less than that "the Christian religion is the ultimate religion for the earth's whole future."

Rudolf Steiner advocated a new perception of Christianity that is really also a new perception of reality itself. He drew an analogy with Copernicus, whose ideas altered the very way we look at nature, rather than reshaped its order: "Nature stayed as it was, but people learned to think about nature in a way that accorded with the new view of the world." Like natural science, Steiner argued, Christianity is rooted in reality; it is "mystical fact." Barfield believed that this central point of Steiner's anticipated the discovery Lewis made at his conversion to Christianity, where Tolkien persuaded him that the gospel narratives have all the qualities of a good story and yet also actually happened in history; in Lewis's terms, "myth became fact."* Although there does at first sight seem to be a strong parallel here between Steiner and Lewis, the similarity is based only on the ambiguity of the word *fact*, a notoriously difficult term. For both Lewis and Tolkien, the factual nature of the gospel narratives was understood in terms of normal historical documents, whereas Steiner allowed himself to be free and easy in his interpretation of the four Gospels according to the esoteric "spiritual" and "scientific" discipline of anthroposophical meditation.

Barfield drew inspiration from anthroposophism and Rudolf Steiner for his many writings. His adherence to this view formed the basis for the "great war"* between Lewis and himself. Barfield's influence on Lewis and Tolkien was mainly through his early work, *Poetic Diction*,* and concerned the nature of poetic language and a theory of an ancient semantic unity, which require no commitment to anthroposophical interpretations of Christianity. Even though Barfield influenced Lewis through this "great war" of ideas in the 1920s, the debate helped prepare Lewis for accepting orthodox Christianity rather than any anthroposophist ideas. Significant differences remained between the close friends until the end of Lewis's life despite Lewis's great intellectual debt to his friend.

FURTHER READING

Rudolf Steiner, *Anthroposophy and Christianity* (English translation, 1985).

Anvard The capital of Archenland,* the seat of King Lune* in *The Horse and His Boy.** Anvard is a small, many-towered castle at the foot of the northern mountains. The city is protected from the north wind by a wooded ridge. The ancient castle is built of a warm reddish brown stone. Pleasant green lawns extend to the front of the entrance gate. See also: NARNIA, GEOGRAPHY.

Anya (1940) A novel by Joy Davidman, who later married C. S. Lewis (see: LEWIS, HELEN JOY DAVIDMAN). The book was completed in 1938 and published in 1940, by which time Joy, then an atheist, was a convinced Marxist and member of the Communist Party. She was twenty-five.

The first novel received good reviews. It narrates the life of a Ukrainian Jewish woman from her youth to middle age. The events and characters are based upon real people and incidents that were part of the living memory of Joy's mother. However, the themes and concerns of the novel sprang from Joy's developing view of the world. Like Joy, Anya is a free spirit. She is determined not to be overpowered by the dominant forces of a society in radical change. The original dust jacket proclaimed: "Like its heroine, this novel is glowing, sensuous, alive. It is written in a vein suggesting D. H. Lawrence, with poetic artistry and with all five senses awake to the warmth, color, and feel of things."

Aphallin Also called Abhalljin. A distant island beyond the seas of Lur in *Perelandra,** the Third Heaven. It is a cup-shaped land that contains the House of Kings, in which sits King Arthur, taken there by God to be in the body until the end of time, along with the Old Testament characters Enoch, Elijah, Moses, and Melchizedek—the mystical king.

Aravir In *Prince Caspian,** the morning star of Narnia.* See also: NARNIA, GEOGRAPHY.

Aravis Only daughter of Kidrash Tarkaan, lord of the Calormene* province of Calavar, and descended from the god Tash.* She is the heroine of Lewis's Narnian Chronicle *The Horse and His Boy.** Aravis runs away from home when her mother arranges a marriage to Ahoshta, who is sixty years old, with a face like an ape. She meets up with and eventually marries Cor,* and becomes queen of Archenland.*

Archenland Found in Lewis's Narnian Chronicles. To Narnia's* south, and connected by a high mountain pass, Archenland was ruled by King Lune* from Anvard* during the time of the co-regency of Peter and Edmund, Susan and Lucy Pevensie.* Leading to the high mountains were pine-covered slopes and narrow valleys. The highest peaks were Stormness Head and Mount Pire. In Archenlandian mythology the twin-peaked Mount Pire was once a two-headed giant turned to stone. Archenland's southern boundary is marked by Winding Arrow River. Beyond this lies a vast desert that separates Archenland and the troublesome Calormen.* Travelers en route to Archenland from Calormen could use the conspicuous double peak of Mount Pire as a landmark. Archenland's wine was highly regarded, and it was so potent that water had to be mixed with it before drinking. See also: NARNIA, GEOGRAPHY; NARNIA, HISTORY; *THE HORSE AND HIS BOY.*

Archon See: ELDIL.

Argan Prince of Phars* in *Till We Have Faces,** and troublesome to neighboring Glome.* Eventually he is defeated in single combat by Queen Orual,* allowing a peaceful alliance between the kingdoms. He had straw-colored hair and beard, and was thin and yet somehow bloated, with pouting lips.

Argoz In the Narnian* Chronicle *The Voyage of the "Dawn Treader"** he is one of the seven lords* of Narnia sought by Caspian* X. He was eventually discovered slumbering a deep sleep of years at Ramandu's Island.*

Arlian In the Narnian* Chronicle *Prince Caspian** one of the Telmarine* lords of Caspian* IX, executed for treason by the usurper Miraz.*

Arnom In *Till We Have Faces** the progressive new priest of Ungit,* whose "new theology" takes in ideas from Greek rationalism. He was a dark man, no older than Queen Orual,* and "smooth-cheeked as a eunuch."

Arsheesh In *The Horse and His Boy** an unpleasant Calormen* fisherman who raises the apparently orphaned Shasta.*

Arthurian Torso (1948) This book contains an unfinished prose work by Charles Williams* on the Figure of Arthur and a commentary by C. S. Lewis on his friend's unfinished cycle of Arthurian poems, *Taliessin Through Logres* and *The Region of the Summer Stars*. The title refers to the geographical image of the female human body that Williams employs in the poems. Lewis intended his commentary to be complementary to Williams's prose work in helping the reader to appreciate the difficult poetry. He also suggests an order for reading the poems that establishes a narrative continuity.

Lewis robustly defends his friend's poems, arguing that their obscurity is valid. He points out their biblical orthodoxy and expounds their implicit Christian themes of incarnation and love. Lewis also shows Williams's belief that, even when great empires collapse, a faithful remnant survives.

Charles Williams's thought and poetry had a deep and lasting influence on C. S. Lewis's thinking and on a number of his postwar writings. It was because of Lewis's popularity in the United States that in 1974 William Eerdmans was able to publish, in one volume, *Arthurian Torso* and Williams's Arthurian poems.

Askins, John Hawkins (1877-1923) Known as "Doc" to Lewis, Askins was the younger brother of Mrs. Janie King Moore,* Lewis's adopted mother. Deeply affected and destabilized by his war service in the Royal Army Medical Corps, Askins studied the new psychoanalysis and may have dabbled in the occult. He and his family moved near to his sister in 1922, settling in Iffley near Oxford.* Lewis was shocked by his ravings and eventual death in 1923. Prior to that the two had had many conversations in which the subject of immortality figured. It is likely that these experiences influenced what has been dubbed the "Easley Fragment,"* Lewis's unfinished Ulster novel.

Aslan Lewis's invented world of Narnia* contains many talking lions, the kings of beasts. Aslan is not only this, but he is also the creator and ultimate sovereign of the land. His father is the Emperor-over-sea, dwelling beyond the Eastern Ocean, past Aslan's Country* and the World's End. Aslan (Turkish for "lion") is intended to be a symbol of Christ, Christ not as he appeared and will appear in our world (as a real man), but as he appears in Narnia (as a "real" Narnian talking lion). The symbol of the lion (a traditional image of authority) perhaps owes something to Lewis's friend Charles Williams's novel *The Place of the Lion*. In his *The Problem of Pain** Lewis writes: "I think the lion, when he has ceased to be dangerous, will still be awful."

Lewis didn't intend Aslan to be an allegory of Christ. He explained why in a letter written a few days after Christmas, 1958: "By an allegory I mean a composition (whether pictorial or literary) in which immaterial realities are represented as feigned physical objects; e.g., . . . in Bunyan, a giant represents Despair. If Aslan represented the immaterial Deity in the same way in which Giant Despair represents Despair, he would be an allegorical figure. In reality however he is an invention giving an imaginary answer to the question, 'What might Christ become like, if there really were a world like Narnia and He chose to be incarnate and die and rise again in that world as he actually has done in ours?' This is not allegory at all."

All seven of The Chronicles of Narnia* teem with Christian meanings found also in Lewis's other writings, such as the true character of God,* mankind, nature,* heaven,* hell, and joy* (*Sehnsucht*). The key to these meanings lies in the fact that Aslan is a figure of Christ, out of many possible figures of him. If a reader is unaware of this, he or she can still enjoy the stories in their own right; if he or she is aware, the meaning of Christian truths often come strangely alive. For instance, many readers, who are so familiar with the gospel narratives as to be unmoved by the accounts of Christ's death, are moved to tears at the death of Aslan.

As a child Lewis attended St. Mark's (Anglican) Church in Dundela, on the outskirts of Belfast. The traditional symbol of St. Mark is the lion, a fact reinforced by the name of the church's magazine, *The Lion*. See also: ALLEGORY.

Aslan's Country This land lies high up and beyond Narnia's* Eastern Ocean. It features in Lewis's *The Voyage of the "Dawn Treader."** Also

Jill Pole* and Eustace Scrubb* arrive there when they are drawn out of our world in the story known as *The Silver Chair.** Seen from World's End Island,* Aslan's Country appears to be made up of mountains of enormous height, yet forever free of snow, clothed in grass and forests as far as the eye can glimpse. The highest peak is known as the Mountain of Aslan. Viewed from its summit, clouds above the Eastern Ocean look like small sheep. The distinctive water of Aslan's Country quenches hunger and thirst. Approaching visitors find a deepening and splendid brightness that confers increasing youthfulness to those long exposed to it. Its brightness is like that experienced by Elwin Ransom* in Deep Heaven in Lewis's science-fiction trilogy. The quality of light in Deep Heaven and near Aslan's Country reminds us that Lewis was very much inspired by the medieval imagination, with its marked response to brightness, rather than the modern imagination, with its awe at the vastness of deep space or large quantities.

In *The Voyage of the "Dawn Treader,"* Aslan* in his Country appears to the children, Edmund and Lucy Pevensie* and Eustace, first as a lamb and then as the familiar great lion.

Aslan's How A huge mound in Lewis's story *Prince Caspian,** which during the course of the ages has been built over the Stone Table* where Aslan,* the great talking lion, was sacrificed. It is located in the Great Woods of Narnia,* and it has hollowed-out galleries and caves.

Atlantis In Lewis's *That Hideous Strength,** a lost world that is the origin of Logres, the spiritual and true Britain, established during the time of King Arthur and Merlin. Merlin's magical art was a surviving remnant of the older and different realm of Atlantis, or Numinor, as it is sometimes called, which existed in the pre-glacial period before primitive druidism. Merlin's magic was brought to Western Europe after the fall of Atlantis, and it differed greatly from the Renaissance magic with which we are familiar. Merlin was a member of the Atlantian Circle and retained an instinctive feel for the powers of nature,* lost to modern science.

The Atlantian heritage retains something of Eden, mankind's unfallen state, captured mythically in Lewis's planetary world of Perelandra.* This heritage was passed on through the succession of the Pendragon of Logres to Elwin Ransom.* It was also preserved in the language of Old Solar,* spoken before the fall of mankind and beyond the moon's orbit. The N.I.C.E.* wished to utilize this power through reviving the sleeping body of Merlin, preserved through the ages by a spell, for its own satanic ends.

In *The Magician's Nephew,** the magical rings that allowed Polly Plummer* and Digory Kirke* to travel to other worlds, including Narnia* and Charn,* were made from Atlantian dust. Then Lewis employs the image of Atlantis overwhelmed by a flood to describe the impact of his mother's death in his autobiography *Surprised by Joy.**

Atlantis also features prominently in Tolkien's *The Silmarillion** as Númenor.*

FURTHER READING

J. R. R. Tolkien, *The Silmarillion* (1977) and "The Notion Club Papers" (in *Sauron Defeated*, 1992).

Charles Williams, *Taliessin Through Logres* (1938) and *The Region of the Summer Stars* (1944).

Stephen Lawhead, *Taliesin* (1988).

Plato, *Critias* and *Timaeus.*

Pierre Benoit, *L'Atlantide* (1919).

Sir Arthur Conan Doyle, *The Maracot Deep* (1929).

Augray In *Out of the Silent Planet,** a sorn* whom Dr. Elwin Ransom* meets on his way across the high harandra* to Meldilorn.* Augray gives him oxygen, for the atmosphere on Malacandra is thin, and shelters him in his cave. Later Augray carries Ransom on his high shoulders to his destination.

Avra A sparsely inhabited island in the Narnian* Chronicle *The Voyage of the "Dawn Treader,"** the third of a group known as the Lone Islands, and the location of the estates of Lord Bern.* See also: NARNIA, GEOGRAPHY.

Awe An emotion that Lewis considered close to fear, but implying no consideration of danger. It was caused by the presence of the numinous.* Lewis expresses his belief in *The Problem of Pain** that awe was a direct experience of the supernatural.*

Axartha Tarkaan In *The Horse and His Boy,** he is Grand Vizier of Calormen* before Ahoshta.*

Azim Balda To the south of the capital of Calormen,* a town at the junction of many roads, in the Narnian Chronicles. It was an important center of communications and the core of the country's postal system. Mounted messengers of the House of Imperial Posts carried letters throughout the vast country. See also: NARNIA, GEOGRAPHY; *THE HORSE AND HIS BOY.*

B

Baker, Leo Kingsley (1898-1986) A contemporary and friend of Lewis, Leo Baker was a fighter pilot with the RFC (RAF) during the First World War. He was awarded the Distinguished Flying Cross after being severely wounded in August 1918. The following year he returned to Oxford as an undergraduate, and he introduced Owen Barfield* to Lewis. Leo Baker was a frequent visitor to the Lewis-Moore household, as recorded in Lewis's *All My Road Before Me.**

After graduation Baker became an actor, a profession he eventually had to give up because of his war wounds. He and his wife set up a weaving business in Chipping Campden. During the Second World War he taught in a Rudolf Steiner* school in Gloucester. After this he became Drama Advisor for the Regional Authority in various senior roles. The Bodleian Library, Oxford, houses Lewis's letters to him.

Balder In Scandinavian mythology, Balder (or Baldur) was the god of light and joy. He was the son of Odin and Frigg, king and queen of the gods. In a dream Frigg was warned that Balder's life was threatened. Frigg made all the forces and beings in nature swear that they would not harm Balder, with one exception—the mistletoe. When the gods hurled darts and stones at Balder, Loki placed mistletoe in the hands of his twin brother Hoder, the blind god of darkness. Balder was slain. Odin sent Hermod, another brother, to the underworld to plead for his return. If everything in the world would weep for him, he could return from death. Everything did so but for one ancient giantess (said to be the mischievous Loki in disguise). Balder could not therefore return to life.

In *Surprised by Joy,** Lewis records the impact this story had upon him even in its barest form: "Instantly I was uplifted into huge regions of northern sky, I desired with almost sickening intensity something never to be described (except that it is cold, spacious, severe, pale, and remote)" (chapter 1).

Lewis confessed that he loved Balder before he loved Christ. He came to see, however, that Christ's incarnation in history made abstract reality tangible to human beings much more successfully than mere myth (see: MYTH AND FACT). See also: PAGANISM AND MYSTICISM.

Balfour, Arthur James (1848-1930) British prime minister between 1902 and 1905. His Conservative policies were important for Unionists in what eventually became Northern Ireland. As a boy Lewis would have heard Balfour's name mentioned by his father, Albert Lewis,* and his father's friends, for whom politics was a dominant theme of conversation. Balfour joined the coalition cabinet of Prime Minister Herbert Henry Asquith in 1915 as first lord of the Admiralty. When David Lloyd George became prime minister in December 1916, Balfour was transferred to the Foreign Office. In 1917 he published the Balfour Declaration, which stated that Britain would support the creation in Palestine of a national home for the Jewish people. Among his works are *Essays and Addresses* (1893), *The Foundations of Belief* (1895), *Theism and Humanism** (1915), and *Theism and Thought* (1923). *Theism and Humanism* was one of Lewis's chosen list of ten books that particularly had a formative influence on him (see: READING OF C. S. LEWIS).

In his paper "Is Theology Poetry?" (1944), Lewis speaks of *Theism and Humanism* as "a book too little read." Balfour's book was a significant influence on Lewis's seminal *Miracles*,* particularly on his treatment of naturalism.* Like Lewis, Balfour thought of himself as a plain man, with a plain man's common sense. Lewis was keen to employ a plain style in his theological writings.

FURTHER READING

Arthur James Balfour, *Chapters of Autobiography* (1930).

Blanche E. C. Dugdale, *Arthur James Balfour, First Earl of Balfour 1906-1930* (n.d.).

Max Egremont, *Balfour: A Life of Arthur James Balfour* (1980).

Ruddock F. Mackay, *Balfour: Intellectual Statesman* (1985).

Bar In Lewis's *The Horse and His Boy*,* the chancellor of jolly King Lune.* Bar turned traitor and kidnapped the infant Prince Cor* when he heard that Cor would save Archenland.* Later Lord Bar was slain in battle.

Barfield, Owen (1898-1997) A close friend of Lewis and fellow Inkling,* Owen Barfield was a child of "more or less agnostic" parents—one a London solicitor, the other a suffragette. They retained a deep respect for Christianity, however. He was born near Highgate, London, in 1898 and had two sisters and a brother. His mother taught him to read. In high school he was keen on gymnastics. In the spring of 1917 he was called up to the army at the age of eighteen.

Barfield served with the Royal Engineers and joined the Signal Service. In the Wireless Department he studied the theory of electricity. He had already learned Morse code from his elder brother. While he was still training, the armistice was signed, so he had no combat experience at all, though he was sent to Belgium. There he had very little to do, as pigeons were still used for communications.

He had won a scholarship to Oxford,* but he did not get up to the university until October 1919. He first studied at Wadham College, reading English and attempting some of his own writing. At this time he formed a lifelong friendship with Lewis.* He later became an anthroposophist,* an advocate of the religious school of thought developed by Rudolf Steiner. Barfield and Lewis would walk together or ask each other to lunch, but did not really see a lot of each other until after graduation, when the "great war"* started between them.

As an undergraduate, Owen Barfield experienced what has aptly been described as an "intellectual epiphany" (*New York Times* Obituary, December 19, 1997) while studying the Romantic poets. As with Tolkien, his main intellectual stimulus came from language. Owen Barfield recalled in 1966: "What impressed me particularly was the power with which not so much whole poems, as particular combinations of words worked on my mind. It seemed like there was some magic in it; and a magic which not only gave me pleasure but also reacted on and expanded the meanings of the individual words concerned" (*New York Times, op. cit.*). Language, he believed, had the power to transform human consciousness and to embody historic changes in this consciousness.

He married Maud Douie soon after graduation, in 1923. They had met at the English Folk Dance Society where they were both dancers. She had been looking for a male dancer for a concert party around Cornish villages. His wife came into a little money, and for several years he was a free-lance writer, doing various odd jobs to supplement his income. He had started writing poetry while in high school.

After graduation he also began a B.Litt., the thesis of which became his book *Poetic Diction* (1928). This book deeply influenced Lewis and Tolkien, shaking them to the roots. In 1925 Barfield published a children's book, *The Silver Trumpet*, which later was a success in the Tolkien household. In 1926 his study *History in English Words* appeared.

In 1929 Barfield moved back to London to train in his father's firm of solicitors. He would visit Oxford once a term, and this sometimes coincided with an Inklings meeting, and he would then attend. He always saw himself as a fringe member. About 1930 he had finished his "metaphysical argument" with Lewis, the "great war." This roughly coincided with the process of Lewis's conversion to Christianity. After the "war" he had jokingly said to Lewis that while Lewis had taught him to think, he had taught Lewis what to think. Lewis undoubtedly forced him to think systematically and accurately, passing on hard-won skills he had acquired from his tutelage under W. T. Kirkpatrick.* Barfield in his turn helped Lewis to think more imaginatively, to combine his imagination with his formidable intellect. This was a "slow business," remembered Barfield.

His wife, Maud, was an Anglican and somewhat antipathetic to Steiner and anthroposophism. She gradually modified her resistance, and he in turn became an Anglican in 1950, but he was embarrassed by Lewis's "fundamentalism." Christianity for Barfield meant the "working of the Logos in human destiny and human life." Like Rudolf Steiner, he became convinced that the incarnation, life, and death of Christ was at the center of the "evolution of consciousness."* Also like Steiner, he believed in reincarnation. Owen Barfield had no children of his own, but he and Maud adopted two children and foster-parented a third. The daughter Lucy (to whom *The Lion, the Witch and the Wardrobe* is dedicated) had multiple sclerosis.

During his early years as a solicitor—1929 to 1934—he contributed essays, poems, and reviews mostly to anthroposophical journals. There was then a quiet period until a collection of essays, *Romanticism Comes of Age*, was published in 1944. At The Little Theatre, Sheffield, his poetic drama *Orpheus* was performed in 1948. An autobiographical novel appeared in 1950, entitled *This Ever Diverse Pair*, under the pseudonym G. A. L. Burgeon. Owen Barfield continued to write essays. A major statement of his philosophy, perhaps as significant as *Poetic Diction*, came out in 1957, called *Saving the Appearances: A Study in Idolatry*. The book dealt with the implications of a scientific perception of reality upon ordinary human consciousness.

Two years later Owen Barfield retired from his legal profession, and his writing output significantly increased, including *Worlds Apart* (1963), *Unancestral Voice* (1965), *Speaker's Meaning* (1967), *What Coleridge Thought* (1971), *The Rediscovery of Meaning* (1977), *History, Guilt and Habit* (1979), and *Owen Barfield on Lewis* (1990). In 1994 *A Barfield Sampler* was published. His reputation steadily grew in the American academic world, and he gave a number of lectures there. He was for many years Lewis's literary executor, soon joined by Walter Hooper. When he originally started advising Lewis legally, Lewis faced a major catastrophe over his income tax, an episode captured in a chapter in *This Ever Diverse Pair* (1950).

Lewis's debt to Owen Barfield was enormous. He paid tribute to Barfield in *Surprised by Joy** and earlier in *The Allegory of Love** ("the wisest and best of my unofficial teachers"). More recently Owen Barfield has been appreciated as a leading twentieth-century thinker by figures as diverse as Saul Bellow, Theodore Roszak, G. B. Tennyson, and Norman O. Brown. Barfield outlived Lewis by thirty-four years and Tolkien by twenty-four, dying peacefully on December 14, 1997, in Forest Row, East Sussex. His wife, Maud, thirteen years older than he, had died in 1983 (nearly making her century).

FURTHER READING

G. B. Tennyson, ed., *Owen Barfield on Lewis* (1989)

Lionel Adey, *Lewis's "Great War" with Owen Barfield* (1978)

C. S. Lewis, *Surprised by Joy* (1955, chapter 13).

Batta In Lewis's *Till We Have Faces*,* the big-boned, fair-haired, hardheaded foreigner from the north who is the nurse of Orual* and Redival.* When Orual becomes queen, as part of her reforms she has Batta hanged, because of her troublemaking.

Baynes, Pauline Diana (b. 1922) Lewis chose her to illustrate his Narnia* books apparently after seeing her illustrations for a story by his friend Tolkien,* *Farmer Giles of Ham** (1949). Commenting on her work for *The Silver Chair*,* Lewis observed: "There is, as always, exquisite delicacy." As George MacDonald* had done with the artist Arthur Hughes, Lewis found an illustrator whose imagination complemented his own.

Pauline Baynes played an important part in visualizing the world of Narnia, working from a basic sketch map by Lewis—she drew a Narnia map for the end papers of the original hardback books, a popular poster map (1968), and a map of the voyage of the *Dawn Treader*. In addition to the Narnia stories, Pauline Baynes illustrated other books by Tolkien.

BBC (British Broadcasting Corporation) As well as recording several series of wartime talks in 1941, 1942, and 1944, which became *Mere Christianity*,* Lewis occasionally recorded other talks for the BBC. He read the text of his "*De Descriptione Temporum*"* for instance over the air. Most of the wartime recordings seem to have been deleted by the BBC, but several of the other talks are available on audiotape from the Episcopal Radio-TV Foundation.

Mr. and Mrs. Beaver Loyal Narnian talking beavers who lead Peter, Lucy, and Susan to the meeting point with Aslan in *The Lion, the Witch and the Wardrobe.** See also: ANIMALS, TALKING.

Behmenheim Region depicted in the Mappa Mundi* of *The Pilgrim's Regress,** after Jakob Boehme, or Behmen (1575-1624). He was a German mystic whose influence spread to Germany, Holland, and England. He published a treatise, *Aurora*, in 1612. He saw the origin of evil as a necessary opposition to good and posited that God's eternal nature contained a principle to reconcile good and evil.

Belbury In *That Hideous Strength*,* "a florid Edwardian mansion that had been built for a millionaire who admired Versailles." Acquired by the N.I.C.E.* for their headquarters, it contrasted directly with the household community run by Elwin Ransom* at St. Anne's.

"Belsen" Wynyard School, Watford, Hertfordshire, was so named by Lewis in his autobiography, *Surprised by Joy** (see chapters 2 and 3). The young Lewis brothers attended it. The brutal headmaster, Rev. Robert Capron (1851-1911), was later certified insane. One speculation is that Uncle Andrew,* the mad scientist in *The Magician's Nephew*,* was based on Capron.

Bennett, J. A. W. (1911-1981) A New Zealander, Inkling, and colleague of Lewis's at Magdalen College, Oxford, from 1947. In 1964 he took on Lewis's post as Professor of Medieval and Renaissance Literature at Cambridge. His inaugural lecture was devoted to the subject of Lewis, entitled "The Humane Medievalist" (1965).

Bern Also spelled Berne. In *The Voyage of the "Dawn Treader,"** a chronicle of Narnia,* one of the seven lords* of Caspian* IX. He is discovered living on one of the Lone Islands,* and Caspian X makes him a duke.

Bernagh The home of Lewis's friend Arthur Greeves,* near Little Lea,* at the time they first became acquainted. *The Pilgrim's Regress** was written here during a two-week holiday with Greeves. The building is now a private nursing home (called Red Hall) located on Circular Road in northeast Belfast.

Beruna, Fords of Fords over the River of Narnia,* later bridged, near the Stone Table* (Aslan's How*). During the night of Aslan's* terrible death, his loyal forces encamped there. At the time of the events recorded in *The Silver Chair*,* the town of Beruna was there. See also: *THE LION, THE WITCH AND THE WARDROBE*..

Betjeman, Sir John (1906-1984) Lewis was Betjeman's tutor in English language and literature, a period in which antipathy grew between the two, expressed at times in the latter's poetry. Lewis was impatient over Betjeman's reluctance to work, while the poet blamed Lewis for his leaving Oxford without a degree. Many years later the two were reconciled and became friends. Sir John was chosen as Poet Laureate 1972.

FURTHER READING

John Betjeman, *Collected Poems* (1958).

Bible The debate about the authority and infallibility of the Bible is a complex one. Generally, Lewis may be taken as orthodox in his high view of Scripture, but he offered some tentative views, partly as a response to questions, on inspiration and the Word of God. Michael Christensen, in *C. S. Lewis on Scripture* (1979), has tried to extend these tentative observations logically to present what Lewis's views might have been on the inerrancy debate (the discussion about whether or not the Bible is always accurate where it touches on science or history). For Christensen, Lewis stands between the position of theological liberalism (which lessens biblical authority in favor of religious experience or rationalism) and Evangelicalism (for which the Bible is the final authority on all of life). Evangelicalism, which has a great debt to Lewis's writings, particularly in America, is confused by Christensen with Fundamentalism.

Christensen helpfully observes: "To get . . . to his fundamental assumptions regarding the nature of Scripture, we must give thoughtful analysis to (1) his provocative theological persuasions and speculative sentiments, which suggest his view of Scripture, (2) his theory of the function of literature and the role of literary criticism, which largely determine his approach to biblical literature, and (3) his appreciation of myth (properly defined) and understanding of revelation, which apply directly to the Bible" (p. 23).

Though Christensen's book contains many valuable insights, it is flawed in drawing Lewis into a debate he never addressed. Two evangelicals who were in correspondence with Lewis, Clyde S. Kilby and Kathryn Lindskoog, have commented helpfully on Lewis's view of Scripture in relation to Evangelicalism. It is clear that while Lewis sharply attacked theological liberalism, he had little or nothing critical to say about Evangelicalism. To Clyde Kilby he offered a series of detailed difficulties that he had with an evangelical view of inspiration. These were offered in a spirit of helpfulness, in the expectation that anyone grappling with the authority of Scripture must give honest answers to such questions. None of the questions is incapable of solution. Lewis however treated theological liberalism as the antithesis of all that he stood for as a supernaturalist and a "mere Christian." Thus it would be wrong to say that Lewis stood in opposition to both theological liberalism and Evangelicalism.

For evangelicals and other orthodox groups sharing common ground, Lewis offers a great deal that is helpful. As a literary critic,* Lewis's insights are valuable in approaching the Bible as a literary text (though Lewis was skeptical of a simple "the Bible as literature" approach). His book *Reflections on the Psalms** provides a useful model. Lewis's observation about inspiration, that truth is scattered in many myths around the world, and not only in the Bible, deserves attention. It bears similarity with Calvin's view that truth is to be welcomed where it is to be found in non-Christian thinking. Lewis's *Miracles** provides fascinating insights into the wider implications of the doctrine of the Incarnation, God's* supreme revelation of himself. Language, story, and myth can, in God's grace, be incarnations of truth, anticipating or echoing the incarnation of truth himself. A seminal essay, "Transposition," attempts to show the logic of incarnation, as the richer level of meaning is transposed or translated into a lower, poorer level. In the gospel records, true history and the greatest of all stories are one; myth becomes fact.

It is easy to see the Bible only in terms of propositional truth, as if the Bible first and foremost encouraged looking at reality in a theoretical, systematic way. It is undoubtedly true that the Bible can generate a consistent theoretical model that has far-reaching consequences for all of human knowledge, in the sciences as well as the arts. This can be seen, for instance, in Thomist and in Reformed thought. The Bible is propositional revelation from a person to persons; it is objective truth, representing what is the case. It is easy to focus only on this in an age of radical relativism.

Seen as a whole, however, the Bible in a very basic, straightforward, and ordinary way looks *at* reality *through* the frame of narrative, story, image, and symbolic elements. The Bible begins with a seven-day creation and the events in the Garden of Eden and ends with the visions of the book of Revelation and the denouement of the Holy City, within which is the Tree of Life introduced in Genesis. The hero of heroes of Scripture is the lamb that was slain from the creation of the world. In a profound sense such symbols are not merely poetic but solidly real. The lamb that was slain, for instance, is linked in myriad ways to actual events in documented history, such as the crucifixion and resurrection of Christ.

Preeminently, such symbols are linked to events and facts, not in the first place to concepts, even though they provide subject matter for thought (for example, the symbol of the lamb that was slain helps our thinking about the achievement of the cross). Their primary function is to bring us into contact with significant events in history, selected events in our space-time, events of historical importance.

Lewis (deeply influenced by his friend Barfield*) suggests that comparatively recently we have lost an ancient unity between the poetic and the prosaic, the symbolic and the literal. In the Bible, to give an example, "spirit" is equally "spirit" and "breath" and "wind." Again, the *logos* of John's Gospel is a profound unity integrating many meanings that we today have to separate out. The same would be true of early Genesis; the common dichotomy of facticity and poetry in reading these chapters is misleading.

When we saturate ourselves in the Scriptures, a healing of this division, a restoration of a basic human unity of consciousness, can begin to take place. We find this far harder than, for instance, a seventeenth-century English, German, or Dutch reader of the Bible. For this reason Lewis advocated a diet of old books, i.e., books belonging to the period he called the Old West.* The Bible insists, by its very nature, on looking at the natural and human worlds through its multifaceted appeal to our imaginations. It blatantly appeals to our human taste for a story and to our delight in other unifying symbolic elements such as archetypes.

Lewis's imaginative work reinforces such a biblical emphasis upon a symbolic perception of reality. His symbolic worlds of Narnia* and Perelandra,* Glome,* and the allegorical world of *The Pilgrim's Regress,** even though fictional, are in some sense solidly real. For this reason they take us back to the ordinary world that is an inevitable part of our human living and experience, deepening both the wonders and the terrors of our world. Our awareness of the meaning of God's creation and his intentions for us is enlarged. Lewis guides us in seeing this world with a thoroughly Christian understanding. His invented worlds also illuminate what is revealed of God in the natural order.

Though fantasy was Lewis's preferred medium, it is not the only valid symbolic mode for winning truth. The Bible, guide to truth-gaining as well as the truth, employs numerous modes: historical, poetic, apocalyptic, story, motif, archetype, master image, and prophecy. In the natural sciences, imaginative models play an important part in winning truth, both at the macro and micro level (see: *THE DISCARDED IMAGE).*

Perhaps the dominance of realistic literature has coincided with the reign of modernism—the inherited pattern of the Enlightenment—that squeezed fantasy on to the periphery of the canon of literature. Now that we are increasingly in a postmodernist culture, the character and social role of fantasy might change and become more central, as it was before the Enlightenment became dominant. The continued popularity and thus cultural relevance of the fantasy fiction of Lewis (and of course his friend Tolkien—both avowedly anti-modernist) are surely significant. They might be called premodernist rather than postmodernist authors who have outstanding contemporary appeal, an appeal that continues to grow.

Lewis saw the symbolic appeal of the Bible most focused in the Gospels. These, in form and in substance, have an extraordinary imaginative draw. Indeed, W. H. Auden* points out in *Secondary Worlds* (pp. 120, 121) that they subverted classical ideas about the imagination.* The incarnation of Christ and the other events of the gospel story locate the imagination in the ordinary world of creation, or nature:

> In a magico-polytheistic culture . . . poets are the theologians, the sacred mouthpieces of society; it is they who teach the myths and rescue from oblivion the great deeds of ancestral heroes. That to which the imagination by its nature responds with excitement, namely, the manifestly extraordinary and powerful, is identified with the divine. The poet is one whose words are equal to his divine subjects, which can happen only if he is divinely inspired. The coming of Christ in the form of a servant who cannot be recognized by the eye of flesh and blood, only by the eye of faith, puts an end to all such claims. The imagination is to be regarded as a natural faculty, the subject matter of which *is* the phenomenal world, not its Creator. . . . The poet is not there to convert the world.

Auden goes on to point out the remarkable contrast between "the claim of the gospel narratives to be the Word of God, and the outward appearance and social status of the characters in them." He argues that, if the claim is believed, this abolishes the "assumptions of the classical aesthetic." In evidence he quotes Eric Auerbach's *Mimesis,* where he speaks of the account of Peter's denial:

> Both the nature and scene of the conflict [writes Auerbach] also fall entirely outside the domain of classical antiquity. Viewed superficially the thing is a police action and its consequences; it takes place entirely among everyday men and women of the common people; anything of the sort could be thought of in antique terms only as farce or comedy. A scene like Peter's denial fits into no antique genre. It is too serious for comedy, too contemporary and everyday for tragedy, politically too insignificant for history, and the form which was given it is one of such immediacy that its like does not exist in the literature of antiquity. This can be judged by a symptom which at first glance may seem insignificant—the use of direct discourse. Direct discourse is generally restricted in the antique historians to great continuous speeches delivered to the senate or before a popular assembly, but here in the scene of Peter's denial—the dramatic tension of the moment when the actors stand face to face has been given an immediacy compared with which the stichomactry of antique tragedy appears highly stylized.

Lewis (persuaded by Tolkien and Dyson*) became convinced that the events documented in the Gospels, located in the real world of first-century Palestine, nevertheless retain the quality of myth—that is, they are the epitome of human storytelling. But just as they retain the quality of myth, equally they are true history. Though this combination was alien to a Greco-Roman mentality, it was fully consistent with the logic and imagination of a theology steeped in the Bible. See also: MYTH BECAME FACT.

Bide, The Reverend Peter (1912-) An Anglican (Episcopalian) clergyman and friend who performed the Christian marriage between Lewis and Joy Davidman Gresham, and who also prayed for her healing from cancer at Lewis's request. Prior to this Peter Bide had discussed the efficacy of prayer for healing with Lewis, as in some cases he had experienced healing after praying for people and sometimes not. Lewis regarded his wife's recovery as miraculous, and indeed she had over three years of remission after being in a hopeless state.

In performing the wedding ceremony Rev. Bide chose to ignore the reluctant refusal of the Bishop of Oxford to give Lewis and his wife a Christian ceremony, a refusal on the grounds that Joy Lewis was a divorcee, even though she was the innocent party in the event.

Bird and Baby See: THE EAGLE AND CHILD.

Bism An underground world deep below Narnia,* not to be confused with the Green Witch's* perverted Underland,* which lies above Bism. The children in *The Silver Chair** catch a glimpse of Bism through a chasm in the earth. Here the bright gems of all colors are alive, and it is the home of gnomes. Through Bism runs a river of fire inhabited by Salamanders. See also: NARNIA, GEOGRAPHY.

Black Woods In *Prince Caspian,** woods near the ruins of Cair Paravel* and the sea. It was rumored by the Telmarines* that the woods were full of ghosts. Telmarines feared the sea, and they let the woods grow to protect them from it.

Blamires, Harry (1916-) A former pupil of Lewis's, Harry Blamires is a literary critic and author of a kind of divine comedy in the genre of *The Screwtape Letters.** His trilogy is *The Devil's Hunting Ground* (1954), *Cold War in Hell* (1955), and *Blessing Unbounded* (1955).

Bodleian Library, Oxford See: READING OF C. S. LEWIS.

Boxen An imaginary kingdom created by Lewis as a young child, in collusion with his brother, W. H. "Warnie" Lewis.* The stories have been collected and edited by Walter Hooper into a book of the same name (1985). In his autobiography, *Surprised by Joy,** Lewis describes the origin of Boxen. The first stories were written and illustrated "to combine my two chief literary pleasures—"dressed animals" and "knights in armor." As a result, "I wrote about chivalrous mice and rabbits who rode out in complete mail to kill not giants but cats." In creating an environment for the tales, a medieval Animal-Land was born. In order to include Warnie in its creation and shaping, features of the modern world such as trains and steamships had to be included. Thus a history had to be created, and so on.

Bracton College In *That Hideous Strength,** by Lewis, one of several university colleges at Edgestow,* owning Bragdon Wood,* later acquired by the N.I.C.E.* for sinister purposes. Edgestow and its colleges is modeled on Durham, though Lewis disclaimed any definite connection. In his preface to the book he tells us that he selected his own profession as the setting for his tale because he naturally knew it best. It was not because he thought fellows of colleges more likely to be corrupted than anyone else! The other colleges were St. Elizabeth's College, a nineteenth-century women's college beyond the railway, Northumberland, standing below Bracton on the river Wynd, and Duke's, opposite the Abbey. Jane Studdock* had studied at St. Elizabeth's and was now a postgraduate at the university.

Bragdon Wood Owned by Bracton College* in Lewis's *That Hideous Strength,** the wood was enclosed by a high wall with only one entry, a gate by Inigo Jones within the college. The wood was perhaps a quarter of a mile broad and a mile from east to west, with the river Wynd flowing by it. In the center of the wood was a well with worn steps going down to it and the remains of an ancient pavement about it, built in the time of King Arthur. "Merlin's Well" was situated by Merlin's subterranean tomb, where the ancient magician lay in suspended animation.

Bramandin In *The Magician's Nephew*,* a city of the ancient dead world of Charn.*

Bricklethumb In *The Horse and His Boy*,* a Red Dwarf who, with his brother Duffle, feeds Shasta (Cor*) when he first comes into Narnia.*

Bright People Inhabitants of heaven who travel to the outer lands to meet shades from hell allowed a visit in *The Great Divorce*.* Lewis imagines himself one of the visitors, meeting the solid figure of his mentor, George MacDonald.*

Mr. Broad An allegorical figure in *The Pilgrim's Regress** representing a modernizing religion which "is friends with the World and goes on no pilgrimage."

Brothers and Friends: The Diaries of Major Warren Hamilton Lewis (1982) The late Clyde S. Kilby and Marjorie Lamp Mead edited these diary extracts from over a million words filling twenty-three journals. The result is a fascinating and indispensable portrait of W. H. "Warnie" Lewis* that also vividly pictures the day-to-day life of Lewis and his household at The Kilns. Warnie's own biography of his brother was never published, and it exists in typescript at The Marion E. Wade Center of Wheaton College. As Warnie reread his journals up to 1949 on September 6, 1967, nearly four years after Jack's death, he records: "I find these notebooks do amount to something of a biography in which I see myself much as I have lived, and often with pangs of remorse for my own selfishness and ill-living. On the other hand with much vividly recalled happiness. . . . One thing that stands out from these books is that the great pleasures of my life have been J[ack]'s society, books and scenery in that order. . . . One thing I now bitterly regret about these diaries is that I preserved hardly any of my innumerable conversations with J. If only I had known that he was to leave me to end my life in loneliness, with what jealous care I would have Boswellised him."

The diaries are also notable for the rare records of meetings of the Inklings* and of Lewis's friendship with and marriage to Joy Davidman,* a person Warnie wholly and unjealously admired.

Bulgy Bears In *Prince Caspian*,* three sleepy bears who are among the loyal Old Narnians. They offer Caspian* honey. See also: ANIMALS, TALKING.

Mr. Bultitude A bear in *That Hideous Strength** who, along with a jackdaw and other animals, makes up the household of Elwin Ransom* at St. Anne's. Mr. Bultitude had escaped from a provincial zoo after a fire. Lewis seems particularly fond of this character, basing him upon a bear at Whipsnade Zoo* that his brother Warnie* and he knew as "Bultitude." Lewis had, according to Warnie's diary, dreamed of adding a bear to their private menagerie at The Kilns.

In the story Jane Studdock* encounters Mr. Bultitude unexpectedly occupying most of her bathroom, "a great, snuffly, wheezy, beady-eyed, loose-skinned, gor-bellied brown bear." Later the bear was captured by the N.I.C.E.* and narrowly escaped vivisection.

Lewis takes the name from a character, Paul Bultitude, in the humorous *Vice Versa*, by F. Anstey, the pseudonym of Thomas Anstey Guthrie (1856-1934). Lewis read the book in childhood. In 1947 the story was made into a film, directed by Peter Ustinov, starring Petula Clark and James Robertson Justice. Anstey writes: "Mr. Bultitude was a tall and portly person, of a somewhat pompous and overbearing demeanour." As a widower, who found the company of his son "an abominable nuisance," Bultitude may have reminded Lewis of his father. Like Lewis senior, Mr. Bultitude was baffled by his son's request to leave his miserable boarding school. The relation between father and son is dramatically altered when the two swap bodies through the power of an Eastern talisman, and the father is forced to attend his son's school.

Bulverism A common phenomenon in argument, where an opponent's case is reduced to causes and therefore dismissed, as in "You only say that because you are a woman." Psychological interpretations are particularly prone to this fallacy—for instance, the view that belief in God is wish-fulfillment. Naturalism, discussed in *Miracles*,* reduces all thinking and thus beliefs to causes, and in the process eliminates the validity of its own truth claims.

"Bulverism" is Lewis's name for this widespread view, a view that typically explains why a person is wrong before demonstrating that a person is wrong. This view marks the death of reason. Lewis points out, "Either we can know nothing *or* thought has reasons only, and no causes." Much of *Miracles* consists of a sophisticated rebuttal of this attitude. His essay, "Bulverism, or, The Foundation of 20th Century Thought," can be found in *God in the Dock*, *Undeceptions*, and *First and Second Things*.

Burnt Island In *The Voyage of the "Dawn Treader"** a low, green island within sight of Dragon Island.* Here the only living creatures the travelers discover are rabbits and goats. Ruins of stone huts, several bones, and broken weapons between the fire-blackened areas suggested that it had been inhabited fairly recently. See also: NARNIA, GEOGRAPHY.

C

Cabby Name given to a London horse-and-cab driver. See FRANK, THE CABBY. See also: *THE MAGICIAN'S NEPHEW.*

Cair Paravel Capital of Narnia,* the beautiful castle stands on the estuary of the Great River. In *The Lion, the Witch and the Wardrobe,** it was the seat of High King Peter and the other ruling kings and queens. Originally it was situated between two streams, but erosion turned its location into a small island. When the children return to Narnia ages later (as told in *Prince Caspian**), the castle is in ruins. Caspian* X rebuilds it to its former splendor. In their subsequent visit, recounted in *The Silver Chair,** Eustace Scrubb* and Jill Pole* hear the ancient tale of *The Horse and His Boy.** See also: NARNIA, GEOGRAPHY.

Calabria, Giovanni (1873-1954) Founder of a Roman Catholic order, the Poor Servants of Divine Providence, Don Giovanni began a correspondence with Lewis in Latin, after reading *The Screwtape Letters.** The letters have been collected and translated into English by Martin Moynihan, a former student of Lewis's, under the title *Letters: C. S. Lewis and Don Giovanni Calabria* (see: LETTERS OF C. S. LEWIS).

Calavar In *The Horse and His Boy,** a province of Calormen* ruled by Kidrash Tarkaan, Aravis's father.

Caldron Pool In *The Last Battle,** a large pool under the cliffs at the western end of Narnia.* It owes its name to the bubbling and dancing movement of its churning water. See also: NARNIA, GEOGRAPHY.

Calormene Inhabitant of Calormen.*

Calormen A huge land to the far south of Narnia,* Calormen is ruled by a dark and cruel people. Its capital is Tashbaan, and it has many provinces, each ruled by a Tarkaan, or lord. Calormen is the setting for *The Horse and His Boy.** To its north lies Archenland,* from which it is separated by a large desert.

Tashbaan city is one of the wonders of the world. It is situated on a river island with a many-arched bridge leading to it from the southern river bank. The city is gated, with high walls. Within them, buildings are crowded together and climb to the top of a hill. At its summit is displayed the magnificent palace of the Tisroc* and the great temple of Tash* with its silver-plated dome. From the city hill, it is possible to see the masts of ships at anchor at the river's mouth. To the south of Tashbaan a range of low wooded hills is visible.

Unlike democratic Narnia and Archenland to its north, Calormen has a strictly hierarchical, caste society. The dark-skinned peasant majority have few or no rights, and slavery is common. The society is basically agricultural, though fishing, crafts, and trade have an important place. A troublesome country, Calormen historically has coveted the northern lands of its peaceable neighbors, and it particularly becomes a threat in the period described in *The Last Battle.** Calormen originated in the Narnian year 204, when outlaws fled south from Archenland. See also: NARNIA, HISTORY.

Campbell College A public (i.e., private) school near Lewis's childhood home of Little Lea,* on the outskirts of Belfast, Northern Ireland. Lewis attended the institution briefly after the closure of "Belsen,"* his former school. The institute has a fine reputation, and Lewis's lifelong friend Jane McNeil* was the daughter of a former head teacher there. The College's War Memorial lists pupils who served in World War One, including Lewis.

Cancer Lewis records in his poignant *A Grief Observed**: "Cancer, and cancer, and cancer . . . my mother, my father, my wife; I wonder who is next in the queue." His mother died of the disease when he was the tender age of nine; his father when Lewis had not long turned thirty; his wife, Joy, when she was in her mid-forties.

Canyon, The An important region in *The Pilgrim's Regress,** which John the pilgrim must cross in order to fulfill his quest and be saved.

Caphad In *Till We Have Faces,** a kingdom south of Glome* from which King Trom* obtained his short-lived and delicate second wife, mother of Psyche.*

Caspian The name of the first ten of the Telmarine* kings. In the story *Prince Caspian** that Caspian is the one who becomes Caspian X, after defeating the usurper Miraz.* Caspian X appears also as a central figure in *The Voyage of the "Dawn Treader"** and, in old age, in *The Silver Chair.** He is succeeded by his son Rilian.* Caspian X married the daughter of Ramandu,* later murdered by the Green Witch* of the line of Jadis.*

The first of the kings of Telmar, Caspian I, conquered Narnia* and silenced the talking animals,* its proper inhabitants. Caspian IX was murdered by his brother Miraz. See also: NARNIA, HISTORY.

Centaur The half-human, half-horse creature of classical mythology appears in Lewis's Narnian Chronicles. Lewis saw the centaur as an appealing illustration of how nature* might one day be harmonized with spirit (*Miracles*, chapter 14).

The mingling of human and natural delighted Lewis's imagination,* which was oriented towards the premodern period—particularly the medieval and ancient world. For Lewis the characteristic feature of the modern world is the machine. It is perhaps significant that the modern imagination mingles the machine and humanity, rather than nature and humanity—a process Lewis prophetically explored through the growth of a sinister technocracy in *That Hideous Strength.**

Charity Agape, or gift-love. See: *THE FOUR LOVES.*

Charn In *The Magician's Nephew,** a dead world that is the domain of Jadis,* later known as the White Witch. Charn was once the city of the King of Kings, and wonder of all worlds. It was a gloomy world, dominated by a giant red dying sun. As far as the eye could see, ruins extended. A great river had once flowed through Charn, but now only a wide ditch of gray dust remained. In Charn Digory Kirke* awoke Jadis and all her evil by striking a forbidden bell. Through him she was drawn first into our world and then into Narnia.*

"Chartres" Lewis's name for Cherbourg School, Malvern, in his autobiography *Surprised by Joy.** He attended the school from January 1911 till 1913 after briefly attending Campbell College,* Belfast. The school moved to the town of Evesham in 1925, but the school building can still be found on Abbey Road, Malvern, now named Ellerslie.

Chervy the Stag In *The Horse and His Boy,** he informs Corin* of the Calormen* attack on Anvard.*

Chest The seat of balance in the mature human being, according to Lewis (drawing on ancient thought). The chest harmonized our cerebral and visceral aspects. For Lewis, modern people increasingly lack chests—a process he warned would eventually lead to the abolition of humanity (see: *THE ABOLITION OF MAN*). Lewis pictured the human soul, with its "north" and "south" regions of head and heart, in the Mappa Mundi* of his *The Pilgrim's Regress.**

Chesterton, Gilbert Keith (1874-1936) A celebrated convert to Christianity who influenced C. S. Lewis's thinking. "I liked him for his goodness," Lewis observed in *Surprised by Joy.** Chesterton wrote, like C. S. Lewis, in defense of Christian faith and fantasy. An essayist, critic, novelist, and poet, his best-known writings include *The Everlasting Man,** *Orthodoxy*, the Father Brown stories, *The Man Who Was Thursday*, *The Napoleon of Notting Hill*, and biographies of Robert Browning and others. Typical of his astuteness as a critic is his comment on George MacDonald* in his *The Victorian Age in Literature*: "a Scot of genius as genuine as Carlyle's; he could write fairy-tales that made all experience a fairy-tale. He could give the real sense that every one had the end of an elfin thread that must at last lead them into Paradise. It was a sort of optimist Calvinism."

Chesterton's *The Everlasting Man** was listed by Lewis as one of the ten most influential books that shaped his thinking and vocational attitude (see: READING OF C. S. LEWIS).

Chief Voice In *The Voyage of the "Dawn Treader"** the leader of the Dufflepuds,* who tells brave Lucy Pevensie* their history. All the other Dufflepuds repeat what he says with approval.

Chlamash In *The Horse and His Boy,** a Tarkaan or lord of Rabadash's.*

Christian Reflections (1967) Published after C. S. Lewis's death, this collection of essays represents the breadth of his popular theology. One essay, "Christianity and Literature,*" had previously appeared in *Rehabilitations and Other Essays.**

The contents are as follows:

"Christianity and Literature." An early attempt by C. S. Lewis to relate his faith to literature.

"Christianity and Culture." In this, the value or otherwise of culture is considered, against those who try to make culture into a religion. Lewis is considering high culture, not culture as distinct from nature, where culture includes all human formative activity, including society and politics, as well as the sciences and humanities. However, he affirms the value of all human employments when offered to God. "The work of a charwoman and the work of a poet become spiritual in the same way and on the same condition."

"Religion: Reality or Substitute?" Lewis considers the question of whether our faith is a substitute for some real well-being we have failed to achieve on earth.

"On Ethics." As in *The Abolition of Man,** C. S. Lewis argues for the objectivity of moral values. Mankind cannot create a new system of values, only obey or disobey values that all human beings acknowledge. "Those who urge us to adopt new moralities are only offering us the mutilated or expurgated text of a book which we already possess in the original manuscript." A so-called new morality would deprive us of our full humanity.

"*De Futilitate.*" Lewis examines the modern sense that life is futile and meaningless.

"The Poison of Subjectivism." Similar in theme to *The Abolition of Man.**

"The Funeral of a Great Myth." An attack on popular ideas of evolution and progress, as distinct from evolution as a biological theory of change.

"On Church Music." C. S. Lewis asks if church music has any particular religious relevance.

"Historicism."* A key essay on the belief that people can, by the use of their natural powers, discover an inner meaning and pattern in the historical process—a view Lewis repudiates.

"The Psalms." Contains ideas filled out in *Reflections on the Psalms,** including reflections on the theme of judgment.

"The Language of Religion." Religious language has been a central debate in philosophy of religion. C. S. Lewis's conclusion is that there is no specifically religious language. In the process, he rejects the notion that poetic language is merely an expression or a stimulant of emotion. Rather, he argues that it is a real medium of information, though with necessary limitations. Religious language is not a special language, but ranges between ordinary and poetic talk.

"Petitionary Prayer: A Problem Without an Answer." Prayer is a theme that constantly preoccupied C. S. Lewis, and he returns to it in *Letters to Malcolm: Chiefly on Prayer.**

"Modern Theology and Biblical Criticism." This is a paper Lewis read at a Cambridge theological college in 1959, giving his criticisms of modern, liberal theology.

"The Seeing Eye." In this magazine article, Lewis's thoughts were sparked by a Russian astronaut's report that he had not found God in outer space. This report revealed much about modern misconceptions of reality. "Looking for God—or Heaven—by exploring space," wrote C. S. Lewis, "is like reading or seeing all Shakespeare's plays in the hope that you will find Shakespeare as one of the characters or Stratford as one of the places. Shakespeare is in one sense present at every moment in every play."

"Christina Dreams" For Lewis and his friends in the early 1920s this was a shorthand for the idea that dreams of love can make a person incapable of true loving, dreams of heroism inculcate cowardice, etc. Lewis as a young atheist firmly supported the idea, and his friend Barfield, in the process of converting to anthroposophy,* did not, linking such dreams to the material of art (*Letters,* June 30, 1922). The age was saturated by the new psychology,* and such introspection as theirs was characteristic. Lewis explained, in his preface to the 1950 edition of *Dymer,** that he and his friends wrestled with the problem of wishful thinking or fantasy: "The 'Christina Dream,' as we called it, after Christina Pontifex in Butler's novel, was the hidden enemy whom we were all determined to unmask and defeat." The Samuel Butler novel referred to was *The Way of All Flesh* (1903), a brilliant satirical attack on religious smugness and its devastating impact on family life.

"Christianity and Literature" (1939) An essay that first appeared in *Rehabilitations and Other Essays,** it represents C. S. Lewis's early thinking on the subject. For his fully developed views on the place of literature in human life, see his book *An Experiment in Criticism** (1961).

C. S. Lewis begins his essay by pointing out that Christian literature as such has no literary qualities peculiar to itself—it depends on the basic qualities of structure, suspense, variety, diction, and the like. By these norms a work is good or poor literature. Furthermore, poor Christian writing—for example, a bad hymn—will consist to some degree in confused or erroneous thought and unworthy sentiment. It is not so much these structural norms about which he is concerned. Rather, he disagrees violently with the circle of ideas used in modern literary criticism. This conflict is more of attitudes than of clearly defined concepts. He asks what the key words of modern criticism are. They are words such as *creative* (as opposed to *derivative*), *spontaneity* (as opposed to *convention*), and *freedom* (as opposed to *rules*). Great authors are innovators, pioneers, explorers. Bad authors bunch in schools and follow models.

In contrast, while the New Testament says nothing explicitly about literature, it does reveal quite a different emphasis. For Lewis, this emphasis is tellingly suggested in the apostle Paul's passage about the woman being the glory of a man, as a man is the glory of God. The idea is that man is derived from God in Adam, and woman is derived from man in Eve. Man imitates God, and woman imitates man. There is a hierarchy here of imitation.

Lewis says that, in pointing out this theme of imitation, he is not building a theological system. As a layman, not a theologian, he has no intention of doing this. He does feel, however, that he can suggest that the stages of this hierarchy (Father over Son in the Trinity, angels over human beings, a husband over his wife) are connected by imitation, reflection, and assimilation. This is why we are commanded to imitate, or put on, Christ—that is, to model ourselves upon him. Thus, we are told in Galatians 4:19, Christ is to be formed or portrayed inside each believer. Furthermore, Christ on earth seemed to speak of copying or modeling himself upon what he sees the Father doing.

In the New Testament, the art of life is the art of imitation. The mentality this generates, Lewis argues, rules out the dominant values of modern criticism, such as originality. "'Originality,' in the New Testament," he writes, "is quite plainly the prerogative of God." Lewis points out: "Our whole destiny seems to lie in the opposite direction, in being as little as possible ourselves, in acquiring a fragrance that is not our own but borrowed, in becoming clear mirrors filled with the image of a face that is not ours . . . the highest good of a creature must be creaturely—that is, derivative or reflective—good." C. S. Lewis couches this idea of reflection or imitation in terms of a literary theory. "Applying this principle to literature, in its greatest generality, we should get as the basis of all critical theory the maxim that an author should never conceive himself as bringing into existence beauty or wisdom which did not exist before, but simply and solely as trying to embody in terms of his own art some reflection of eternal Beauty and Wisdom. . . . It would be opposed to the theory of genius as, perhaps, generally understood; and above all it would be opposed to the idea that literature is self-expression."

See also: LITERARY CRITIC, C. S. LEWIS AS A; MEANING; *THE PERSONAL HERESY.*

Christmas, Father In *The Lion, the Witch and the Wardrobe,** this familiar figure appears in Narnia* as the White Witch's* curse of perpetual winter begins to break with Aslan's reappearance. Her boast had been that it would be ever winter but never Christmas. Father Christmas is a portent of change. Also he gives magical presents to three of the four Pevensie* children who will become kings and queens of Narnia.

Chronicles of Narnia, The See: NARNIA, THE CHRONICLES OF.

Chronological snobbery C. S. Lewis believed that one of the strongest myths of our day is that of progress. Change is considered to have a value in itself. We are increasingly cut off from our past (and hence from a proper perspective on the strengths and weaknesses of our own age). He expressed this concern with the myth of progress in his inaugural lecture at Cambridge University, "*De Descriptione Temporum.*"* From his friend Owen Barfield he gained the concept he himself dubbed "chronological snobbery" to characterize this attitude. He explains this snobbery in *Surprised by Joy.**

> Barfield . . . made short work of what I have called my "chronological snobbery," the uncritical acceptance of the intellectual climate common to our age and the assumption that whatever has gone out of date is on that account discredited. You must find out why it went out of date; was it ever refuted (and if so by whom, where and how conclusively), or did it merely die away as fashions do? If the latter, this tells us nothing about its truth or falsehood. From seeing this, one passes to the realization that our age is also "a period," and certainly has, like all periods, its own characteristic illusions. They are likeliest to lurk in those wide-spread assumptions which are so ingrained in the age that no one dares to attack or feels it necessary to defend them.

Church, the As a child Lewis was baptized into the Anglican (Episcopal) communion, attending St. Mark's—belonging to the Church of Ireland—in Dundela, on the outskirts of Belfast. After a period as a confessing atheist, Lewis gradually returned to a faith in

Christ (as told in his autobiography, *Surprised by Joy**). He resumed worshiping in the Church of England until his death. Lewis was careful to avoid promoting any one denomination in his public writing, lecturing, and broadcasting, championing what Richard Baxter called "mere Christianity."* This led him to emphasize common ground or "great-tradition" Christian faith. As a result, all orthodox Christian groupings have benefited from his writings, most dramatically Evangelicalism, but also Roman Catholic and Eastern and Russian Orthodox believers.

In private the Anglican Lewis saw himself as not especially High nor especially Low Church. Features of his devotional life belonged to both High and Low. His close Roman Catholic friend J. R. R. Tolkien* noticed elements of his Northern Irish Protestant upbringing in his constitution, dubbing this his "Ulsterior motive." Lewis had affinities with Puritanism, in its richest sense, and also with a restrained High Church sacramentalism. He attended his local church regularly.

City Ruinous In *The Silver Chair*,* a ruined city close by Harfang* in the northern wastelands. The Green Witch's Underland* lay beneath it. According to the witch,* a king who once dwelt there had the following words inscribed on the ruins:

Though under Earth and throneless now I be,
Yet, while I lived, all Earth was under me.

See also: NARNIA, GEOGRAPHY.

Classical Honor Moderations As part of the four-year humanities course, the *Literae Humaniores*, or "Greats,"* taken by Lewis at Oxford,* he was required to undertake a public examination midway in his second year. This was the Classical Honor Moderations, or "Mods," an examination in Latin and Greek, involving translation, composition, key works such as those of Homer and Virgil, and special subjects.

Clipsie In *The Voyage of the "Dawn Treader"** the little daughter of the Chief Voice,* the leader of the Dufflepuds.* She spoke the spell that made the Dufflepuds invisible.

Clodsley Shovel In *Prince Caspian*,* a loyal Old Narnian mole met by Caspian.*

Cloudbirth In *The Silver Chair*,* a centaur and renowned healer who tends the burned foot of Puddleglum.*

Coalblack In *The Silver Chair*,* the horse of Prince Rilian.*

Coghill, Nevill (1899-1980) Nevill Coghill was Professor of English Literature at Oxford 1957-1966. After serving in the First World War, he read English at Exeter College, Oxford, and in 1924 was elected a fellow there. He was a friend of C. S. Lewis's from undergraduate days and like Lewis hailed from Ireland. His Christianity influenced Lewis as a young man. Coghill was admired for his theatrical productions and for his translation of Chaucer's *Canterbury Tales* into modern English couplets.

Colin In *The Horse and His Boy*,* he fights, together with his brother Cole, for King Lune* against the troublesome Calormenes.*

Collected Poems of C. S. Lewis , The (1994) A collection, compiled by Walter Hooper,* of *Spirits in Bondage** (1919), *Poems* (1964), and seventeen other short poems. Eleven previously unpublished poems appear in the collection. Most of the latter are reproduced from the Lewis Family Papers.* Included in the work is a previously unpublished introductory letter by Lewis that valuably sums up his attitude to his own poetry, particularly the isolation he felt as a poet. See: POETRY OF C. S. LEWIS.

***Consolation of Philosophy, The,* Boethius** Lewis listed this ancient work as one of ten books that particularly influenced his thinking and vocational attitude (see: READING OF C. S. LEWIS). Boethius wrote while in prison awaiting execution. Theodoric put him to death in 525. The *Consolation*'s objective is to prove from reason the existence of Providence. A woman appears to the prisoner and tells him she is his guardian, Philosophy, come to console him in his misfortunes and to point out their remedy. A dialogue follows, exploring the questions that have troubled humanity, such as the origin of evil, God's omniscience, and human free will. The "Consolations" are alternately in prose and verse—a method afterwards imitated by many authors (including Lewis in *The Pilgrim's Regress**). Most of the verses are suggested by passages in Seneca, considered at that time the greatest moral authority in the West outside of Christianity. The success of the work was enormous; it was soon translated into Greek, Hebrew, German, French, and Anglo-Saxon (the latter version by Alfred the Great); it became an important work of Anglo-Saxon prose. The *Consolation* was one of the most important works in the medieval world. Its Christian author explored how far the virtuous pagan mind could reach without special revelation in the form of Christianity. The book displays an enormous respect for philosophy.

The *Consolation*, described as "the last work of Roman literature," is made up of five books. In the first, the vision of Boethius the philosopher is recounted. A woman appears before him, in one hand holding a book and in the other a scepter. She offers him the promise of consolation. He recognizes her as his lifelong companion, Philosophy. As he pours out his woeful tale, she listens with sympathy. In Book II Philosophy chides the prisoner for the folly of his ambition to be a great statesman and philosopher, pointing out that such greatness has no enduring value. Book III discusses the Supreme Good. It concludes that such Good consists neither of riches, nor power, nor pleasure; rather, it resides in God. In Book IV the problems of evil and human freedom are considered. The subject of the freedom of the will is taken further in the final book, showing its reconciliation with Providence.

Context, Lewis in The subject of Lewis's context is a complex one. Key elements come out if we focus upon Lewis's formative years, roughly the 1920s and 1930s. His work is illuminated by his biographical context and by the intellectual currents surrounding his scholarship. Lewis's uniqueness might easily suggest that he concocted his ideas with a minimum of help from others. In fact, he benefited from several key contemporaries such as Owen Barfield,* from the wider scholarly community, and from long, searching hours spent in Oxford's Bodleian Library (see: READING OF C. S. LEWIS). What emerges from Lewis's bookish background is a richness of thought, imagination, and writing that has influenced literary criticism (see: LITERARY CRITIC, C. S. LEWIS AS A), science fiction, children's literature, literary approaches to the Bible, and Christian apologetics throughout the West.

In the 1920s, particularly in Lewis's Oxford, idealism* predominated in philosophy, with realists counterattacking. As an atheist at that time, Lewis was at first staunchly opposed to idealism. He was an out-and-out realist and naturalist (see: NATURALISM AND SUPERNATURALISM). Naturalism permeates his early poetry, *Spirits in Bondage** (1919) and *Dymer** (1926).

Lewis taught philosophy for the year 1924 to 1925 in University College, before getting his teaching post at Magdalen College in English Literature. It was not only in philosophy that Oxford in the twenties had an affinity with the nineteenth century. It was also, on the language and literature side, still gripped by the paradigm of philology, with its historical emphasis and zest for source hunting. The philologist at his best was embodied in J. R. R. Tolkien,* who left Leeds University in 1925 to take the Chair of Anglo-Saxon at Oxford. Lewis and he met in 1926 and soon became fast friends. It was this friendship, and Lewis's friendship with Hugo Dyson and Owen Barfield, that was the basis of the Inklings.* Lewis took on many of Tolkien's concerns, such as the serious writing of fantasy, and shared his passionate love of language, evidenced in his *Studies in Words** (1960). At one time Lewis and Tolkien planned to collaborate on a book on language. Lewis affectionately was to fictionalize his philologist friend in the figure of Elwin ("Elf-friend") Ransom in *Out of the Silent Planet** (1938).

Perhaps the most radical intellectual current crossing the twenties was what Lewis and his colleagues tended to dub "the new psychology," stemming particularly from the insights of Sigmund Freud (satirized as Sigismund Enlightenment in Lewis's *The Pilgrim's Regress** [1933]). This trend had a devastating impact that exists in various forms to this day. Lewis's narrative poem *Dymer* was published in 1926. In his preface to the 1950 edition, explaining the context of its writing, he comments: "In those days the new psychology was just beginning to make itself felt in the circles I most frequented at Oxford. This joined forces with the fact that we felt ourselves (as young men always do) to be escaping from the illusions of adolescence, and as a result we were much exercised about the problem of fantasy or wishful thinking." (See: "CHRISTINA DREAMS"). A new literary criticism, stemming from Cambridge and associated with I. A. Richards, was underpinned by a psychological approach.

The "new psychology" created a distrust of the Romanticism that had so marked the nineteenth century, reinforced by bitter memories of the First World War. Lewis was, as he says, affected by this distrust, forcing him to rethink the whole basis of Romanticism and literary fantasy, a process that eventually led to his move from atheism, via a modified idealism, to theistic belief in 1929 and to his conversion to Christ in 1931.

In the preface to *The Allegory of Love** references are made to three members of the Inklings—Tolkien, Hugo Dyson,* and Owen Barfield (to whom the book is dedicated and to whom Lewis acknowledges the greatest debt, after his father):

> There seems to be hardly anyone among my acquaintances from whom I have not learned. The greatest of these debts—that which I owe to my father for the inestimable benefit of a childhood passed mostly alone in a house full of books—is now beyond repayment; and among the rest I can only select. . . . Above all, the friend to whom I have dedicated the book, has taught me not to patronise the past, and has trained me to see the present as itself a "period." I desire for myself no higher function than to be one of the instruments whereby his theory and practice in such matters may become more widely effective.

Lewis pays tribute to Barfield particularly for demolishing what he calls elsewhere his "chronological snobbery."* As undergraduates, Lewis and Barfield had often walked together or asked each other to lunch, but they did not really see a lot of each other until after graduation, when their "great war"* began.

Lewis's other friends who shaped his thinking and approach to literature in this period were Dyson and Tolkien, particularly in the thirties and forties. Tolkien was of colossal importance to Lewis. Indeed, their friendship is comparable to that between Wordsworth and Coleridge. In the formative years of the twenties, however, Barfield's influence was much greater. Dyson was a friend from undergraduate days who played a key role in helping Tolkien to persuade Lewis of the truth of Christian belief. Tolkien's influence increased in the thirties as Barfield's declined.

The first important area of Tolkien's influence on Lewis was his decision to accept Christianity. When they first met, Lewis was not a

Christian and previously had been a naturalist (as recorded in *Surprised**). Tolkien's Christian faith is a complex matter, and Lewis inherited some of its cast. Essential to Tolkien's Christianity is his view of the relation of myth* and fact, and how myth became fact.* The view can be seen as a theology of romance.*

Related to Tolkien's view of myth-become-fact is his distinctive doctrine of subcreation,* the view that the highest function of art is the creation of convincing secondary or other worlds. Without the impact of Tolkien's view of subcreation, I do not think we would have had Malacandra,* Perelandra,* or Glome,* particularly Perelandra, one of Lewis's most successful creations. Along with their mutual friend Owen Barfield, Tolkien was responsible for helping along the process that led Lewis to become aware of a dramatic shift from the Old to the Modernist West (see: OLD WEST), a shift that made the change from medieval to Renaissance culture insignificant by comparison. Tolkien was responsible for pointing out to Lewis that the values of pre-Christian paganism* were not merely of aesthetic interest, but were life and death matters reflecting an objective state of affairs.

In the later 1920s, Tolkien began sharing his early versions of *The Silmarillion.* Tolkien's tales in their own manner embody antimodernist themes as powerfully as any stories written by Lewis, disclosing his Old Western values. Antimodernism can be seen clearly, for instance, in Tolkien's treatment of the related themes of possession and power, themes central to his work.

In the young scholar's mental geography, Barfield's *Poetic Diction** had a vital place. Lewis's own work on *The Allegory of Love** over many years is of equal importance. This work expresses his characteristic interest in the Christianization of paganism* (in this case, romantic love), an interest deeply shared by Tolkien.

The thirties and forties saw a minor renaissance in Christian literature, a movement not reflected in theology, which then was in the grip of modernist liberal theologians. Lewis's own popular theological writings were against the stream of this liberalism, but as a writer of literary criticism and Christian fiction, he was part of a wider countermovement. He was not as isolated and disconnected with contemporary culture as he thought. Even then, modernism was not everything.

This point is summed up admirably by Lewis's former pupil, the literary historian Harry Blamires*:

> Lewis began writing just at the point when this minor Christian renaissance in literature was taking off. His *Pilgrim's Regress* came out in 1933. And the 1930s were a remarkable decade in this respect. Eliot's *Ash Wednesday* came out in 1930, *The Rock* in 1934, *Murder in the Cathedral* in 1935 and *Burnt Norton* in 1936. Charles Williams's *War in Heaven* was published in 1930, *The Place of the Lion* in 1931, *The Greater Trumps* in 1932, and his play *Thomas Cranmer of Canterbury* in 1936. Helen Waddell's *Peter Abelard* came out in 1933. Meanwhile

> on the stage James Bridie had great popular successes with his biblical plays *Tobias and the Angel* (1930) and *Jonah and the Whale* (1932). Then by 1937 Christopher Fry was launched with *The Boy with a Cart*. That same year saw Dorothy Sayers's *The Zeal of Thy House* performed, and David Jones's *In Parenthesis* and Tolkien's *The Hobbit* published. Lewis's *Out of the Silent Planet* followed in 1938, along with Williams's *Taliessin Through Logres* and Greene's *Brighton Rock*. Eliot's *Family Reunion* followed in 1939, Greene's *The Power and The Glory* in 1940. During the same decade Evelyn Waugh was getting known and Rose Macauley was in spate. Edwin Muir, Andrew Young and Francis Berry appeared in print.
>
> So when the literary historian looks back at the English literary scene in the 1930s and 1940s he is going to see C. S. Lewis and Charles Williams, not as freakish throwbacks, but as initial contributors to what I have called a Christian literary renaissance, if a minor one.

Lewis's uniqueness and particularity is not easy to capture. It is easier to show him as a child of his times—an upper-middle-class Ulsterman, reluctant product of the British public school system, and a brilliant scholar of the type best nurtured by a traditional university setting such as Oxford, which encouraged cross-disciplinary exploration. There are contemporaries similar to him, like Barfield and Tolkien, and many other Christian writers that belong to Blamires's "minor Christian literary renaissance." However, like Tolkien and Barfield, his great friends and mentors, he is remarkably relevant to the context that confronts us at the cusp of the millennium. The increasing shift to postmodernism has created a greater sympathy for the unique antimodernism of Lewis and his closer mentors.

FURTHER READING

Harry Blamires, "Against the Stream: C. S. Lewis and the Literary Scene," *Journal of the Irish Christian Study Centre*, Vol. 1, 1983, 15. Further insight into the presence of Christian belief in Oxford circles in particular at this period is given in "Is there an Oxford 'School' of Writing?: A discussion between Rachel Trickett and David Cecil," *The Twentieth Century*, June 1955, 559-570.

Doris T. Myers, *C. S. Lewis in Context* (1994).

Cor A twin son of King Lune* of Archenland, who was lost in Calormene,* to the south, for many years. There he had the name Shasta. The famous Narnian tale of how he returned to Archenland, learned his true identity, and gained his Calormene wife, Aravis,* is retold in *The Horse and His Boy.** To them was born Ram the Great, the most notable of all the kings of Archenland. Cor's identical twin was named Corin.*

Coriakin In *The Voyage of the "Dawn Treader"** a magician who, like Ramandu,* is a retired star of the sky. As a punishment, Aslan* gave him the task of governing the Dufflepuds.*

Corin In *The Horse and His Boy,** the younger twin brother of Cor.* He would have been heir to the Archenland* throne had Cor not been restored, but Corin was quite content not to become king. He was nicknamed "Thunder-fist" because he was a great boxer.

Cornelius, Doctor In *Prince Caspian,** a half-dwarf who is the tutor of Caspian,* later King Caspian X. He is loyal to the "Old Narnia" and teaches the young prince the true history of Narnia.*

Correspondence See: LETTERS OF C. S. LEWIS.

Cosmic war In a letter written on May 8, 1939, Lewis observed: "My memories of the last war haunted my dreams for years." War for him was an image of a permanent cosmic war between good and evil. In "Learning in Wartime"* he commented: "War creates no absolutely new situation; it simply aggravates the permanent human situation so that we can no longer ignore it."

It is not surprising that this perpetual cosmic war features prominently in Lewis's writings, particularly in his first theological fantasy, *The Pilgrim's Regress.** Significantly John Bunyan's *The Pilgrim's Progress* and *The Holy War* influenced this work. These allegories reflect a similar belief in the great battle for a person's soul.

The central figure in *The Pilgrim's Regress* is John, loosely based on C. S. Lewis himself. As in *The Pilgrim's Progress*, the quest can be mapped. Indeed, Lewis provides his reader with a Mappa Mundi,* in which the human soul is divided into north and south, the north representing arid intellectualism and the south emotional excess. A straight road passes between them. The story powerfully illuminates the intellectual climate of the 1920s and early 1930s, and its geography of thought applies much more widely.

On the Mappa Mundi provided by Lewis, it is significant that there are military railways to both the north and south. He observes in his preface to the third edition that "the two military railways were meant to symbolize the double attack from Hell on the two sides of our nature. It was hoped that the roads spreading out from each of the enemy railheads would look like claws or tentacles reaching out into the country of Man's Soul."

Lewis's map of the human soul anticipates his reflections in *The Abolition of Man,** given fictional form in *That Hideous Strength,** in which he points out the danger of "men without chests" (see: CHEST). He comments in the preface that "we were made to be neither cerebral men nor visceral men, but Men. Not beasts nor angels but Men—things at once rational, and animal."

Relevant to Lewis's theme of cosmic war is a phenomenon pointed out by Professor Tom Shippey, author of *The Road to Middle-earth*. He showed links between several apparently disparate writers just after the Second World War. The writers were linked in struggling with the appalling reality of evil in the modern world, a theme that forced them to create new forms and abandon the received canons of what constitutes a proper novel and fiction. The writers and their books, as highlighted by Shippey, are William Golding's *The Lord of the Flies* (1954), Tolkien's *The Lord of the Rings* (1954-1955), Lewis's *That Hideous Strength* (the final part of his science-fiction trilogy), George Orwell's *Animal Farm* (1945) and *1984* (1949), and T. H. White's *The Once and Future King* (published 1958 but written long before).

FURTHER READING

T. A. Shippey, "Tolkien as a Post-War Writer," in *Scholarship and Fantasy: Proceedings of The Tolkien Phenomenon* (Turku, Finland: University of Turku, 1993).

Cowley Fathers A religious community in the Church of England founded in 1866. The Fathers met in their Mission House next to the Church of St. John the Baptist, in the Oxford* suburb of Cowley, to the south of the city. Lewis, as part of his private devotions, made regular confessions to one of the Fathers, Walter Adams, between 1940 and 1952, when Adams died.

Cruelsland A northern region depicted on the Mappa Mundi* in *The Pilgrim's Regress.**

Cullen, Mary Cook-housekeeper at the Lewises' Belfast home, Little Lea, between 1917-1930. She was affectionately nicknamed by the Lewis brothers "The Witch of Endor."

Cupid and Psyche See: *THE GOLDEN ASS;* PSYCHE; *TILL WE HAVE FACES.*

Cure Hardy In *That Hideous Strength,** a picturesque village with sixteenth-century almshouses and a Norman church. The steam train on the branch line from Edgestow* passed through here on its way to the terminus at St. Anne's.* Its existence was jeopardized by a N.I.C.E.* plan to divert the Wynd River into a reservoir in the narrow valley in which the village lay. The idea was to supply water to Edgestow when it was expanded into a major center of population. The plan was another example of the Institute's disregard for "outdated" values such as beauty.

D

Daaran In *Till We Have Faces,** a nephew of Queen Orual* of Glome.* He is a prince of Phars.*

Dancing Lawn In *Prince Caspian,** the setting of the Great Council of Caspian* and his Narnian friends.

Dark Island In *The Voyage of the "Dawn Treader"** an island that appeared to the voyagers as a dark spot in the ocean. Here dreams come true.

Dark Tower and Other Stories, The (1977) A collection of two unfinished narratives and three short stories, two of which appeared in *The Magazine of Fantasy and Science Fiction.* One fragment, "The Dark Tower," seems to have been written after *Out of the Silent Planet** and before *Perelandra,** and is about time rather than space travel. It owes much to David Lindsay's* *A Voyage to Arcturus.* Lewis abandoned it as unsatisfactory. Some have doubted the genuineness of the bulk of the text, a view I do not share. The other fragment, "After Ten Years," was unfinished because of illness and age and also perhaps his grief over the death of Joy Davidman* Lewis. This fragment is a historical fiction that shows the promise of his great novel *Till We Have Faces.**

Davidman, Joy See LEWIS, HELEN JOY DAVIDMAN.

Dawn Treader In *The Voyage of the "Dawn Treader"** the galleon in which the children, Eustace Scrubb* and Jill Pole,* sail almost to Aslan's Country* at the World's End. Shaped like a dragon, the vessel had green sides and a purple sail. Pauline Baynes* provided a useful cutaway illustration of the ship for the book.

Deathwater Island In *The Voyage of the "Dawn Treader"** this island, not more than twenty acres in size, lay to the east of Burnt Island.* The voyagers discovered that it was rocky and rugged with a tall central peak. Its only flora was perfumed heather and coarse grass. Only seagulls appeared to live there.

Two streams were found, one of which flowed from a small mountain lake guarded by cliffs. To the horror of the visitors, anything dipped into the lake turned to solid gold. This explained the naked gold statue lying in its waters. It was the transformed body of one of the missing seven lords,* Restimar. As a result of this grisly discovery, Reepicheep* gave the island its name. See also: NARNIA, GEOGRAPHY.

Demons See: ANGELS; *THE SCREWTAPE LETTERS.*

"*De Descriptione Temporum*" (1954) This was C. S. Lewis's inaugural lecture as Professor in the newly formed Chair of Medieval and Renaissance English Literature at the University of Cambridge. Delivered November 19, 1954, the lecture reveals his sympathies with an earlier age, even though he was ever concerned to communicate as a writer to a modern reader. He recognized that his assumptions and ideas were distasteful to many modern people. Lewis argued that he was in fact a relic of Old Western Man, a museum piece, if you like; that even if one disagreed with his ideas, one must take account of them as being from a rare (and therefore valuable) specimen of an older world.

Lewis's "*De Descriptione Temporum*," which has some striking parallels with Francis Schaeffer's book *Escape from Reason* (1968), argues that the greatest change in the history of the West took place around the beginning of the nineteenth century, and ushered in a characteristically modern mentality. Christians and ancient pagans have more in common with each other than either has with the modern world. The change can be observed in the areas of politics, the arts, religion, and the invention of the machines. The machine had in fact been absorbed into the inner life of modern people as an archetype. Just as older machines are replaced by new and better ones, so too (believes the modern) are ideas, beliefs, and values replaced when outdated. This notion that newer is better, the myth of progress, owes much to the "the myth of universal evolutionism," which predated Darwin.

The theme of this lecture complements his book *The Abolition of Man*,* and like that book is illustrated by his science-fiction story *That Hideous Strength*.* See: OLD WEST.

***Descent into Hell*, Charles Williams** (1937) Writing to his friend Charles Williams on September 9, 1937, Lewis remarks that *Descent into Hell* is "a thundering good book and a real purgation to read." Williams's publisher T. S. Eliot wrote on the dust jacket of the Faber Standard Edition of the novel (words he took from a BBC broadcast):

> [Williams] had a kind of extended spiritual sense: he was like a man who can perceive shades of color, or hear tones, beyond the ordinary range. The theme of all his novels is the struggle between good and evil; and as an interpreter of the mystical experience he was unique in his generation. He excels in descriptions of strange experiences such as many people have had once or twice in their lives and have been unable to put into words. There are pages also which describe, with a fright-

ful clarity, the deterioration and damnation of a human soul; and pages which describe the triumphant struggle towards salvation.

Lewis included his friend's novel among a list of the top ten books that influenced his thinking and vocational attitude (see: READING OF C. S. LEWIS). This book explores Williams's characteristic themes of exchange and substitution, themes worked out in the parallel stories of one individual's salvation (Pauline Anstruther's) and another's damnation (the historian Lawrence Wentworth's). Lewis identified with the particular temptations that afflict the academic. Williams's novels, poetry, and personality had an enormous impact upon Lewis's thinking and writing (on, for instance, *A Preface to Paradise Lost,** *That Hideous Strength,** and *Till We Have Faces**). Williams's preoccupation with the theological implications of love also, no doubt, partly influenced the choice of subject and writing of *The Four Loves,** an interest Lewis had shown pre-Williams in *The Allegory of Love.**

Denniston, Arthur and Camilla In *That Hideous Strength*,* a young Christian couple who join the company of Elwin Ransom* at St. Anne's. They provide an important contrast with the marriage of Mark and Jane Studdock.* Arthur is a brilliant sociologist and fellow of Northumberland College at the University of Edgestow.* According to one of the "progressive element" at Bracton College,* he "seems to have gone quite off the rails . . . with his Distributivism and what not." He was the chief rival for Mark Studdock's job when he had applied to Bracton several years earlier—but wasn't the "right sort of man" for the progressive element. Mark and he had originally been friends as undergraduates but had grown apart because of Mark's desire for success and the lure for him of the "inner ring."* Like Lewis, Arthur and Camilla liked weather of all descriptions. Jane was surprised to discover this when she was invited on a picnic with them on a foggy autumn day. Arthur explained: "That's why Camilla and I got married. . . . We both like Weather. It's a useful taste if one lives in England."

Desire (the dialectic of desire) See: JOY.

Destrier In *Prince Caspian*,* the horse of Caspian.*

Determinism See: NATURALISM AND SUPERNATURALISM.

Devil, devils See: ANGELS; *THE SCREWTAPE LETTERS.*

Devine, Dick (Lord Feverstone) In *Out of the Silent Planet** Professor Weston's* fellow conspirator in a plan to kidnap a human sacrifice for the rulers of Malacandra.* The two lived at The Rise, a country house near Sterk,* where a rocket ship had been built in Weston's laboratory. By coincidence, Devine had been at school at Wedenshaw with Ransom,* his victim (where Ransom had disliked him as much as anyone he could remember, a dislike that was mutual). Devine was also at Cambridge at the same time as Ransom. Ransom had been puzzled at the appointment of this flashy and overconfident man to a fellowship at Leicester College, Cambridge, and further puzzled by his ever-increasing wealth.

Devine eventually became "something in the city" and later an M.P. He funded Weston's experiments in space travel and had plans for an ocean-going yacht, expensive women, and a big place on the Riviera with ill-gotten wealth from Malacandra's mineral resources. Behind his wasted life were genuine abilities, revealed when he saved the spacecraft returning from Mars by his persistence at the controls during its perilous flight.

More emerges about him when he reappears in *That Hideous Strength** after the war as Lord Feverstone, M.P., now a fellow of Bracton College* and deeply implicated in the evil plots of the N.I.C.E.* Though apparently likeable with his infectious laugh, his ruthlessness is revealed in his verbally brutal treatment of elderly Canon Jewel in the committee meeting that determined the fate of ancient Bragdon Wood.* Politically, he was totalitarian to the heart, taking, he said, Clausewitz's view that total war is most humane in the long run (redefining *humane* in the process). He graphically represents Lewis's theme of the abolition of mankind and human values. To Jane Studdock* he was "that man with the loud, unnatural laugh and a mouth like a shark, and no manners." There was something shifty about him. Mark Studdock* noticed that he never looked a person in the face.

As the stranglehold of the N.I.C.E. tightened, Devine was appointed Emergency Governor at Edgestow.* He enjoyed the spectacle of the massacre at the great banquet at Belbury.* After slipping away to Edgestow, he was fittingly engulfed in its destruction.

Dialectica A region charted in the Mappa Mundi* in *The Pilgrim's Regress.**

Diaries Both Lewis and his brother, Major Warren ("Warnie") Lewis,* kept diaries, though the latter did much more, penning over a million words filling twenty-three journals (see: *BROTHERS AND FRIENDS*). Lewis himself appears to have kept a significant diary only between 1922-1927 (see: *ALL MY ROAD BEFORE ME*). A significant record of Lewis's early domestic life appears in the unpublished Lewis Family Papers.*

Dick A spirit, one of the solid heavenly inhabitants in *The Great Divorce.** The narrator (Lewis) overhears a conversation between Dick and a wraith of a bishop who was visiting the hinterlands of heaven. Dick had been a clergyman on earth. Ironically the bishop chides him for entertaining the "narrow-minded" belief in a literal heaven and hell toward the end of his life. When Dick replies, "Wasn't I right?" .the bishop is shocked.

Digory Kirke See: KIRKE, DIGORY.

Dimble, Dr. Cecil In *That Hideous Strength,** a fellow in literature of Northumberland College in the University of Edgestow.* He was a Christian who, like C. S. Lewis, didn't suffer fools gladly. An elderly man, he had lived in Edgestow for twenty-five years and was a close friend of Elwin Ransom.* He had been Jane Studdock's* tutor during her last years as an undergraduate. In his house there was a constant danger of the conversation taking a literary turn, in which King Arthur* and the Matter of Britain might come up, as Dimble had a deep knowledge of Arthurian legend. He was prone to speculate aloud, letting his thoughts take him wherever their logic led. Cecil Dimble was scrupulously polite, even with those he disliked, such as Mark Studdock.* Even then, his conscience had troubled him for years about his lack of charity toward Jane's husband. He suffered from a habitual self-distrust.

When the N.I.C.E.* requisitioned their cottage, the Dimbles joined Ransom's community at The Manor at St. Anne's. His shrewd mind was a great help to Ransom in interpreting the enemy's moves, and he was also practical, able to search for Merlin* despite knowing better than almost anyone the dangers involved. His fluent knowledge of Old Solar,* the Great Tongue, was especially valuable in communicating with the magician. According to N.I.C.E. intelligence, Dimble posed no threat—they saw him as purely academic in a worthless discipline, and impractical, unknown to anyone except a few scholars in his own subject, a nonentity. In this respect Cecil Dimble parallels the humble hobbit Frodo Baggins in J. R. R. Tolkien's* *The Lord of the Rings*, confounding the wisdom of wicked powers by having a strategic role in the battle of good against evil.

Dimble, "Mother" Margaret ("Margery") In *That Hideous Strength,** the wife of Cecil Dimble,* a humorous, easy-natured, and childless woman who mothered generations of women students. She was able to like her husband's pupils of both sexes in the University of Edgestow.* Their homely house consequently "was a kind of noisy salon all the term." Lewis draws her character with affection—an archetypal mother-figure, gray-haired and double-chinned, with affinities with the young Green Lady* of Perelandra,* essentially "grave, formidable, and august . . . a kind of priestess or sibyl." She helped Jane Studdock* and introduced her to the community at St. Anne's.

Discarded Image: An Introduction to Medieval and Renaissance Literature, The (1964) C. S. Lewis's study of medieval allegory suggested to him the writing of an allegory himself, *The Pilgrim's Regress.**

This study also resulted in his writing *The Allegory of Love** and led him to think hard and deeply about the truth status of the main medieval picture of reality. He considered the position of various world models in our thinking about truth, knowledge, and reality.

The Discarded Image arose out of a series of lectures Lewis gave many years earlier on the medieval world image that provided a background to literature up to the seventeenth century. The lectures did the same sort of thing that Basil Willey's books did for the background to seventeenth- to nineteenth-century literature.

C. S. Lewis came to the conclusion that a world model is not meant to represent reality literally (though obviously people have identified such models with reality). If it did represent reality, some element from the real world could be substituted for the model; the model did not really matter. (In a parallel way, in imaginative literature, nothing can be substituted for a good image or allegory—the image is, in some sense, necessary for there to be meaning.*) Like John Milton before him, C. S. Lewis saw that if the medieval world model did not literally portray reality, if it was fictional, then it could still be used imaginatively. Milton employed it in his *Paradise Lost*, even though he was well aware of the scientific revolution in thought created by Galileo and Copernicus. In the twentieth century, Lewis employed the medieval world model in his science-fiction trilogy and The Chronicles of Narnia.* Lewis helps his readers (of all ages) to feel the imaginative power of this model. It has an integrated picture of the heavens, the earth, and mankind itself, with the human being as a miniature world, a microcosmos.

C. S. Lewis concludes *The Discarded Image* by hoping that no one thinks that he is recommending a return to the medieval model. He has only sought a proper regard of world models, respecting each and making an idol of none. Each age inevitably has its own "taste in universes." Thinking of chronological snobbery,* Lewis added: "We can no longer dismiss the change in Models as a simple progress from error to truth. No Model is a catalogue of ultimate realities, and none is a mere fantasy. Each is a serious attempt to get in all the phenomena known at a given period, and each succeeds in getting in a great many. But also, no less surely, each reflects the prevalent psychology of an age almost as much as it reflects the state of that age's knowledge."

Our world model will eventually change, like others before it. Lewis suggested that the shift was more likely to come from a change in the mental temper of a future age than from some dramatic discovery about the physical universe. This change in mentality will shape questions asked of nature,* and thus influence what is considered evidence in support of a world model. Lewis points out:

> The new Model will not be set up without evidence, but the evidence will turn up when the inner need for it becomes sufficiently great. It

> will be true evidence. But nature gives most of her evidence in answer to the questions we ask her. Here, as in the courts, the character of the evidence depends on the shape of the examination, and a good cross-examiner can do wonders. He will not indeed elicit falsehoods from an honest witness. But, in relation to the total truth in the witness's mind, the structure of the examination is like a stencil. It determines how much of that total truth will appear and what pattern it will suggest.

See also: LITERARY CRITIC, C. S. LEWIS AS A; IMAGINATION.

Divine love See: *THE FOUR LOVES.*

Doorn In *The Voyage of the "Dawn Treader"** the chief among the Lone Islands, a group of islands some 400 leagues to the east of Narnia.* These islands had been under Narnian rule since the tenth King of Narnia, Gale, freed the islanders from a dragon.* The town of Narrowhaven is Doorn's major settlement. Caspian* and the other voyagers were displeased to discover Narrowhaven to be a center of a slave trade to Calormen.* After skillfully deposing the governor, despite inferior forces, Caspian gave Lord Bern* the post.

Dragon In *The Voyage of the "Dawn Treader"** an old and dying dragon is discovered by Eustace Scrubb* on Dragon Island.* (The dragon later turns out to be one of the lost Narnian lords—Octesian*—for whom the party of voyagers is searching. He has been transformed into this hideous shape.) Upon the dragon's death, the unpleasant Eustace himself becomes a dragon, and only Aslan* is able to restore him to his boy nature.

Dragon Island Discovered and named by Caspian* of Narnia* in *The Voyage of the "Dawn Treader,"** it lies to the east of the Lone Islands.* The island is named after a sad dragon* who lived there, who was the transformed shape of the missing Narnian lord, Octesian.* The mountainous island had deep bays rather like Norwegian fjords, ending in steep valleys that often had waterfalls. Cedars and other trees covered what little level land existed. Besides the ill-fated dragon, a few wild goats lived there. See also: NARNIA, GEOGRAPHY.

Drinian In *The Voyage of the "Dawn Treader"** Caspian's* loyal captain of the ship. Later in *The Silver Chair*, he is a part of Caspian's Court and a friend of the young Prince Rilian.*

Dufflepuds Encountered on the Island of Voices* in *The Voyage of the "Dawn Treader,"** these monopods (one-footed creatures) had been made invisible by a spell. Lucy Pevensie* is persuaded to find the spell in the magician's book to make them visible again. They have a humorous way of talking about the obvious. The name is a contraction of their original title, "duffers," and the new name of "monopods" given them by the voyagers.

Dumnus In *Prince Caspian,** a faun.

Dwarf, The A wraith on a trip from the Gray Town to the outskirts of heaven* in *The Great Divorce.** Back on earth he had been Frank, husband of Sarah Smith* from Golder's Green. The Dwarf is accompanied by a tall ghost, the "Tragedian," representing the theatrical, posing side of Frank. Sarah fails to persuade The Dwarf to enter heaven, and all that remains is the tall, unreal ghost.

Dying God See: BALDER.

Dymer (1926; new edition, 1950) An antitotalitarian poem that has some similarities with *Spirits in Bondage.** Written while Lewis was still an unbeliever in Christianity, the poem is included in *Narrative Poems.** The hero, Dymer, escapes from a perfect but inhuman city into the soothing countryside. Various adventures overtake him. In contrast to Dymer's idealism, a revolutionary group rebel against the Perfect City in anarchy, claiming Dymer's name. Fresh in Lewis's mind when he wrote were the bloody events of the Russian Revolution and of his native Ulster. He regarded popular political causes as "daemonic."

D

In *Dymer* the young C. S. Lewis attacks Christianity bitterly, regarding it as a tempting illusion that must be overcome and destroyed in one's life. Christianity is lumped together with all forms of supernaturalism, including spiritism.

Old Theomagia, Demonology,
Cabbala, Chemic Magic, Book of the Dead,
Damning Hermetic rolls that none may see
Save the already damned—such grubs are bred
From minds that lose the Spirit and seek instead
For spirits in the dust of dead men's error,
Buying the joys of dream with dreamland terror.

By the time Lewis wrote *Dymer*, he had rejected atheism and naturalism* in favor of idealism,* hence the reference to losing "the Spirit."

Dyson, H. V. D. "Hugo" (1896-1975) A member of the Inklings,* Dyson was seriously wounded at Passchendaele before reading English at Exeter College, Oxford.* He was scarred both physically and mentally by war, as Lewis observed: "a burly man, both in mind and body, with the stamp of war on him" (letter to WHL, November 22, 1931). As an undergraduate, Dyson heard Tolkien* read "The Fall of Gondolin" (part of *The Silmarillion*) to the Essay Club at Exeter College. On a night in 1931, he helped Tolkien to persuade Lewis of the truth of Christianity. He initially lectured in English at Reading University, near enough to Oxford to keep in touch with fellow Inklings.* There he pioneered a Combined Humanities course in

1930. He also encouraged the development of a School of Fine Arts, and was considered a distinctive and outstanding lecturer. Like Charles Williams,* he gave lectures to the Workers' Educational Association. He poured more of himself into teaching than into his writing—he was involved in very few publications. He was, in 1945, elected Fellow and Tutor in English Literature at Merton College. He retired in 1963.

Dyson was cool toward Tolkien's constant reading of *The Lord of the Rings* to the Inklings. He appears in fictional form as Arry Loudham in Tolkien's unfinished "The Notion Club Papers." Dyson's theatrical nature contributed an important dimension to the Inklings, and he was very important to Lewis in providing emotional support. He was featured as an aging writer in John Schlesinger's film *Darling*, starring Julie Christie and Dirk Bogarde. He also gave several lectures for BBC television on Shakespeare.

E

Eagle and Child, The Familiarly known as The Bird and Baby, this central Oxford Public House was frequented by the Inklings* on Tuesdays, and later Mondays, over many years. The pub still exists, adorned with Inklings memorabilia. Although the Inklings also visited other pubs in central Oxford, this one has entered Oxford folklore and is a necessary venue for all on the C. S. Lewis trail. In Edmund Crispin's crime novel, *Swan Song* (1947) his detective-professor observes, "There goes C. S. Lewis; it must be Tuesday." Inspector Morse, in Colin Dextor's thrillers, frequently visits The Eagle and Child.

Earthmen In *The Silver Chair*,* gnome creatures who live in the Green Witch's* realm of Underworld—called by them the Shallow Lands.* They originally came from Bism,* deep below the earth's surface. At the time of their slavery to the Witch, they all looked sad. Physically, they differed greatly from each other—some had horns on their foreheads, tails, round faces, long, pointed or trunk-like or blobbed noses, or beards.

"Easley Fragment" This is a fragment, around 5,000 words, of what has been dubbed Lewis's "Ulster novel," never completed. Warren Lewis included it in the Lewis Family Papers.* The central character is a young medical doctor, Easley, facing illusion and reality. Apparently poor relatives in Belfast have misused him and his widowed mother. On the ferry crossing to Belfast he learns from a cheating businessman that the relatives are in fact people of substance, living among "the most substantial people." Later Easley argues in Belfast with the perverted Rev. Bonner about evil and hell. The plot is likely to have been inspired by Lewis's distressing experiences with Dr. John Askins,* who was subject to ravings and delusions as his death approached.

Eastern Mountains In *The Pilgrim's Regress** John (the pilgrim) is born on the western edge of the Eastern Mountains in Puritania.* His visions of an island lead him across the world depicted in the Mappa Mundi.* When John at last finds the island of his vision, he discovers that it is, in fact, the other side of the Eastern Mountains he knew in childhood.

Eastern Ocean In The Chronicles of Narnia,* a great ocean washing the shores of all the countries on the east. See also: NARNIA, GEOGRAPHY.

Edgestow In *That Hideous Strength,** a small midland university town more beautiful, in C. S. Lewis's opinion, than either Oxford or Cambridge. Before the arrival of the N.I.C.E.,* "no maker of cars or sausages or marmalade ha[d] yet come to industrialize the country town." The university itself was tiny, having only four colleges, including Bracton,* and had a fine Norman church. Mark and Jane Studdock* lived in a flat on a sandy hillside suburb above the central and academic part of Edgestow. The Dimbles* also lived there. Their typically English country cottage was requisitioned by the N.I.C.E., along with Bracton College property south of the river Wynd, including Bragdon Wood.* The Birmingham road lay to the east, Worcester in the other direction. Stratford to the east and Oxford were not great distances away. Edgestow lay at the heart of ancient Logres, and Merlin* had once worked in what was now Bragdon Wood. The N.I.C.E. engineered a great riot in the town, allowing their institutional police to take control. At this time, and later, very many of its citizens fled as refugees, saving themselves from the destruction that purged the evil that the N.I.C.E. had brought. The scene of destruction was like an event from a novel by Charles Williams* and like the judgment on Gwyntystorm in *The Princess and Curdie* by George MacDonald.*

Edmund, King See PEVENSIE, PETER, SUSAN, EDMUND, AND LUCY.

Education C. S. Lewis makes many references to education in his fiction. Experiment House,* for instance, in the story of *The Voyage of the "Dawn Treader"** embodies his dislike of modern educational methods. Mark Studdock,* in *That Hideous Strength,** is characteristic of many of today's intelligentsia—actually uneducated by classical standards. Judged only by his satire, however, Lewis would seem intensely prejudiced. This is misleading. His powerful essay *The Abolition of Man** revealed antihuman values being unwittingly embodied in some typical recent school textbooks.

Lewis nowhere more clearly put forward his vision of education than in his early essay, "Our English Syllabus," in *Rehabilitations and Other Essays*. He confesses:

> Human life means to me the life of beings for whom the leisure activities of thought, art, literature, conversation are the end, and the preservation and propagation of life merely the means. That is why education seems to me so important: it actualizes that potentiality for leisure, if you like for amateurishness, which is man's prerogative. You have noticed, I hope, that man is the only amateur animal; all the others are professionals. . . . The lion cannot stop hunting, nor the beaver

making dams, nor the bee making honey. When God made the beasts dumb He saved the world from infinite boredom, for if they could speak they would all of them, all day, talk nothing but shop.

Eldila In C. S. Lewis's science-fiction trilogy, angel-like beings who serve the Old One through Maleldil the young. Dr. Elwin Ransom* first comes across them on Malacandra* in *Out of the Silent Planet.** They are barely discernible to human eyes, though their voices are audible. Ransom learns from a sorn* that the eldila were placed on Malacandra from its creation to rule it. The overall ruler of the eldila on a planet is called the Oyarsa, and has some similarity to classical gods associated with Mars, Venus, Mercury, and other planets. The Oyarsa also steer their planets through Deep Heaven. Earth (or Thulcandra, the Silent Planet) is atypical in having a Dark Oyarsa who has turned away from Maleldil. Earth is consequently in quarantine from the rest of the universe.

Emeth the Calormene Emeth is Hebrew for "truth," and Emeth in *The Last Battle** symbolizes what is best in human knowledge unenlightened by Christ. He is a Calormene* who attains to the New Narnia* because he is able to acknowledge Aslan* when the moment of truth arises. Orual* is a somewhat similar figure in *Till We Have Faces.** See: PAGANISM.

Emperor-over-sea In The Chronicles of Narnia,* a metaphorical term for the father of Aslan,* representing God* the Father of the biblical Trinity.

English Literature in the Sixteenth Century (Excluding Drama) (1954) Volume three of *The Oxford History of English Literature.* The book is based upon Lewis's embryonic lectures given at Cambridge University in 1944. As well as providing a thorough history of the period, the book is notable for its introduction, "New Learning and New Ignorance," which adds to the themes laid out in *The Discarded Image** and Lewis's inaugural lecture to the Chair of Medieval and Renaissance Literature at Cambridge, "*De Descriptione Temporum.*"* Lewis points out, for example, a transformation in the concept of magic that happened with the influence of a new empiricism. This new empiricism is what eventually led to the rise of modern science.

Lewis's introduction is of great interest to theologians, philosophers, and historians of ideas, as well as to literary students. He points out that in this period "a Protestant may be Thomistic, a humanist may be a Papist, a scientist may be a magician, a sceptic may be an astrologer." He regards the idea of historical periods as a mischievous conception but a methodological necessity, and he points out the grave dangers of historicism.*

Writing this volume allowed him to expound one of his favorite authors, Edmund Spenser, though space severely restricted him. Where he quotes from neo-Latin authors, he translates into sixteenth-century English, not simply "for the fun of it" but to guard against false impressions created by reading modern attitudes into the past.

C. S. Lewis concludes that the period "illustrates well enough the usual complex, unpatterned historical process; in which, while men often throw away irreplaceable wealth, they not infrequently escape what seemed inevitable dangers, not knowing that they have done either nor how they did it."

The book's contents are as follows:

Introduction: New Learning and New Ignorance.

Book I. Late Medieval. The Close of the Middle Ages in Scotland. The Close of the Middle Ages in England.

Book II. "Drab." Religious Controversy and Translation. Drab Age Verse. Drab and Transitional Prose.

Book III. "Golden." Sidney and Spenser. Prose in the "Golden" Period. Verse in the "Golden" Period.

Epilogue: New Tendencies.

See also: LITERARY CRITIC, C. S. LEWIS AS A.

Enjoyment and contemplation A technical distinction key to Lewis's thinking that he derived from the philosophy of Samuel Alexander.* He expounds it briefly in *Surprised by Joy** to explain a basic mistake he made in understanding joy.*

Mr. Enlightenment An allegorical figure in *The Pilgrim's Regress,** representing the pilgrim John's encounter with nineteenth-century rationalism. The Enlightenment itself emerged in eighteenth-century France, its agenda to institutionalize a belief in naturalism (see: NATURALISM AND SUPERNATURALISM).

Erimon In *Prince Caspian,** a lord of Caspian* IX, executed by the usurping Miraz* on a trumped-up charge of treason.

Erotic love; eros See: *THE FOUR LOVES.*

Essays Presented to Charles Williams (1947) This posthumous tribute brings together essays by a number of Charles Williams's friends, mainly from the Inklings.* The preface by Lewis superbly assesses Williams. Dorothy L. Sayers (the only non-Inkling) contributes "And Telling You a Story," recounting her discovery of Dante through Williams's *The Figure of Beatrice.* The next chapter is J. R. R. Tolkien's seminal paper "On Fairy-Stories," first delivered at St. Andrews in 1938. Equally important is Lewis's "On Stories," and Owen Barfield follows it with a lucid account of the importance of metaphor, "Poetic Diction and Legal Fiction." Gervase Mathew adds "Marriage and

Amour Courtoise in Late Fourteenth-Century England," and Warren Lewis writes about "The Galleys of France."

Lewis's preface valuably speaks about his friendship with Charles Williams, describing him as a "Romantic theologian"; that is, someone who considers the theological implications of Romanticism. See: THE INKLINGS.

Essur In the novel *Till We Have Faces,** a kingdom lying west of Phars,* separated from it by a high mountain range. Great forests and rushing rivers and its richness in game distinguish the country. It is also notable for a hot spring close to its capital. In recent times the worship of Istra* has been introduced. The legends of Istra follow closely the events in the life of Princess Psyche* of Glome.* Apuleius's account of the myth of Cupid and Psyche is virtually identical to that of the Istra legends.

Ettinsmoor In *The Silver Chair,** a desolate region of moorland north of Narnia* and the Shribble River. Beyond Ettinsmoor lies the region of giants. Years before the events recounted in the story, Caspian* X had fought the giants and forced them to pay tribute. See also: NARNIA, GEOGRAPHY.

Evacuees The children at the center of events in *The Lion, the Witch and the Wardrobe** are wartime evacuees from the city and are billeted with Professor Digory Kirke.* During the war Lewis, his brother, Mrs. Moore, and Maureen Moore lodged evacuees at different times in their Oxford home, The Kilns.* The first two—Patricia Boshell (later Heidelberger) and Marie Bosc—arrived in September 1940. Patricia Boshell remembered, "My first impression of C. S. Lewis was that of a shabbily clad, rather portly gentleman, whom I took to be the gardener, and told him so. He roared—boomed! — with laughter. And then with a twinkle in his eye, he said, 'Welcome, girls.'" Later in the war June Flewett (later Freud) was billeted there and eventually stayed nearly two years. She was just sixteen when she arrived, with no opinion, as she put it, of her intellectual ability. "Lewis," she recalls, "was the first person who made me believe that I was an intelligent human being, and the whole time I was there he built up my confidence in myself and in my ability to think and understand."

FURTHER READING

Stephen Schofield, ed., *In Search of C. S. Lewis* (1983).

***Everlasting Man, The,* G. K. Chesterton** G. K. Chesterton* was a significant influence upon Lewis, and *The Everlasting Man* was one of ten books that particularly shaped Lewis's thought and vocational attitude (see: READING OF C. S. LEWIS).

Like Lewis in many of his writings, Chesterton was concerned to undeceive modern people, restoring a true view of things (see: UNDE-

CEPTION AND RECOGNITION). Lewis found that this process worked well in fantasy, as he found that any amount of theology could be "smuggled into people's minds" through it. In *The Everlasting Man*, Chesterton sought such a restoration through the medium of prose argument that soon transforms into vision.

The Everlasting Man is an attempt to stand outside the human race and thus to see humans as the strange beings we really are, and to step outside Christianity and see for the first time its uniqueness among the religions of the world. (Lewis and Tolkien had a similar aim in exploring paganism,* allowing their readers to step outside the modern world and thus see it in its true light.) We do not see these uniquenesses because we do not look at either our humanity or Christian faith properly. Familiarity has dulled our consciousness. Chesterton's book succeeds in helping its reader to see both as if for the first time.

Chesterton explains his purpose: "I desire to help the reader to see Christendom from the outside in the sense of seeing it as a whole against the background of other historic things; just as I desire him to see humanity as a whole against the background of natural things. And I say that in both cases when seen thus, they stand out from their background like supernatural things." With this purpose in mind he divides his book into two parts. The first concerns "the main adventure of the human race in so far as it remained heathen; and the second [is] a summary of the real difference that was made by it becoming Christian."

The first part, therefore, is really a preparation for the second. It shows the Christian faith not as one religion among many but as the religion without rival. It uniquely binds into one both philosophy (or thought) and mythology (or poetry), by giving us a Logos who is the central presence in the strangest story in the world. These ideas of Chesterton in *The Everlasting Man* lay behind the arguments used by Tolkien* and Dyson* to persuade Lewis of the truth of Christian faith—they convinced him that myth had become fact in the Gospel (see: MYTH BECAME FACT). The Christian story completes both human thought and human imagination*; either is incomplete without the light of the Gospel.

Ewart, Sir William Quartus and Lady Cousins of Lewis's mother, Flora, who lived near Little Lea* in Glenmachan (called "Mountbracken" in *Surprised by Joy*).* Sir William was a Belfast linen manufacturer. The young C. S. Lewis fancied one of their daughters, Grundeda. She and her sisters, Hope and Kelsie, would often visit Little Lea and play with the Lewis brothers. They also gave tennis parties at Glenmachan attended by Lewis and Warnie.

Experiment House In *The Silver Chair*,* the experimental school attended by Eustace Scrubb* and Jill Pole.* It partly presents a satire on modern educational* methods and is partly based on grim memories of Lewis's own school experiences.

Experiment in Criticism, An (1961) Though literary criticism, this book should be read by all who take reading seriously. As C. S. Lewis's mature reflections on fiction, story, and myth,* it helps us to understand what he was trying to do in his own fiction and poetry. He is also concerned with the function of the imagination.*

C. S. Lewis argues that literature exists for the enjoyment of readers, and books therefore should be judged by the kind of reading that they evoke. Instead of judging whether a book is good or bad, it is better to reverse the process and consider good and bad readers. When you have an idea of what a good reader is, you then can judge a book by the way in which it is read. A good book cannot be read in the same way as a bad one.

Good reading has something in common with love, moral action, and the growth of knowledge. Like all these, it involves a surrender, in this case by the reader to the work being read. A good reader is concerned less with altering his or her opinion than in entering fully into the opinions and worlds of others.

"The good reader," argues C. S. Lewis, "reads every work seriously in the sense that he reads it whole-heartedly, makes himself as receptive as he can." Shelley had said: "What is love? Ask him who lives, what is life? Ask him who adores, what is God?" C. S. Lewis adds, "Ask him who is a reader, what is literature?"

Lewis presents the evidence of a good reader himself in *An Experiment in Criticism*. He concludes talking about the specific good or value of literature in terms of its content or meaning.* (He had previously discussed literary qualities, including narrative ones.) This value or good is that:

> it admits us to experiences other than our own. . . . Those of us who have been true readers all our life seldom fully realize the enormous extension of our being which we owe to authors. . . . The man who is contented to be only himself, and therefore less a self, is in prison. My own eyes are not enough for me, I will see through those of others. Reality, even seen through the eyes of many, is not enough. I will see what others have invented. Even the eyes of all humanity are not enough. I regret that the brutes cannot write books. . . . In reading great literature I become a thousand men and yet remain myself. Like the night sky in the Greek poem, I see with a myriad eyes, but it is still I who see. Here, as in worship, in love, in moral action, and in knowing, I transcend myself; and am never more myself than when I do.

See also: LITERARY CRITIC, C. S. LEWIS AS A.

F

Fact See: MYTH BECAME FACT.

Fantasy See: IMAGINATION.

Farrer, Austin (1904-1968) A distinguished theologian and friend of C. S. Lewis. He was chaplain and fellow of Trinity College, and warden of Keble College, Oxford,* and considered to be one of the most brilliant people at Oxford in his day.

FURTHER READING

P. Curtis, *A Hawk Among Sparrows: A Biography of Austin Farrer* (1985).

Farrer, Katherine (1911-1972) Wife of Austin Farrer* and friend of C. S. Lewis, and particularly of Joy Davidman Lewis.*

Farsight In *The Last Battle,** the talking eagle who reports the downfall of Narnia to King Tirian.*

Father Time In *The Silver Chair,** the children discover a sleeping giant in Underland. He had a snowy beard that covered him to his waist. They are told that he is old Father Time, once a king in Overland. He has sunk into the Deep Realm and there dreams of the happenings in the upper world. He will not wake until the end of the world. Father Time appears again in *The Last Battle,** having been given a new name, and he helps to end the old Narnia* by blowing his horn.

Felimath See: LONE ISLANDS.

Felinda In *The Magician's Nephew,** a city of the long-dead world of Charn.*

Fenris Ulf See: MAUGRIM.

Final Honor School The second part of *Literae Humaniores* (see: "GREATS") taken by Lewis, the Oxford undergraduate. The school combines history and philosophy, requiring the student to study Greek or Latin historians and philosophers in their original texts. As well as teaching classical thought, the school involves study of modern philosophy, originating in Descartes.

Fledge See: STRAWBERRY.

Four Loves, The (1960) The four loves distinguished by C. S. Lewis are affection, friendship, eros, and charity (divine love). This anatomy of love was written during the period of his short but happy marriage to Joy Davidman.* He shows how each love is able to merge into another or even become another. It is vital however not to lose sight of the real differences that give each love its valid character.

He argues that "we must join neither the idolaters nor the 'debunkers' of human love. . . . Our loves do not make their claim to divinity until the claim becomes plausible. It does not become plausible until there is in them a real resemblance to God, to Love Himself."

Affection is the humblest and most widespread of the four loves. Most of whatever tangible and consistent happiness we find in our lives can be explained by affection. It is not a particularly appreciative love. This very lack of discrimination gives it the potential to broaden the mind and to create a feeling for other people of all shapes and sizes. Lewis approved of a comment made by someone: "Dogs and cats should always be brought up together. It broadens their minds so." Affection seeps through the whole texture of our lives. It is the medium of the operation of the other loves.

C. S. Lewis constantly explored the virtues and dangers of affection in his fiction. In *The Great Divorce,** for example, the ghost of a mother still desires to possess her son after death. In the novel *Till We Have Faces,** the deep affection Orual* feels for her sister Psyche* turns into a destructive jealousy that she cannot distinguish from love.

Friendship is the least instinctive, biological, and necessary of our loves. Today it is hardly considered a love, and C. S. Lewis is virtually unique among contemporary Christian thinkers in devoting so much of his attention to this theme. Lewis points out that the ancients put the highest value upon this love, as in the friendship between David and Jonathan. The ideal climate for friendship exists when a few people are absorbed in some common, unnecessary interest. Lovers are usually imagined face to face; friends are best imagined side by side, their eyes ahead on their common interest. Friendship, as the least biological of the loves, refutes sexual or homosexual explanations for its existence. It is also sharply different from membership in an inner ring.*

Friendship was deeply important to C. S. Lewis throughout his life. Arthur Greeves* was a lifelong friend, as was Owen Barfield.* Friendship formed the basis of the association of the Inklings,* core figures that included J. R. R. Tolkien* and Charles Williams.* Lewis's brother, "Warnie" (W. H. Lewis*), was also his friend from childhood, and in Joy Davidman* he found a friend as well as a wife. He had other female friendships, too, including Sister Penelope* and Jane McNeil.* Friendship, reckoned C. S. Lewis, made good people better and bad people worse. Sharing a disinterested point of view was not itself good.

Eros is the kind of love that lovers are within or "in"—the state of being in love. It is different from mere physical, sexual desire in that eros primarily wants the beloved, not sex as an end in itself. In eros love, a person is taken out of him or her self, and thus enlarged as a person. Eros would value the beloved above happiness and pleasure and would wish to retain the beloved even if the result was unhappiness. Lewis characteristically felt that, were we not human beings, we should find eros hard to imagine. As it is, we find it difficult to explain.

Lewis's friend Charles Williams explored eros, and in his thought, fiction, and poetry, he developed a theology of romantic love. This deeply influenced Lewis, and eros is an important theme in *That Hideous Strength** (in the marriage of Jane and Mark Studdock*) and in *Till We Have Faces** (in Psyche's* love for the god of the mountain, the West-wind*). It was to have been a theme of the unfinished novel "After Ten Years."

Charity, or divine love, the fourth love, transcends all earthly loves in being a gift-love. All human loves are by nature (even unfallen nature) need-loves. As created beings we, by necessity, have to turn to God for our fulfillment and meaning. This pattern is repeated throughout creation, in our dependence on other people and upon nature.* Our human loves are potential rivals to the love of God, and they can only take their proper place if our first allegiance is to him. All God's love for us and for his creation is gift-love, as he has no need of the universe and its inhabitants for his existence and personal fulfillment.

As with several other of his books of popular theology, Lewis concludes by looking to heaven* as the ultimate context of human life. It is the divine likeness in all our human loves (affection, friendship, and eros) that is their heavenly, and thus permanent, element. It is only what is heaven-like that can enter heaven; all else, when shaken, will fall. Thus any love for someone or something that is allowed to be a proper love has a heavenly element and is, in fact, also a love for God. Our own loves, like our moral choices, judge us. When those that enter heaven see God, they will find that they know him already. See also: *THE ALLEGORY OF LOVE.*

The Fox The Greek slave in *Till We Have Faces** engaged by King Trom* to teach his daughters. "The Fox" is one of his nicknames (others include "word-weaver" and "Greekling"). His real name is Lysias, and he has sons and a daughter in far-off Greece. The Fox is short, thick-set, and very bright-eyed, always full of great intellectual curiosity. His nickname derives from the fact that when he arrived in Glome,* whatever of his hair and beard was not gray was reddish. The Fox became Queen Orual's closest advisor and taught her to think like a Greek, as well as to read and write the language. She never, however, allowed this to make her lose touch with the common people of Glome and their worship of Ungit.*

The Fox followed the philosophy of the Stoics, and particularly Zeno and other Greek philosophers of the third century B.C. He dismissed the stories of the gods as "only lies of poets. . . . Not in accordance with nature." The world, The Fox believed, can be understood by the principles of right reason. He opposed the supernaturalism* that filled the very air of Glome.

Fox, Adam (1883-1977) A member of the Inklings,* and fellow of Magdalen College, Oxford,* and Dean of Divinity there from 1929. In 1938 he was elected Professor of Poetry at Oxford. He became Canon of Westminster Abbey in 1942. Among his publications were *Plato for Pleasure* (1945), *Meet the Greek Testament* (1952), and *Dean Inge* (1960).

Frank In *The Great Divorce** (see: THE DWARF).

Frank the Cabby In Lewis's *The Magician's Nephew*,* an Edwardian London cabby. The character perhaps owes something to Diamond's father in *At the Back of the North Wind* by George MacDonald.* Frank is accidentally drawn into Narnia* as it is being created and, with his cockney wife, Helen, is the first to rule there. His second son was the first King of Archenland.* All humans in Narnia or its surrounding countries descended either from Frank and Helen or from the Telmarines* who stumbled into its world. Aslan commanded that Narnia be ruled by sons and daughters of Adam. See also: NARNIA, HISTORY.

Friendship See: *THE FOUR LOVES.*

Friendship of J. R. R. Tolkien and C. S. Lewis J. R. R. Tolkien and C. S. Lewis had childhoods strikingly dominated by their imaginations. Typically, Lewis in Belfast created Boxen and Animal Land while Tolkien in the English Midlands invented languages and fell under the spell of existing languages such as Welsh and later Gothic. Significantly, both lost their mothers—Lewis at the age of nine, Tolkien when just into his teens. Both started writing seriously during the First World War, in which Lewis was wounded and Tolkien lost two of his closest friends. Tolkien was several years older than Lewis and had already taught in Leeds University before returning to Oxford to be a professor and meeting Lewis in 1926. With H. V. D. Dyson, Tolkien was responsible for persuading Lewis of the truth of Christianity (see: MYTH BECAME FACT). C. S. Lewis's conversion deepened the friendship, a friendship only later eclipsed by Lewis's acquaintance with Charles Williams and what Tolkien called his "strange marriage" to Joy Davidman.

Tolkien was a central figure in the Inklings* from the beginning, a literary group of friends held together by Lewis's zest and enthusiasm. Tolkien's influence on Lewis and the importance of Lewis to Tolkien is a great and rich subject. Their association is comparable in importance to that of Wordsworth and Coleridge.

1. The first element of influence was Tolkien's Christianity. When they first met, Lewis was not a Christian and previously had been an atheist (as recorded in *Surprised by Joy**). Tolkien's Christian faith is a complex matter, and Lewis inherited some of its cast, to which was added the influence of Owen Barfield's view of the imagination on the two men.

The essence of Tolkien's Christianity is captured in lines he wrote to Lewis at the time of their early acquaintance, lines familiar through their quotation in Tolkien's essay "On Fairy Stories":

The heart of man is not compound of lies,
but draws some wisdom from the only Wise,
and still recalls him. Though now long estranged,
man is not wholly lost nor wholly changed.
Dis-graced he may be, yet is not dethroned,
and keeps the rags of lordship once he owned,
his world-dominion by creative act:
not his to worship the great Artefact,
man, sub-creator, the refracted light
through whom is splintered from a single White
to many hues, and endlessly combined
in living shapes that move from mind to mind.
Though all the crannies of the world we filled
with elves and goblins, though we dared to build
gods and their houses out of dark and light,
and sow the seed of dragons, 'twas our right
(used or misused). The right has not decayed
We make still by the law in which we're made.

The poem gives fascinating insight into the discussions that went on between Tolkien and Lewis at that period.

2. The second element of Tolkien's influence is his view of the relation of myth and fact. Tolkien had a sacramental view of story. The gospel story of Christ's incarnation, death, and resurrection—a story told by God himself in the real events of history—has broken into the "seamless web of story." Story—preceding and subsequent to the Gospel—is joyfully alive with God's presence. Lewis has a key essay "On Stories" (1947) in *Essays Presented to Charles Williams*,* which he expanded with his seminal *An Experiment in Criticism*.* This book reveals how integral a theology of romance* was to his thinking and imagination.

3. The third related element is Tolkien's distinctive doctrine of subcreation,* the view that the highest function of art is the creation of convincing secondary or other worlds. The concept of secondary worlds is very versatile and is likely to continue to be fruitful in many varieties far beyond the mode of obvious fantasy.

4. The fourth influence is speculation. Tolkien distinctively says that "all tales may come true" (because of the link between human and divine making). This idea was conveyed to Lewis by Tolkien. In the matter of Digory's apple, in *The Magician's Nephew** (the apple that gave life to Digory's mother), Lewis was doing more than indulging in wish-fulfillment. The story for him embodied the possibility that his own mother might one day live again in a fully human physical-spiritual existence.

Turning the other way now, what was Lewis's importance to Tolkien? Lewis clearly didn't influence Tolkien in the way Tolkien influenced him. In Lewis, rather, Tolkien found a ready listener and appreciator. In fact Tolkien confesses that without C. S. Lewis's encouragement, it is unlikely that he would have finished *The Lord of the Rings*. Sadly, Lewis did not persist in encouraging the completion of *The Silmarillion*, especially the great tales such as *Beren and Lúthien*. The gradual falling apart of the two friends later in life has probably had far-reaching consequences.

Considering the two men together, however, there were a great number of shared beliefs deriving from their common faith, which, though orthodox, had an original cast, to say the least.

1. They saw the imagination* as the organ of meaning rather than of truth (which made their Romanticism distinctive).

2. They also both valued a sense of "otherness"*—or otherworldliness.

3. This all-pervasive sense of the other is focused in the quality of the numinous* in both men's writings.

4. There are other key similarities. One is the central importance of imaginative invention, most obviously expressed in Tolkien's doctrine of subcreation. Other similarities include a desire to embody a quality of joy* in their work. Though associated with Lewis, joy is strong too in Tolkien, and valued by him, as his essay "On Fairy Stories" makes clear. Finally, both men were preoccupied with pre-Christian paganism.* Most of Tolkien's fiction is set in a pre-Christian world, as was his great model *Beowulf*. Similarly Lewis explored Tolkien's pagan world in his superb novel *Till We Have Faces.**

There were important differences between Tolkien and Lewis. Preeminently Lewis was much more earthy than Tolkien in his view of art. He was closer to the radical Puritanism of John Bunyan. Tolkien inclined to a spiritual view of art. He regarded some of Lewis's work, particularly The Chronicles of Narnia, as too allegorical, i.e., too conceptually and explicitly loaded with Christian beliefs. Tolkien struggled to have Christian meanings incarnate in his work, giving it an inner radiance. Yet when Lewis explored a pre-Christian world in *Till We Have Faces*, he achieved a depth of symbolism rather than allegory. Significantly too Tolkien approved of *Out of the Silent Planet.**

One does get the feeling that Lewis portrays God* as much more approachable than Tolkien does. This may only be because Tolkien's work lies in a pre-Christian setting. His world is certainly alive with God's providence. Lewis's fiction is much more literally Christ-centered. The only real exception is his novel *Till We Have Faces*. In Narnia, the creator-lion Aslan is mediator. In *Perelandra** the death of Maleldil on Thulcandra—our Silent Planet*—means that the fall of humankind cannot simply repeat itself. In Tolkien's world, it is the Valar who mediate between the Children of Ilúvatar and Ilúvatar himself. Eärendil is the closest to a Christ-figure, perhaps, in his intercession. But he is more a herald of Christ—a John-the-Baptist-figure from old English literature—than a Christ-figure.

For Tolkien art was tied up with his conception of the elves. Elves were at the center, for him, of the fairy story, among the highest achievement of art. He saw such spiritual art as having been verified by the greatest story of all—the Gospel. Tolkien argued: "God is the Lord, of angels, and of man—and of Elves. Legend and history have met and fused." Art—and language, to which it is ultimately related—represents an elfin quality of humankind, embodied in the biblical teaching of people being in God's image, making still by the law in which we're made.

G

Gale In The Chronicles of Narnia,* the ninth king of Narnia* in descent from King Frank.* He delivered the population of the Lone Islands* of the Eastern Ocean* from a dragon. In gratitude they gave the islands over to Narnian sovereignty.

See also: NARNIA, HISTORY.

Galma In *The Voyage of the "Dawn Treader"** an island off the coast of Narnia* and about a day's sailing northeast of Cair Paravel.* King Caspian* X of Narnia stopped here on his great journey across the Eastern Ocean.* Galma's governing duke marked the occasion by a great tournament.

Giant Allegorical figure in *The Pilgrim's Regress,** signifying the Spirit of the Age,* who captured John.

Ginger the Cat An evil and clever cat who joins forces with the perverse Shift,* a talking ape, in *The Last Battle.** After meeting Aslan* face to face, he loses the ability to speak.

Girbius In *Prince Caspian,** a faun.

Glamaria A region charted on the Mappa Mundi* in *The Pilgrim's Regress.**

Glasswater Creek Mentioned in *Prince Caspian,** a creek that leads to the hill of the Stone Table.*

Glenmachan House See: "MOUNTBRACKEN."

Glenstorm A centaur in *Prince Caspian** who lives in a mountain glen. He is a particularly noble creature with glossy chestnut flanks and a golden red beard, as befits a prophet and star-gazer.

Glimfeather A talking owl in *The Silver Chair** who is as big as a dwarf. In the service of the now elderly King Caspian* X, he takes under his wing Jill Pole* and Eustace Scrubb.* Glimfeather aids them in their endeavor to find the lost Prince Rilian* by carrying them one by one to a Parliament of Owls and then, with another owl, to marsh-wiggle* country to the north of Narnia.*

Glome Glome was a kingdom bordering on Phars* and Caphad,* described in the novel *Till We Have Faces*.* The country's cattle and its silver mines played a leading role in its economy. The capital, also called Glome, was situated well back and west of the river Shennit, and a day's journey northwest of the border town of Ringal. The royal palace stood on a hillside above the city. The older part of the building was made of wood and the rest of painted brick. On the second floor was a small five-sided room sometimes used as a prison.

Near the city lay stretches of mud, reeds, and plenty of wildfowl on each side of the river Shennit, which tended to flood during heavy rain.

About a mile beyond a ford that served the city was the temple of Ungit,* deity of Glome, whom the far-off Greeks called Aphrodite. Four great stones, twice the height of a man, were erected there in an egg-shaped ring. Within the ring, and in the brick and thatched temple, stood a shapeless stone, representing Ungit. She was considered to be the mother and sometimes wife of the West-wind,* god of the mountain, who dwelt on the Gray Mountains. The foothills of these lay farther northeast of the city, past the temple. Here Psyche* (or Istra) was left as a sacrifice to the god. Psyche was the half-sister of Orual,* who became queen of Glome. See also: SUBCREATION; ESSUR.

Glozelle In *Prince Caspian*,* one of the lords of the usurper Miraz* who plans the tyrant's defeat by getting him to accept Peter Pevensie's* challenge to a duel.

Glubose In *The Screwtape Letters*,* the tempter assigned to the crabbed mother of the patient looked after by the inexperienced Wormwood.* Wormwood's uncle, Screwtape,* urges him to liaise with Glubose to induce all the characteristics the patient dislikes in his mother.

Gnomes In *The Silver Chair*,* the inhabitants of Underworld* and Bism.* They are short, fat, white-faced, goblin-like creatures, but with no malice toward "overlanders," as they call those who live above the world's crust.

God

> Men are reluctant to pass over the notion of an abstract and negative deity to the living God. . . . An "impersonal God"—well and good. A subjective God of beauty, truth, and goodness inside our own heads—better still. A formless life-force surging through us, a vast power we can tap—best of all. But God Himself, alive, pulling at the other end of the cord, perhaps approaching at an infinite speed, the hunter, king, husband—that is quite another matter. There comes a moment when the children who have been playing burglars hush suddenly: Was that a real footstep in the hall? There comes a moment when people who have been dabbling in religion ("Man's search for God"!) suddenly

> draw back. Suppose we really found Him? We never meant it to come to that! Worse still, supposing He had found us? (*Miracles*, chapter 11).

Throughout his life C. S. Lewis loved particular things, distinctiveness in people and places, books and conversations. This was an affinity he shared with his mentor, George MacDonald.* In Lewis's book *Miracles*,* which is key for understanding his view of God, many connections are made between the deep reality of particular things and the underlying factuality—the utter concreteness—of God.

Lewis pointed out that it is one thing to speak about beauty, truth, or goodness, and about God as a great force of some kind. People will listen in a friendly manner. But it is quite another matter if you talk about a God who commands, acts, and who has definite ideas and a pointed character.

Many non-Christians, Lewis points out, say that God is beyond personality, and they mean that God is impersonal, less than a person. If you want that kind of God, there are many religions to choose from. Christians, on the other hand, find God beyond personality because he is more than a person. Only Judeo-Christianity has this kind of God.

Lewis felt that people often hide from the idea of a definite, personal God by calling it crude or primitive. In fact, they reject the idea very often because the thought of a God who does things and makes demands is distasteful. Lewis became convinced that, far from being impersonal, God is far more personal than we can imagine, more than we are ourselves.

We realize God's concreteness and reality best not by merely thinking about him but by obeying and worshiping him. Lewis accepts St. Paul's appeal to "put on Christ." At first, this has to be rather like pretending to be Christ, as a child might pretend to be a nurse or fireman; but by this conscious effort we eventually begin to enter into the life of Christ. The prime purpose of life is to "lose" ourselves and to enter the divine life. Of course it is the easy way out (for there is no cost) to think of God as a formless life-force surging through us, as Lewis was tempted to do when he contemplated the possibility that God existed after all.

For Lewis, God is therefore fact, rather than the result of a rational argument. To this fact of God we bring to bear views of life and the world that we already hold. We interpret this divine fact or even explain him away. Unlike modern theologians such as Paul Tillich or Don Cupitt, Lewis was not afraid to call God a fact that is given to us, a definitive thing. Rather than being an abstract concept or a human symbol, God is overwhelmingly concrete and real. Lewis felt that if we fully understood what God is, we should see that there is no question whether he is. He is the center of all existence. In Lewis's vivid phrase, he is the "fountain" of facthood. To some people he is discoverable everywhere, to some nowhere—depending on whether we are blind or see.

We often make a basic mistake when trying to imagine God as unchangeable, invisible, infinite, and eternal. We are prone to miss his overwhelming life, energy, joy, and concreteness, to fall into the folly of conceiving him as less definite than ourselves. This is why the central statement we can make about God is that he is.

Lewis's view of God as the utterly concrete thing, the basic fact, was part and parcel of the supernaturalism that marks all his writings. In an age of increasing secularization, where the supernatural becomes more and more implausible, Lewis stands out in holding to the reality of the unseen world. He, like Francis Schaeffer, has refreshed and renewed the reality of God for many people in the modern world.

Soon after his conversion to theism, Lewis wrote about his progress and later gave a fuller account in *Surprised by Joy.** He claimed that he was an "empirical theist." He meant that he had come to theism as a result of uncomfortable facts, not merely by reasoning in a theological or philosophical manner (though he did plenty of that). Lewis always stressed the danger that our theoretical reasoning—which has to be abstract—can easily draw us from the particularity of the world. God is present to us first of all in given things, facts that resist being grasped fully in abstractions. Often, Lewis felt, picture language and stories came closer to grasping the concreteness of reality.

The pre-Christian Lewis felt the concreteness of God first of all through stories and myths—but his reason demanded that God's existence must be perceived in literal facts and events. This prepared him for finding God through the literal facts of Christ's incarnation, life, death, and resurrection. These events were not merely a story, though they were like many good stories that God had been pleased to give to the human race. Such "good stories," felt Lewis, were real though unfocused shafts of divine light and truth. He fashioned one such "good story" himself, *Till We Have Faces*,* based upon an ancient myth.*

C. S. Lewis believed that God has done three basic things to reveal himself to mankind. The first was to install within people a conscience. The second was to send what Lewis dubbed "good dreams." By these he meant "those queer stories scattered all through the heathen religions about a god who died and comes to life again and, by his death, has somehow given new life to men." The third was to give the Scriptures to the Jewish people, climaxed in the incarnation of Christ and the writings of the New Testament. These three acts of God were closely related in Lewis's mind. For example, he believed that the Genesis creation story might possibly have been derived from earlier pagan myths, although he believed that the biblical retelling was the one chosen by God, the "vehicle of the earliest sacred truth." The creation account was not less true than history as we know it, but more so. Its symbols portray the essence, the meaning, of the historical event. We have a three-dimensional rather than a two-dimensional picture of creation.

God as revealer is tied up for Lewis with our innate sense of the fittingness of things. We are meant to be moral, rational creatures, but rationality is hard work—a lifetime's training of our thinking, emotions, imagination, and behavior. We have a sense of order that needs cultivating with loving care. The greatest objective fact we have to attend to is God himself. Like life, literature, those we love, our needy neighbor, and other aspects of reality, he as the source of reality makes right and proper demands upon our attention. These aspects of reality cannot, however, be his rivals, no matter the strength of their demands.

It was vital for C. S. Lewis that belief in God does not undermine our whole system of thinking, which leads us to regard certain things as true—unlike naturalism.* He states that a system that has no place for thought cannot itself be true. Such a system undermines the validity of the very process of thinking that leads to the conclusion that it is true.

Like George MacDonald, Lewis saw God essentially as "the glad creator" and hence regarded the Incarnation as the central miracle, springing from God's involvement with his creation. Christian faith, beginning as it does with concrete historical events, endorses and delights in the reality and "thereness" of the universe.

> Christian teaching by saying that God made the world and called it good teaches that Nature or environment cannot be simply irrelevant to spiritual beatitude in general, however far in one particular Nature, during the days of her bondage, they may have drawn apart. By teaching the resurrection of the body, it teaches that Heaven is not merely a state of the spirit but a state of the body as well: and therefore a state of Nature as a whole. . . . God . . . is the glad creator. He has become Himself incarnate (*Miracles*, chapter 16).

For many readers of C. S. Lewis, he is most memorable for the fresh images of God and Christ that he created, enabling people in our modern world to see again the meaning of God's reality. These images include Aslan,* the Emperor-over-sea, Maleldil, the Old One, the Landlord, and even the pagan insights of the character of West-wind,* the god of the mountain in *Till We Have Faces*. Lewis's delight in God's creation was at the heart of his fantasy writing (see: IMAGINATION) and his theology of romance.

See also: THEOLOGY, C. S. LEWIS AND; MYTH; NATURE; JOY.

God in the Dock See: UNDECEPTIONS.

God of the Gray Mountains In *Till We Have Faces*,* a god, in the mythology of the land of Glome,* who dwells in the Gray Mountains. He is also referred to as the Shadowbrute and the West-wind. As son of the goddess Ungit,* he is a debased image of Cupid, who appears in the classical myth of Cupid and Psyche.* The people of Glome sacrifice princess Psyche to the god in appeasement for various calamities, and he takes her as his bride, placing her in his palace. He turns out to be a god of beauty rather than a hideous monster. See also: PSYCHE'S PALACE.

***Golden Ass, The,* Apuleus** A collection of stories divided into eleven books, written in Carthage, not later than A.D. 97. The plot is simple. A young man sees an old sorceress transform herself into a bird after drinking a philter. He also wishes for such a transformation, but he mistakes the vial and turns into an ass. To become a man again, he must eat a certain species of roses. The pilgrimage of the donkey in search of them is the author's device for knitting together a number of fantasies and stories. The most famous of all is "The Loves of Psyche." This inspired Lewis's *Till We Have Faces,** in which he retells the haunting myth. In Apuleus the tale occupies two entire books and has inspired poets, painters, and sculptors in many periods and countries.

Golg A gnome* in *The Silver Chair** originally from Bism* but met by Puddleglum* and the others in Underworld.*

Golnesshire The country of lechery charted on the Mappa Mundi* in *The Pilgrim's Regress.**

"Greats" *Literae Humaniores.* This is the study undertaken by Lewis as an undergraduate of the classics, philosophy, and ancient history. Unlike the other Oxford* schools, *Literae Humaniores* was a four-year course, the first and most esteemed of the humanities courses at the university. It included Classical Honor Moderations* or "Mods" and the Final Honor School* (also called "Greats"). Lewis achieved First Class Honors in both and then went on to take a First in English language and literature in 1923.

Great Divorce, The (1945) Like *The Screwtape Letters,** this story was first serialized in a religious periodical and also concerns the relation of heaven* and hell. C. S. Lewis casts his story in the form of a dream, with himself as narrator, and does not wish his reader to think that information is being presented about the actual state after death. This of course does not mean that Lewis denies an actual heaven and hell. He is in fact concerned in this story to show their plausibility and reality.

The story opens in hell, with C. S. Lewis standing in a bus queue on a pavement in a long, shabby street. He had wandered for hours in similar mean streets. Hell is an endless conurbation of perpetual twilight, where people move farther and farther away from each other. A new building just has to be thought to be made, but lacks sufficient reality to keep out the rain that constantly falls.

Anyone in hell who wishes can take a bus trip to heaven, or at least to its outlands. Lewis takes such a trip with a varied collection of ghosts. Upon arrival in heaven, the passengers find it painfully solid, hard, and bright in comparison to hell. Solid People who have traveled vast distances to meet the ghosts try to persuade them to stay, pointing out that they will gradually adjust to heaven and become more solid as they forsake particular follies that hold them back from heaven. Much of the story is taken up with encounters between Solid People and ghosts, who were friends, relations, or spouses on earth.

Lewis himself meets his mentor, George MacDonald,* who explains many mysteries of salvation and damnation to him. Lewis particularly questions him about his apparent universalism, the belief that all people will be saved. For Lewis, universalism is ruled out by the reality of human will. Hell is in fact chosen by the damned. Lewis's portrayal of the damned adds to Sartre's brilliant comment, "Hell is other people," the reality that hell is also oneself.

C. S. Lewis handles the question of salvation and damnation very sensitively. Out of all the bus passengers, only one accepts the invitation to stay in heaven, after allowing a red lizard of lust perched on his shoulder to be destroyed by a colossal angel. Lewis's portrait of an apostate bishop strikes home painfully, exposing theological liberalism. The bishop returns to hell to read a paper to its Theological Society.

In both *The Screwtape Letters** and *The Great Divorce*,* Lewis highlights practical matters of the Christian life such as family problems, selfishness, disagreement, greed, and the persistence of bad habits. Fantasy proves a powerful medium for examining such matters, remembered long after a sermon is forgotten.

"Great Knock" See: W. T. KIRKPATRICK.

Great River In *Prince Caspian*,* the river leading to Aslan's How,* for which the children search. The river runs its course from Lantern Waste* in the west, across Narnia,* into the Eastern Ocean.* See also: NARNIA, GEOGRAPHY.

"Great War" (between C. S. Lewis and Owen Barfield) What Barfield called "an intense interchange of philosophical opinions" and Lewis described as "an almost incessant disputation, sometimes by letter and sometimes face to face, which lasted for years." The dialogue ensued soon after Barfield's acceptance of anthroposophism* around 1922 and trailed off by the time of Lewis's conversion to Christian faith in 1931. The dispute centered on the nature of the imagination* and the status of metaphor. This dialogue cured Lewis of his "chronological snobbery,"* making him hostile to modernism, and provided a rich background of sharpened thought for Barfield's important study *Poetic Diction** (1928).

Green, Roger Lancelyn (1918-1987) Biographer, with Walter Hooper,* of Lewis, friend, and sometimes visitor to the Inklings.* Lewis and his wife, Joy Davidman Lewis,* visited Greece with Green and his wife shortly before Joy's death. Green was a pupil of Lewis's who became a friend, and the two had a common taste in reading. Green wrote an authoritative study of children's literature, *Tellers of Tales* (1946, updated 1953), and composed many books for children himself. After hearing Lewis read early chapters of *The Lion, the Witch and the Wardrobe,** Roger Lancelyn Green encouraged him to complete it. Many of Green's books introduce children to myth* and legend. *The Land Beyond the North* (1958) follows the Argonauts to the realm of Britain. His other fiction includes *From the World's End* (1948), his most mystical piece.

Green Lady See: *PERELANDRA*.

Green Witch In *The Silver Chair,** the witch who tries to dominate Narnia* during the reign of King Caspian* X. She appears to the travelers Jill Pole,* Eustace Scrubb,* and Puddleglum* as a tall, beautiful young woman wearing a green kirtle. The witch enchanted and dominated Caspian's son Rilian* in her Shallow Lands.* Eventually she reveals her true nature as she transforms into a green serpent. See also: WHITE WITCH.

Greeves, Joseph Arthur (1895-1966) A friend of Lewis's from teenage years who shared the secret of joy* and a similar taste in reading and all things "northern," such as Old Norse mythology. Arthur's skill was in visual art rather than words, though he was an appreciative reader of a lifelong correspondence from Lewis (collected in *They Stand Together**). Arthur lived at a house called Bernagh,* almost opposite Lewis's home on the outskirts of Belfast. Until his death, Lewis continued to meet with Arthur. Between 1921 and 1923 Arthur Greeves studied at the prestigious Slade School of Fine Art in London. Later he exhibited with the Royal Hibernian Academy in Dublin. Lewis did not share his faith (Arthur came from a Christian Brethren background) until 1931, and later Arthur explored varieties of faith, concluding his life as a Quaker. See: *THEY STAND TOGETHER*.

Gresham, David (1944-) Older son of Joy Davidman (see: LEWIS, HELEN JOY DAVIDMAN) and stepson of Lewis. In 1956, with his younger brother Douglas, he joined the Lewis brothers living in The Kilns.* His mother was then seriously ill with cancer. He stayed on at The Kilns after her death in 1960 and gradually explored his Jewish roots. He continues to pursue the study of the Hebrew Bible and the Talmud, and he is involved in furthering Jewish education.

Gresham, Douglas (1945-) Douglas Gresham tells the story of his life, including his memories as Lewis's stepson, in *Lenten Lands* (1994). He is the younger son of Joy Davidman (see: HELEN JOY DAVIDMAN LEWIS), and he features in the films and play *Shadowlands*, scripted by William Nicholson. After his mother's death from cancer, Douglas eventually studied agriculture and moved to Tasmania with his wife, Meredith (Merrie). The family moved to County Carlow, Ireland, in 1993 to create a center for Christian ministry. He is actively involved in the Lewis literary estate and lectures throughout the world.

Gresham, Joy Davidman See: LEWIS, HELEN JOY DAVIDMAN.

Gresham, William Lindsay (1909-1962) Writer and first husband of Joy Davidman (see: LEWIS, HELEN JOY DAVIDMAN). Like Joy, he was for a time a Communist (serving in Spain in the Civil War) and later a convert to Christian faith. Unlike Joy, he did not persist, but later in life moved to Scientology and then to Buddhism. He successfully sold the film rights for his first novel, *Nightmare Alley* (1946). After many marital difficulties Joy eventually agreed to a divorce. After the death of Joy in 1960, Bill Gresham traveled to England to see his two sons and allowed them to stay with their stepfather, Lewis. Tragically, in 1962, after cancer was diagnosed, he took his own life.

Grief Observed, A (1961) Originally published under a pseudonym, N. W. Clerk (see: NAT WHILK), this slim book sets out C. S. Lewis's pilgrimage through bereavement after losing his wife, Joy Davidman.* *A Grief Observed* complements his study *The Problem of Pain.** He says he wrote the former in four exercise books as a kind of journal of grief. Whereas *The Problem of Pain* explores suffering generally and theoretically, the journal observes it specifically and personally (or existentially) with great immediacy. Like the earlier book, *A Grief Observed* affirms the presence of God in the deepest human darkness, even when he for long seems absent. Biographically, *A Grief Observed* reveals the quality of relationship between Lewis and Joy Davidman. He remembers: "She was my daughter and my mother, my pupil and my teacher, my subject and my sovereign; and always, holding all these in solution, my trusty comrade, friend, shipmate, fellow-soldier."

Griffle In *The Last Battle,** the chief of a band of dwarfs who believed that only they themselves were worth believing in and fighting for. They came to this conclusion after being disillusioned by Shift* and his trickery.

Gumpas In *The Voyage of the "Dawn Treader"** the slave-trading and bureaucratic governor of the Lone Islands,* whom Caspian replaces with the worthy Lord Bern.*

H

Hag In *Prince Caspian,** an accomplice of the surly dwarf Nikabrik.* She had dirty gray hair and a nose and a chin that stuck out like nutcrackers.

Handramit The fertile lowlands in the great artificial chasms of Malacandra in *Out of the Silent Planet.**

Harandra The harsh outer surface or highland of Malacandra in *Out of the Silent Planet.** The seroni (or sorns*) liked to live there.

Hardcastle, Major "Fairy" In *That Hideous Strength,** the psychopathic controller of the Institutional Police of the N.I.C.E.* She is a lesbian who enjoys torturing Jane Studdock.*

Harfang The stronghold of wicked giants north of Ettinsmoor* in *The Silver Chair.** The children, and even Puddleglum,* were persuaded the giants were friendly by the Green Witch.* Marshwiggles* and man are considered delicacies for a feast.

Harfang stands on a small hill overlooking the ruins of the giant City Ruinous.* Among the crumbling ruined stone, pillars as tall as factory chimneys can be seen in places. Large sections of pavement can be seen from Harfang to bear the words "UNDER ME," all that remains of a verse about Underland.*

Harwood, Alfred Cecil (1898-1975) A lifelong friend of C. S. Lewis's who first met Owen Barfield* when Barfield was a scholar at Christ Church, Oxford.* Both were introduced to Jack Lewis in 1919 through a mutual acquaintance, Leo Baker. Harwood was, like Barfield, an anthroposophist.* In 1931 Warren Lewis* described him in his diary as a "pleasant, spectacled, young looking man, with a sense of humor of a whimsical kind, to whom I took at sight . . . we found ourselves seeing everything with much the same eye."

Havard, Dr. R. E. "Humphrey" (1901-1985) Affectionately known as the "Useless Quack," he was the doctor of C. S. Lewis and a member of the Inklings.* The son of an Anglican clergyman, "Humphrey" Havard studied medicine after graduating in chemistry at Oxford in 1922. In 1934 he took over a medical practice in Oxford with surgeries in Headington and St. Giles (near The Eagle and Child public house, haunt of the Inklings). It was soon after this that he got to know Lewis and was invited to the Inklings. He and Lewis liked each other instantly. It was years later that Havard says he woke up one morning to find his friends famous. He appears briefly as a character in *Perelandra.** In 1943 he volunteered for the Royal Navy Reserve and became a naval surgeon. When he returned to Oxford (because of his wife's breast cancer), he was dubbed "the Red Admiral" by the Inklings because he now sported a red beard and turned up at a meeting in uniform. "Hugo" Dyson called him "Humphrey" because he couldn't remember his name. Havard converted to Roman Catholicism in 1931, influenced by Ronald Knox. He had five children. His wife succumbed to cancer in 1950.

Havard felt that Lewis's association with Charles Williams* strained the friendship between Lewis and Tolkien. The doctor recalled: "Lewis was fascinated by Williams, and rightly; he [had] a very extraordinary charm. You couldn't be in the same room with him without being attracted to him." Havard felt that Williams had a "curious, rather mixed character." In some way he "wasn't fully integrated." On the friendship of Lewis and Tolkien, and its eventual cooling, Havard observed: "The surprising thing, really, is that they became such close fiends, rather than that differences appeared and separated them."

FURTHER READING

Robert E. Havard, "Philia: Jack at Ease," in *C. S. Lewis at the Breakfast Table*, ed. James T. Como, 1979.

See also the Oral History Project of the Marion E. Wade Center, Wheaton, Illinois, USA.

Heaven Heaven, for C. S. Lewis, is a literal place, though in our present fallen situation, it will not be discovered by searching through the universe in space rockets. It is a new nature* that God has planned, the ultimate context of a fully human life, bodies and all. The theme of heaven's reality runs through Lewis's writings, particularly his fiction, and is closely linked with his characteristic theme of joy* or *Sehnsucht.*

Before his conversion to Christianity, as an atheist, Lewis was uninterested in immortality, and he only became convinced about life after death a year into his Christian life. He desired God himself, and the desire for heaven was a spin-off from this. As heaven is part of creation, it is not worthy to be our ultimate aim. Lewis, however, felt that it was no more mercenary to desire heaven than to wish to marry the person one loves.

In this present life, the situation is like being on the wrong side of a shut door, with heaven on the other side. Morning was one of Lewis's favorite images of heaven. We respond to the freshness and purity of morning, but that doesn't make us fresh and pure.

Lewis isolated five promises about heaven for the believer. One is that we shall be with Christ. Another is that we'll be like him. We shall share his glory, the right to honor and admiration. We shall in some sense be fed, feasted, and entertained. Finally, there will be work to do: We shall be office-bearers of responsibility in the universe.

Heaven is founded upon the paradox that the more we abandon ourselves to Christ, the more fully ourselves we become. Thus, while redemption by Christ improves people in this present life, the consummation of human maturity is unimaginable. In heaven both the individuality and society of persons will be fulfilled, both diversity and harmony. Heaven is varied, hell monotonous. Heaven is brimful of meaning*; hell is the absence of meaning. Heaven is reality itself, hell a ghost or shadow.

C. S. Lewis believed that heaven is probably unimaginable, even though we have the biblical images to take us as far as they can. Parable, allegory, and fiction are the closest that we can come to speaking of heaven. This is why he explored heaven so much through fantasy, as in *The Great Divorce*,* *The Voyage of the "Dawn Treader,"** *The Last Battle*,* and *Perelandra*.* In his prose, he particularly speaks of heaven in *The Problem of Pain*,* *Letters to Malcolm*,* and in the sermon "The Weight of Glory."

In *The Last Battle*, the children see the land of Narnia* die forever and freeze over in blackness. They are filled with regret. Later, as they walked in a fresh morning light in Aslan's Country,* they wondered why everything seemed strangely familiar. At last they realized that this was again Narnia, but now different—larger and more vivid, more like the real thing. It was different in the way that a real thing differs from its shadow, or waking life from a dream.

Lewis's point can be illustrated from the situation that faced Mary in the Gospels. She at first did not recognize her risen Master, but mistook him for the most real of persons, a gardener. When he said her name, she saw that it was he. Yet he was also different. His physical presence was a bit of heaven.

We miss the wonder of such a historical event, our perceptions dulled by familiarity or by carelessness toward the past, but when we see this kind of situation cast into fiction, as Lewis does so consummately well, we glimpse its meaning afresh.

Hegeliana A region charted on the Mappa Mundi* in *The Pilgrim's Regress*,* representing Hegelian philosophy (from Hegel) and absolute idealism.*

Hermit of Southern March In *The Horse and His Boy*,* he looks after the wounded Aravis* and the talking horses while Cor* continues his journey to warn King Lune* of the Calormene* danger. A tall, robed figure with a beard that reaches his knees, the hermit is 109 years of age and has a pool with the properties of a crystal ball.

Historicism See: HISTORY.

History In much of his literary criticism, C. S. Lewis was a literary historian. In an important essay, "Historicism" (1950), first published in book form in *Christian Reflections*,* he expressed his attitude to the study of history. This essay contains both an affirmation and a denial concerning the meaning* of history.

On the one hand, C. S. Lewis believes absolutely that human history is "a story written by the finger of God." On the other hand, he firmly rejects all claims to know the inner meaning and patterns of history by means of mere rational observation of events. Writing history is of course worthwhile, but grand philosophies of history (historicisms) are doomed to futility. Such grand schemes have been worked out by thinkers such as Hegel, Marx, and even Augustine. Lewis comments: "If by one miracle, the total content of time were spread out before me, and if, by another, I were able to hold all that infinity of events in my mind and if, by a third, God were pleased to comment on it so I could understand it, then, to be sure, I could do what the Historicist says he is doing. I could read the meaning, discern the pattern."

C. S. Lewis wanted instead to emphasize trust in God and an openness to ordinary human reality—the "primary history" in which God reveals himself in the moment-by-moment experience of life to each one who seeks him. That this view of history doesn't lead to skepticism about the value of culture is clear from another key essay, "Learning in War-time,"* where he points out the abiding value of scholarship. See also: LITERARY CRITIC, C. S. LEWIS AS A.

Hnohra In *Out of the Silent Planet*,* the hross* who teaches Dr. Elwin Ransom* the language and cultures of the beings on Malacandra.*

Hooper, Walter (1931-) Described by *The Independent* (March 7, 1994) as "Lewis's other American" (the first being Joy Davidman Lewis*), Walter Hooper was born in Reidsville, North Carolina. He was educated at the University of North Carolina in Chapel Hill. After serving in the U. S. Army, he read theology at Virginia Episcopal Seminary. He taught English at Christ School, Arden, North Carolina, 1960-61 and then at the University of Kentucky in Lexington, 1961-63.

After corresponding with Lewis for a while, Hooper was invited to visit him in Oxford. They met on June 7, 1963, and Hooper attended his first meeting of the Inklings* a few days later. That summer, in poor health, Lewis accepted Hooper's offer of secretarial assistance. But the young American's stay at The Kilns proved to be all too brief. "There followed the happiest period of my life," Mr. Hooper told the author, "for Lewis was a thousand times more interesting than his books. But the privilege was of short duration. I was in Kentucky teaching one final term before returning to Oxford when Lewis died."

When Hooper did return to Oxford in 1964, the Lewis estate hired him to collate and edit Lewis's literary legacy. Hooper has been working since 1964 as the literary adviser to the estate, during which time he has edited a number of Lewis's posthumous publications. In 1974 he and Roger Lancelyn Green coauthored the first authorized biography of Lewis. Formerly an Anglican, Walter Hooper became a Roman Catholic in 1988. He is the author of the definitive *C. S. Lewis: A Companion & Guide* (1996). Walter Hooper has undoubtedly contributed more than any other individual to Lewis's popularity throughout the world by his unstinted devotion to the publication of Lewis's works, many of which would have otherwise been neglected.

Horse and His Boy, The (1954) Set in the period of Narnia's* Golden Age, most of the story unfolds in the cruel southern land of Calormen.* Cor,* a lost son of King Lune* of the friendly country of Archenland,* north of Calormen, has been brought up by a poor fisherman. He has the name Shasta and knows nothing of his true origin, but he has a strange longing to travel to the northern lands.

The story also concerns a high-born Calormene girl, Aravis,* who runs away from home to flee an unpleasant marriage. Both children independently encounter Narnian talking horses in captivity in Calormen. The horses tell them about the freedom of Narnia's pleasant land, and they escape with the children.

When passing through Calormen's capital, Tashbaan,* Aravis uncovers a treacherous plot to conquer Archenland and Narnia. The spiteful Prince Rabadash,* foiled in his suit of Queen Susan* of Narnia, leads the plotters. With great courage, and some failures, the children are able to warn the two northern countries of their danger. The Calormene plot fails, Cor is restored to his father, the two horses—Bree* and Hwin*—return to their talking companions in Narnia, and Cor and Aravis marry, to become king and queen of Archenland after Lune's death.

Several of the characters familiar to readers of *The Lion, the Witch and the Wardrobe** appear in this book, including most of the Pevensie* children and the faun, Mr. Tumnus.* Both the skeptical horse Bree and the disdainful Aravis have to encounter Aslan.*

In this tale perhaps more than any other, C. S. Lewis embodies his love of "northernness," which he shared with his friends J. R. R. Tolkien* and Arthur Greeves,* and which is an important element in Tolkien's Middle-earth. The book also reveals some of the extent to which the geography of the world of which Narnia is a part is drawn from the late medieval picture of reality that Lewis loved so deeply, as portrayed in his brilliant study *The Discarded Image.**

House of Correction for Incompetent Tempters In *The Screwtape Letters,** one of the many departments of hell.* Tempters were initially trained at the Tempters' Training College, run by Dr. Slubgob.

Hrossa In *Out of the Silent Planet,** intelligent inhabitants of the planet Malacandra who outwardly look like gleaming black animals, a little like otters or seals, and yet are walking land creatures. From the hrossa Elwin Ransom* learns the language of Old Solar.* They are practical food-gathering beings with a penchant for poetry. See also: TALKING ANIMALS; PLANETS.

Mr. Humanist An allegorical figure in *The Pilgrim's Regress** representing a key player in the intellectual climate in which Lewis, as a young scholar, lived. He is one of the "cerebral" men John the pilgrim meets in the north of the world (see also: MAPPA MUNDI).

Hwin The talking Narnian* mare who plays an important part in the tale known as *The Horse and His Boy.** She helps Aravis* escape an unpleasant marriage. There are many delightful contrasts between her character and that of Bree,* the other talking horse involved in this famous Narnian tale.

Hyaline Splendor In *The Horse and His Boy,** the ship of King Edmund* and Queen Lucy.*

Hyoi In *Out of the Silent Planet,** the hross* whom Dr. Elwin Ransom* first encounters on Malacandra. Much to Ransom's distress, Hyoi is later shot by one of the earth men. See also: TALKING ANIMALS; PLANETS.

I

Idea of the Holy, The, **Rudolf Otto** (1917) Subtitled *An Inquiry into the Non-rational Factor in the Idea of the Divine and Its Relation to the Rational*, this was the chief work of the German Lutheran theologian Rudolf Otto (1869-1937). He was professor of systematic theology at the University of Marburg 1919-1937. In the work he explores our sense of the numinous,* which is, he believed, common to all strong religious experiences and beyond reason, knowledge, or any other term. Lewis powerfully summarizes Otto's main idea in the introduction to his *The Problem of Pain.** Otto's portrayal of the numinous made a major impact upon Lewis's thought and work. Indeed, he listed *The Idea of the Holy** as one of the ten books most influential upon his thinking and vocational attitude (see: READING OF C. S. LEWIS). In the book, as well as providing a phenomenology of the numinous, Otto explores the numinous in the Old and New Testaments, in poetry and art, and in figures such as Luther and John Ruskin.

Idealism, C. S. Lewis and In his journey from atheism Lewis turned at one stage to idealism. In his autobiography, *Surprised by Joy,** Lewis recalls admitting that "the whole universe was, in the last resort, mental; that our logic was participating in a cosmic *logos.*"

In the early years of this century, and in England (particularly in Oxford*), idealism predominated in philosophy, with realists strongly opposing this giant. The philosopher John Mabbott, a colleague of Lewis's during that period, points out the intellectual isolation of Oxford during this period in his *Oxford Memories*. He writes:

> Oxford philosophy, as we found it, was completely inbred. It had practically no contacts with Cambridge, or the Continent, or America. The traditional doctrine was Hegelian idealism, filtered through the great Scottish prophets, [Edward] Caird, Pringle-Pattison, [David George] Ritchie and [William] Wallace, and our own T. H. Green, [Bernard] Bosanquet and [F. H.] Bradley. The basic issue was between the idealists and their view that reality is spiritual and therefore that the world around us is akin to or determined by mind, and our realists, [John] Cook Wilson, [Sir W. David] Ross, [Harold Arthur] Prichard, holding that the objects of knowledge and perception are independent of mind.

Idealism was linked in many minds with Christianity, or with spiritual views that opposed a rapidly spreading secularism and what Lewis in *Miracles** called naturalism. Idealism in England was especially associated with T. H. Green (1836-1882), F. H. Bradley (1846-1924), and J. M. E. McTaggart (1866-1925). The idealists typically held that physical objects can have no existence apart from a mind that is conscious of them. For idealists the divine mind and the human mind have fundamental similarities. As a young atheist in Oxford, C. S. Lewis was at first staunchly opposed to idealism. He was an out-and-out realist and naturalist. He believed, for instance, that the resemblance between human languages was due to the similarities of human throats rather than the result of an innate structure in humans. Naturalism is defined by Lewis as the view that "every finite thing or event must be (in principle) explicable in terms of the Total System." Nature is the whole show. His rejection of naturalism is embedded in everything he wrote after his early poetry, *Spirits in Bondage* (1919) and *Dymer* (1926).

His brilliant friend Owen Barfield,* with whom he had a formative "great war,"* persuaded Lewis eventually to accept some tenets of idealism. C. S. Lewis did not stay long here, however, but moved from idealism, via pantheism, to theism, and eventually to Christian belief.

Lewis taught philosophy for the year 1924 to 1925 in University College, before getting his teaching post at Magdalen College in English Literature. His ability as a philosopher is easily overlooked. In fact his dispute with Barfield was often carried on at a highly sophisticated philosophical level, and his philosophical interests were well known to others. Indeed, he continued teaching some philosophy after taking up his lecturing in English. Mabbott describes the formation of a philosophical discussion club for the young lecturers in which Lewis actively participated, the "Wee Teas" (named by analogy with the breakaway Free Church of Scotland), at the period of his teaching in philosophy. His description gives a remarkable insight into the kind of discussion club in which Lewis thrived and which he always had to have. Even at this stage of his life, Lewis made his mark on his peers.

> Our seniors had an institution called "The Philosophers' Teas." They met on Thursdays at 4 o'clock. Anyone present could raise a point for discussion. We juniors were invited to join, and we found the occasions friendly and unstuffy (again the genuine democracy of the faculty could be clearly felt). But, as a forum for discussion, they were not a success. . . . Tea-time is not a philosophic hour: and, by the time the crumpets had gone round, it would be 4.15 or 4.30. We juniors were under such tutorial pressure that we had to teach daily from 5 to 7 o'clock, so we had to leave at 4.50 to get back to our Colleges. . . . We juniors established a group built on our experience of the "Teas." We agreed that evening is the time for thought. . . . Membership should be limited to the number ideal for a discussion, which we agreed to be six. To avoid competitive luxury, dinners were to be three-course, and with beer, not wine. (This rigor was not pedantically maintained.) Our original mem-

> bership was: Gilbert Ryle, Henry Price, Frank Hardie, C. S. Lewis, T. D. Weldon and myself. C. S. Lewis soon seceded from philosophy to English Literature, popular theology and science fiction; but not before he had assisted in a happy contribution to our proceedings . . . .
>
> It was understood that opening remarks need not be finished papers but rather flying kites (even in note form if desired). We knew each other so well that our basic methods and interests could be taken for granted, and our growing points exposed straightaway to lively, frank and friendly scrutiny. . . . I am sure that everything any of us published would have been considerably less well-argued but for running this gauntlet. . . . Quite apart from its value to our philosophy, I count my membership as, apart from my marriage, the happiest and most refreshing experience of my life.

After his conversion to Christ, C. S. Lewis's position, philosophically, was a modified soft realism. Significantly, he was influenced by the great realist metaphysician, the Australian Samuel Alexander* (1859-1938). Lewis rejected the grand impersonality of idealist systems, and even the goal of a total system of thought. He preferred the individuality of places and people, seasons and times, moods and tones of feeling. God* himself was the most concrete of existences. Christ's incarnation had a joyous logic to it, as did the revelation of God to mankind in the human (yet authoritative) writings of the Bible.*

For all his realism, C. S. Lewis drew imaginative nourishment from idealist systems such as the thought of Plato* or the medieval model of the universe (see: *THE DISCARDED IMAGE*). As a thinker, C. S. Lewis rejected attempts at a natural theology, stressing the importance of presuppositions over where we get to in our knowing. He illustrated this vividly in the case of the miraculous in his book *Miracles*.* Having decided never to rule out the possibility of the miraculous in advance, Lewis's thinking was boldly supernaturalist and yet unflinchingly realistic in tone. His realism is so marked that he appears skeptical in places of the validity of theoretical thinking in view of its inevitable abstraction from concrete things, events, and persons. C. S. Lewis's combination of realism and supernaturalist vision is his hallmark, a combination that is irresistible to numerous readers.

C. S. Lewis's thinking has been described merely in terms of sacramental theology,* for example, by Leanne Payne in her study *The Real Presence*. Such an attempt, however, fails to do justice to the basic realistic tenor of C. S. Lewis's thinking in *Miracles*,* *The Problem of Pain*,* *Mere Christianity*,* and other popular theological writings.

Oxford idealism was dramatically swept away by logical positivism, already weakened by the realism of G. E. Moore (1873-1958) and Bertrand Russell (1872-1970). On the Continent, idealism disintegrated under the attack from secular and religious existentialism. Theologically, existentialism made a deep impression on the thought of Rudolf Bultmann (1884-1976), whose view on myth* in the Gospels was far from that of C. S. Lewis.

C. S. Lewis himself seemed to search for an alternative to the old idealism that was more than his pre-Christian materialism, and which certainly stood in contrast to the new theology of existentialism or the old liberal theology of rationalism. Many forms of realism are compatible with theism, and he found his own. Some of his more creative ideas are summed up in his seminal sermon on what he called "transposition."* His view of reality was fundamentally tied up with a highly original view of meaning,* which he gradually articulated, and in which meaning is associated with, and perhaps identified with, reality. Thinking about meaning strengthened his preoccupation with myth, and with the relationship between myth and fact or reality (see: MYTH BECAME FACT). See also: NATURALISM AND SUPERNATURALISM.

Ilgamuth In *The Horse and His Boy*,* one of the lords of Rabadash,* slain by Darrin of Archenland.*

Ilkeen In *The Horse and His Boy*,* the location in Calormen* of the beautiful palace of Ahoshta Tarkaan.*

Imagination (imaginative fantasy) The imagination is a mental faculty. Fantasy is a power and product of the imagination, as thought is a power and product of the intellect. As thought is the reason in action, fantasy is the imagination at work. Both imagination and fantasy are difficult to define. With both Lewis and his friend J. R. R. Tolkien,* their view of nature implied the reality of the supernatural world and its myriad connections with the natural world. Their Christian fantasy not only concerns the supernatural, but illuminates the natural world, and brings us into contact with it. Hence their fantasy did not always explicitly carry supernatural elements.

As well as a power and product of the imagination, fantasy is also of course a dimension of a number of literary and oral genres, such as science fiction, heroic romance (such as *The Lord of the Rings*), allegory, apocalyptic (such as the biblical book of Revelation), and fairy story. Fantasy always draws attention to its fictional nature, so it has to be well crafted to achieve its effects.

This is why Tolkien saw the high point of fantasy as subcreation,* and Lewis viewed it as imaginative invention. Tolkien had subcreation as its defining feature, whereas Lewis's interest was less structural; for him, fantasy was a prime vehicle for capturing the elusive quality of joy.* But both for Lewis and Tolkien, fantasy had a strong inventive and imaginative component. Fantasies generated in sleep for instance would not in themselves be of interest, nor egocentric daydreaming. The two men were interested in carefully crafted literary fantasy. Lewis particularly saw the imagination as the "organ of meaning" or reality rather than of conceptual truth. See: MEANING AND IMAGINATION.

Inklings These were a group of male friends, all people of talent, who met together at least once a week to talk about ideas, to read to each other for pleasure and criticism pieces they were writing, and to enjoy a good evening of "the cut and parry of prolonged, fierce, masculine argument." The Inklings in fact embodied C. S. Lewis's ideals of life and pleasure. In fact, he was the life and soul of the party. Their important years as a writing group were from the early 1930s to near the end of the 1940s. The war years were especially significant, when Charles Williams* was resident in Oxford.*

The group did not have any consistent documentation such as the careful minuting of the fictional Notion Club, J. R. R. Tolkien's* portrait of an Inklings-type group of friends set in the future. Humphrey Carpenter's excellent study draws on the key sources—the diaries of Major Warren Lewis, C. S. Lewis's letters to his brother in the early months of the Second World War, Tolkien's long letters to his son Christopher while in South Africa with the RAF in that war, Lewis's introduction to *Essays Presented to Charles Williams*, and reminiscences by Inklings such as John Wain,* Commander Jim Dundas-Grant, Christopher Tolkien, and others.

The Inklings expanded from the deep friendship between Tolkien and Lewis, a remarkable association comparable to that between Wordsworth and Coleridge in literary significance. Lewis, in his book *The Four Loves,* explains the process by which friendship, the least jealous of loves, expands:

> In each of my friends there is something that only some other friend can fully bring out. By myself I am not large enough to call the whole man into activity; I want other lights than my own to show all his facets. Now that Charles is dead, I shall never again see Ronald's reaction to a specifically Caroline joke. Far from having more of Ronald, having him "to myself" now that Charles is away, I have less of Ronald. Hence true Friendship is the least jealous of loves. Two friends delight to be joined by a third, and three by a fourth, if only the newcomer is qualified to become a real friend. . . . Of course the scarcity of kindred souls—not to mention practical considerations about the size of rooms and the audibility of voices—sets limits to the enlargement of the circle; but within those limits we possess each friend not less but more as the number of those with whom we share him increases [from pp. 58, 59].

In his book Humphrey Carpenter lists the various Inklings—a long list—but, in a letter to Bede Griffiths in December 1941, Lewis has quite a short list. He is explaining his dedication to the Inklings in his recently published *The Problem of Pain.** He lists Charles Williams, Dyson of Reading (H. V. D. "Hugo" Dyson*), Warren Lewis,* Tolkien, and "Humphrey" Havard.* He explains Tolkien and Dyson as the "immediate human causes of my own conversion" to Christianity. Remarkably, the name of Owen Barfield* does not appear. In fact, Barfield rarely was able to visit. On one occasion, Lewis grumbles that Barfield is visiting on a Thursday, which means he'll attend the

Inklings, and Lewis will have less time alone with him! It was later that the Inklings swelled further to include Colin Hardie, Lord David Cecil, John Wain, and others. Christopher Tolkien attended as soon as he was back from South Africa. It was upon this larger group that Tolkien drew inspiration for "The Notion Club Papers," and it is likely that he read it all to them. Warren Lewis records in his diary, Thursday, August 22, 1946, about "Tollers" reading "a magnificent myth which is to knit up and concludes his Papers of the Notions Club." This would have been "The Drowning of Anadune" (now published with "The Notion Club Papers" in *Sauron Defeated*).

A further complexity of the Inklings is that there were two patterns of meetings: Tuesday mornings in the Bird and Baby pub (The Eagle and Child,* St. Giles)—except when Lewis took the Chair in Cambridge, when Monday mornings were more suitable—and Thursday evenings, usually in Lewis's rooms in Magdalen, but often in Tolkien's in Merton College. The Thursday evenings were of more literary interest, as here members would read to each other work in progress, receiving criticism and encouragement.

The death of Charles Williams was a great blow to the group, particularly to Lewis, and the 1950s marked a gradual cooling of the friendship between Lewis and Tolkien, which was the heart around which the Inklings formed and grew. The situation was not helped by "Hugo" Dyson exercising a veto against Tolkien reading from the unfinished *The Lord of the Rings* at Inklings meetings. A further complexity was introduced by Lewis's (at first only intellectual) friendship with Joy Davidman, but that is another story (see: LEWIS, HELEN JOY DAVIDMAN).

C. S. Lewis describes a typical meeting in a letter to an absent member—his brother—in 1939. The "new Hobbit" is a reference to the first volume of *The Lord of the Rings*. "On Thursday we had a meeting of the Inklings . . . we dined at the Eastgate. I have never in my life seen Dyson so exuberant—'A roaring cataract of nonsense.' The bill of fare afterwards consisted of a section of the new Hobbit book from Tolkien, a nativity play from Charles Williams (unusually intelligible for him, and approved by all), and a chapter out of the book on *The Problem of Pain* from me."

Much of the "new Hobbit," i.e., *The Lord of the Rings*, was read in this way, sometimes by Christopher instead of Tolkien senior. After 1951 the term the Inklings no longer appears in Warren's diaries, and it is probable that about two years before the Thursday meetings dried up, though the Tuesday meetings (or Monday ones) continued until 1962. The key years of the Inklings, in terms of their literary significance, are probably therefore from the late 1930s until near the end of 1949.

The Inklings had a modest and unassuming Boswell, Warnie Lewis. He, more than anyone at the time, seemed aware of the uniqueness and identity of the Inklings, valuing the group at least because of his affection for his brother. Other members were J. A. W. Bennett, Lord David Cecil, Nevill Coghill,* Commander Jim Dundas-Grant, Hugo Dyson, Adam Fox,* Colin Hardie, Dr. "Humphrey" Havard, Gervase Mathew,* R. B. McCallum, C. E. ("Tom") Stevens,* Christopher Tolkien, John Wain,* and Charles Wrenn.

One of the favorite haunts of the Inklings, The Eagle and Child* public house, has since been renovated, but a plaque is now placed there in memory, which reads:

> C. S. LEWIS,
>
> His brother, W. H. Lewis, J. R. R. Tolkien, Charles Williams and other friends met every Tuesday morning, between the years 1939-1962 in the back room of this their favourite pub. These men, popularly known as the "Inklings," met here to drink beer and to discuss, among other things, the books they were writing.

W. H. Lewis was skeptical of the idea of the Inklings representing a school of literature or theology. He was probably right, in view of the diversity of its members at one time or another. However, Lewis hankered for others who shared his core beliefs, and some of the main Inklings such as Williams, Tolkien, and even Barfield did, though Barfield never became an orthodox Christian. Even though Barfield was baptized into the Anglican church, he remained committed to Anthroposophism.*

Speaking in America, Owen Barfield remembered the way Lewis affected all the groups he was part of, including the Inklings. The first way was unconsciously and unobtrusively by the sheer force and weight of his personality, and, as Barfield put it, "a rather loud voice when he was in high spirits." Lewis would set the tone and decide the topic of conversation. Barfield recalled that, on one occasion, when the topic was not of interest to Lewis (it could have been politics or economics), he merely turned aside from the conversation, picked up a book, and proceeded to read it instead of talking.

The second way Lewis affected a group was that, irrespective of the subject brought up, he always turned it around to the point where it was a moral issue or problem. If anyone did not think that a moral issue was involved, Lewis reminded him that there ought to be.

Barfield wondered if something was not happening to "the Romantic Impulse" during the life of the Inklings. He could discern four important threads, each largely identified with Lewis, Tolkien, Williams, or himself: (1) the yearning for the infinite and unattainable—Lewis's *Sehnsucht* or joy*; (2) in Barfield's words, "The conviction of the dignity of man and his part in the future history of the world conceived as a kind of progress towards increasing immanence of the divine in the human" (Barfield's own position); (3) the idealization of love between the sexes, as in Charles Williams's thought and writings; and (4) the opposite of tragedy, the Happy Ending, Tolkien's idea of the eucatastrophe.

As literary artists, Lewis, Tolkien, and Williams certainly seemed to try to redeem the romantic tradition that had been distorted by the

Romantic Movement and its predecessors in the eighteenth century. This early and later Romanticism had reacted against the dominant form of humanism that had made a god out of reason. Romanticism reacted with irrationalism and a nurturing of natural instincts and feeling. It sought the origin of mankind in nature* and rejected traditional philosophy and hierarchical social structure, both of which thought of, and pictured, mankind's origins as being in God. Tolkien, Lewis, and Williams attempted to redeem the romantic tradition by enriching, strengthening, and purifying it with orthodox Christianity and with reason, Lewis following in the footsteps of John Bunyan and his *The Pilgrim's Progress*, nearly 300 years earlier. Reaching back to the periods before the Enlightenment, they were premodernist in orientation (see: THEOLOGY OF ROMANCE).

In their attempt, they rehabilitate an understanding that has almost been lost by modern people. Lewis, Tolkien, and Williams, following Owen Barfield's *Poetic Diction*,* saw that there is a rightness or correctness in the imagination itself. Furthermore, without the enrichment of proper imagining, thought is impoverished and eventually becomes meaningless. Paradoxically, therefore, through fantasy or the play of imagination, thought makes true contact with reality.

Lewis was fond of giving, as an example of the rightness of imagination, the traditional equations of light with truth and of darkness with error. Fairy tales make use of these stock archetypal, "natural," or proper equations. In Bunyan's *The Pilgrim's Progress*, doubt is pictured as the strong Doubting Castle and despair as its owner, Giant Despair. To think of doubt and despair as a castle and a giant is satisfying and "natural" and, in some sense, true and real. The turning of a majority of modern artists and writers to a subjective view of the imagination has helped to create a crisis in meaning.*

The three men attempted in their fiction and poetry to provide true or objective images that had a place in the contemporary world. While a novel, a play, or a poem is not meant primarily to put over Christian or even moral truths, or to be "about life"—imagination has a different function from theoretical thinking—images embodied in such works of literature can enrich and liberate our thinking by enriching and defining our concepts, and can enhance our experience of the world by enlarging our perception of, and sensitivity to, existence.

FURTHER READING

Humphrey Carpenter, *The Inklings: C. S. Lewis, J. R. R. Tolkien, Charles Williams and Their Friends* (1978).

John Wain, *Sprightly Running: Part of an Autobiography* (1962).

Rand Kuhl, "Owen Barfield in Southern California," *Mythlore*, Vol. 1, No. 4, 1969.

Gareth Knight, *The Magical World of the Inklings* (1990).

Diana Pavlac, "The company they keep: Assessing the mutual influence of C. S. Lewis, J. R. R. Tolkien, and Charles Williams" (Ph.D. thesis, 1993, University of Illinois at Chicago).

"Inner Ring" An essay that first appeared in print in *Transposition and Other Addresses.** Its theme is illustrated in C. S. Lewis's science-fiction story *That Hideous Strength.** Lewis saw the lure of the "inner ring" as a perversion of friendship.* Friendship, he wrote, "causes perhaps half of all the happiness in the world, and no Inner Ringer can ever have it." Unlike friendship, the desire to be on the inside of a group leads to a perpetual anxiety, even if achieved, whereas real friendship is "snug and safe" because it is free of this desire. Lewis believed that in most associations of business and professions there were inner rings as well as the official hierarchies. "You are never formally and explicitly admitted by anyone. You discover gradually, in almost indefinable ways, that it exists and that you are outside it; and then later, perhaps, that you are inside it." Inner rings provide a climate in which evil becomes easier. Until a person conquers the fear of being an outsider, an outsider he or she will remain. In *That Hideous Strength*, the lure of the inner ring of Belbury* on Mark Studdock* dramatically illustrates its danger.

Intelligence Department In *The Screwtape Letters,** part of the bureaucracy of hell. Although hell dislikes knowledge, which it regards as hateful and mawkish, a certain amount is necessary to have effective power on earth to upset the Enemy's plans. Devils assigned to human patients pass information back to the Department. Screwtape* laments the inability of the Department to penetrate the purposes of the Enemy.

Island, The Glimpsed by John in *The Pilgrim's Regress,** the cause and object of his sweet desire, a longing involving joy.*

Island of the star See RAMANDU'S ISLAND.

Island of Voices In *The Voyage of the "Dawn Treader"** a low-lying island to the west of Deathwater Island* in the Eastern Ocean.* It has lawns and parks that are noticeably well kept. The only important building is a stone house, approached through an avenue of trees, belonging to the island's governor, Coriakin.*

When the voyagers landed on the island, they at first thought it uninhabited. This mistake is understandable because the main inhabitants, the Dufflepuds,* had been made invisible. Their voices, however, could still be heard, hence the origin of the island's name.

Istra In *Till We Have Faces,** Psyche's* name in her native Glome.* Psyche is the Greek form of her name, preferred by Psyche herself, Orual,* and The Fox.*

J

Jadis See: WHITE WITCH.

Jenkin, Alfred Kenneth Hamilton (1900-1980) As undergraduates attending University College, Oxford, he and Lewis became fast and lifelong friends. He is referred to affectionately in *Surprised by Joy,** and he is mentioned frequently in Lewis's diaries (published as *All My Road Before Me**). Jenkin taught Lewis to enjoy the "thisness" or "quiddity" of things, an enjoyment that became a hallmark of Lewis's thought and writings (see: NATURE). In *That Hideous Strength** Camilla and Arthur Denniston* enjoy all types of weather, as Jenkin did.

Jewel, the unicorn In *The Last Battle,** Jewel, a talking beast, is the dearest friend of Tirian,* last king of Narnia.* They saved each other's lives in war. Jewel's feelings as he enters the New Narnia remade by Aslan* illustrate C. S. Lewis's constant and special theme of joy.*

John John is the contemporary Everyman or pilgrim in *The Pilgrim's Regress,** based loosely upon Lewis himself. The name possibly was borrowed from Lewis's model, John Bunyan.

Joy Joy is a defining characteristic of romance (and thus fantasy) in C. S. Lewis.

His autobiography up to his conversion* at the age of thirty-one is recorded in *Surprised by Joy,** and somewhat in his long allegory, *The Pilgrim's Regress.** These tell us that his lengthy, varied, and reluctant pilgrimage to truth was greatly influenced by a certain distinct tone of feeling that he discovered in early childhood and that stayed with him on and off throughout his adolescence and early manhood.

This longing for beauty or joy he learned from gazing at the Castlereagh Hills of Belfast from his nursery windows. Later reading of northern myths and sagas intensified this restlessness. Significantly, in 1922, while still a nonbeliever, Lewis wrote a poem on this theme, "Joy," reprinted in *Collected Poems.** Toward the end of his life Lewis personified the imaginative longing in a character in *Till We Have Faces.** This character is based upon the Psyche* of an ancient Roman writing. Because myths and otherworldly tales can often define this longing for beauty, Lewis defended and wrote this unrespectable type of literature throughout his distinguished career.

There is a relationship between love and zest for life and the desire for beauty that constantly fascinated Lewis. The stories of George MacDonald,* which shaped Lewis's imagination, are dominated by a joyful quality of holiness or goodness in life—but it was no platonic spirituality. MacDonald's stories (including his novels) concern the homely and ordinary, transformed by a new light. Lewis captured this exactly when he wrote: "The quality which had enchanted me in his imaginative works turned out to be the quality of the real universe, the divine, magical, terrifying and ecstatic reality in which we all live."

C. S. Lewis's own imaginative creations such as The Chronicles of Narnia* sprang from this love of life. He seems to have been very preoccupied with joy, as he called it, throughout the 1940s and early 1950s. The last chapter of *The Problem of Pain** (1940) speaks of it; a sermon, "The Weight of Glory"* (1941), tries to define the desire; *The Voyage of the "Dawn Treader"** (1952) is about the Narnian mouse Reepicheep's quest for Aslan's Country* at the World's End; *Surprised by Joy* (1955) traces the twin threads of Lewis's thinking and his longing for beauty up to his conversion; and in *Till We Have Faces* (1956) Princess Psyche has a love of this beauty that is stronger than death. In *Transposition and Other Addresses** (1949) Lewis wrote: "We do not want merely to see beauty. . . . We want something else which can hardly be put into words—to be united with the beauty we see, to pass into it, to receive it into ourselves, to bathe in it, to become part of it. That is why we have peopled air and earth and water with gods and goddesses and nymphs and elves."

Such joy, thought Lewis, inspired the writer to create fantasy. In fact, *Sehnsucht,* seen as a yearning or longing that is a pointer to joy, was for Lewis a defining characteristic of fantasy. The creation of another world is an attempt to reconcile human beings and the world, to embody the fulfillment of our imaginative longing. Imaginative worlds, wonderlands, are "regions of the spirit." Such worlds of the numinous* may be found in some science fiction, some poetry, some fairy stories, some novels, some myths, even in a phrase or sentence. Lewis claimed in *Of Other Worlds*: "To construct plausible and moving 'other worlds' you must draw on the only real 'other world' we know, that of the spirit."

In a doctoral thesis, *Romantic Religion in the Works of Owen Barfield, C. S. Lewis, Charles Williams, and J. R. R. Tolkien*, Robert J. Reilly sees Lewis as an advocate of "romantic religion," or "the attempt to reach religious truths by means and techniques traditionally called romantic, and . . . to defend and justify these techniques and attitudes of romanticism by holding that they have religious sanction."

Another Ph.D. dissertation specifically concerned the theme of joy in C. S. Lewis's work—Corbin Carnell's "The Dialectic of Desire." He argues that Lewis illuminates a state of mind that has been a recurrent theme in literature. This is the compulsive quest "which brings with it both fleeting joy and the sad realization that one is yet separated from what is desired." Joy for Lewis is the key both to the nature of human beings and to their Creator.

C. S. Lewis saw this unquenchable longing as a sure sign that no part of the created world, and thus no aspect of human experience, is capable of fulfilling fallen mankind. We are dominated by a homelessness and yet by a keen sense of what home means.

In *Surprised by Joy* Lewis reported his sensations of joy, some of which were responses to natural beauty and others of which were literary or artistic responses, in the belief that other people would recognize similar experiences of their own. Even some who cannot identify with this experience in Lewis's autobiographical account, however, will respond when reading his fiction. He claimed that distant hills, seen from his nursery window, taught him longing and made him for good or ill a votary of the "Blue Flower" before he was six years old. The Blue Flower is the symbol of *Sehnsucht* or inconsolable longing in German literature and Scandinavian ballads dating back to the Middle Ages.

For Lewis, joy was a foretaste of ultimate reality, heaven* itself, or, the same thing, our world as it was meant to be, unspoiled by the fall of mankind, and one day to be remade. "Joy," wrote Lewis, "is the serious business of Heaven."

In attempting to imagine heaven, Lewis discovered that joy is "the secret signature of each soul." He speculated that the desire for heaven is part of our essential (and unfulfilled) humanity:

> There are times when I think we do not desire heaven; but more often I find myself wondering whether, in our heart of hearts, we have ever desired anything else. . . . Are not all lifelong friendships born at the moment when at last you meet another human being who has some inkling (but faint and uncertain even in the best) of that something which you were born desiring, and which, beneath the flux of other desires and in all the momentary silences between the louder passions, night and day, year by year, from childhood to old age, you are looking for, watching for, listening for? You have never had it. All the things that have ever deeply possessed your soul have been but hints of it—tantalizing glimpses, promises never quite fulfilled, echoes that died away just as they caught your ear. But if it should really become manifest—if there ever came an echo that did not die away but swelled into the sound itself—you would know it. Beyond all possibility of doubt you would say, "Here at last is the thing I was made for." We cannot tell each other about it. It is the secret signature of each soul, the

> incommunicable and unappeasable want, the thing we desired before we met our wives or made our friends or chose our work, and which we shall still desire on our deathbeds, when the mind no longer knows wife or friend or work. While we are, this is. If we lose this, we lose all. (*The Problem of Pain*, chapter 10).

C. S. Lewis's portrayal of joy can be seen as providing valuable data of a key human experience, data that has philosophical and religious importance. It was also central to his apologetics for the Christian faith. See also: HEAVEN.

K

Ketterley, Andrew See: ANDREW, UNCLE.

Ketterley, Letty In *The Magician's Nephew*,* the aunt of Digory Kirke,* who is caring for his dying mother, sister of his Uncle Andrew.* She is unimpressed by Jadis* the Witch, who hurls her across the room.

Kidrash In *The Horse and His Boy*,* the father of Aravis* who tries to marry her off to the ugly and aged new Grand Vizier, Ahoshta.* It is claimed in Calormen* that he is a descendent of the god Tash.*

Kilns, The Lewis's home from 1930 until his death in 1963. Prior to moving there, he lived at a total of eight Oxford addresses from first arriving in Oxford in 1916. The Kilns occupied eight acres and was eight years old when Lewis established a household in it with Mrs. Janie Moore* and her daughter Maureen. Major Warnie Lewis* also joined them, moving in permanently two years later upon taking early retirement from the British army. At that time the property boasted a tennis court, large unruly grounds including a pond large enough for swimming in, a greenhouse, and the ruins of brick kilns. The pond (which still exists today as part of a nature reserve) is a flooded quarry from which the clay for brick-making had been taken.

The house is now owned by The C. S. Lewis Foundation of Redlands, California, and has undergone extensive renovation, retaining its period character.

Kirke, Digory Digory appears as a boy in *The Magician's Nephew*,* then as a grownup in *The Lion, the Witch and the Wardrobe** and *The Last Battle*.* As a boy, he and his dying mother lodge with his Uncle Andrew* in Edwardian London. With his neighbor, Polly Plummer,* he travels to other worlds by means of magical rings, and is present at the creation of Narnia* by Aslan,* the talking lion. By the beginning of the Second World War, he is an elderly professor who owns a country house of historical interest. The Pevensie* children arrive as evacuees and stumble across a way into Narnia through his wardrobe built of wood from an apple tree that grew from a magical Narnian apple. Later he becomes poor and is forced to sell the house and tutor students, including Peter Pevensie. Digory's surname might be an affectionate tribute to Lewis's own tutor, W. T. Kirkpatrick.* C. S. Lewis uses the name Kirk again in *The Pilgrim's Regress** for Mother Kirk, representing the church.

Kirkpatrick, William T. (1848-1921) Lewis's tutor from 1914-1917 and dubbed by him "the Great Knock" because of the impact of his stringent logical mind on the teenager. Kirkpatrick was then retired as headmaster of Lurgen College in Northern Ireland, where Albert Lewis,* C. S. Lewis's father had attended. Kirkpatrick lived in Great Bookham, Surrey, England, where Lewis lodged happily during the tutelage. Lewis held a great affection for Kirkpatrick, describing him as the person who came closer to being "a purely logical entity" than anyone else he had ever met. Kirkpatrick's method was to combine language study with firsthand experience of major works; he guided Lewis in German, French, Italian, Latin, and classical Greek. His rationalism and atheism reinforced Lewis's own beliefs at that time, though Lewis's imagination* continued to have an independent, contradictory life (for instance, he discovered George MacDonald's* *Phantastes** during this period).

Kirkpatrick made his mark on Lewis's fiction, to be seen in some characteristics of the learned Professor Digory Kirke* and in the skeptical Ulsterman MacPhee in *That Hideous Strength*.*

L

Landlord, The In *The Pilgrim's Regress,** John* first hears of The Landlord in his childhood in Puritania,* and he perceives the giver of rules to be a despot, before his understanding grows as a result of his pilgrimage through the modern world. The Landlord is sovereign over Puritania and the other regions of John's world (depicted in the Mappa Mundi*).

Lantern Waste In *The Magician's Nephew*, the children enter an empty world and see Narnia* created by Aslan. An Edwardian London lamppost grows here from a piece of lamppost brought by the White Witch.* In later years children again enter Narnia near here through a wardrobe in the story, *The Lion, the Witch and the Wardrobe*. Lantern Waste is west of Beaversdam. See also: NARNIA—GEOGRAPHY; NARNIA—HISTORY.

Lasaraleen In *The Horse and His Boy*,* an old friend of Aravis,* who helps her to escape from the great Calormen* city of Tashbaan.

The Last Battle (1956) Based upon biblical prophecies of the end of the world, this story tells the end of one world, the world of which Narnia* is a part, how all worlds are linked, and how the great talking lion Aslan* is the key to this link. Thus The Chronicles of Narnia* draw to their conclusion, and the consistency of their otherworldliness is established. The work won the high-ranking Carnegie Medal for the best children's book of its year.

As in all the stories, children from our world are in Narnia to help or to rule. In this case, Eustace Scrubb* and Jill Pole* come. One of the strangest features of the story, a twist reminiscent of Charles Williams,* is that all the principal characters from our world are already dead as a result of a train accident. There are some similarities with Lewis's *The Great Divorce*,* in that events after death are imagined, and a vision of heaven* is presented.

The Last Battle tells of the passing of Narnia and the beginning of the New Narnia. It recounts the attempt of Shift,* the talking ape, to delude the creatures of Narnia into thinking that Aslan* has returned. Shift drapes Puzzle, a simple donkey, in a lion skin found floating in the river. He then persuades the talking animals that Puzzle is Aslan returned, and that he, Shift, is his spokesperson. Worse, he forms an alliance with Narnia's traditional enemy, Calormen.*

Young King Tirian,* the last of the Narnian rulers and seventh in descent from Rilian,* hears of evil things happening—talking trees cut down, Narnian animals enslaved—and cannot believe that Aslan has returned and that this is his will. With his loyal unicorn Jewel,* he resists the Calormenes and is captured. Like several before him in previous ages, he calls for help from our world. Eustace and Jill are sent in answer to his prayer. The true Aslan also returns.

In our world, Professor Digory Kirke* and Polly Plummer,* the very first visitors to Narnia (as recounted in *The Magician's Nephew**), had called together all those who had been in Narnia. There is a train crash that kills all those who answer the call, both those in an arriving train and those awaiting it at the station. All go into Narnia, though only Eustace and Jill are active participants in the final battle against evil, helping Tirian, Jewel, and the loyal Narnians. The visitors see Aslan's judgment of all the inhabitants of Narnia and its other countries and then are called "further up and further in" to a New Narnia. They discover that it is now permanently linked to their own familiar world of England, also transfigured. They would never again have to part from Aslan, though now they see him in a new form.

"Learning in War-Time" An important essay that first appeared in book form in the collection *Transposition and Other Addresses.** C. S. Lewis argued that nothing—not even war—can rightfully occupy the whole of our lives, except God himself. A person is not defined by any of his or her temporal functions. War might require that we die, but we should never live for it. Since the fall of mankind, war is a permanent human state. All aspects of our lives are to be given to God, including our scholarship. This gives all parts of our lives their proper place and allows them to be good in an ultimate sense. See also: COSMIC WAR.

Mrs. Lefay In *The Magician's Nephew,** the fairy godmother of Uncle Andrew.* She passed on to him a box of dust from Atlantis* to destroy, but he kept it. She is perhaps named after Morgan Le Fay of Arthurian legend.

Letters of C. S. Lewis C. S. Lewis's letters are soon to be published as the *Collected Letters* in three volumes, the first volume of which is complete, edited by Walter Hooper.* The series will be a significant addition to the corpus of Lewis's major writings, because of the quality of his letters. Much of his correspondence has already been published. *Letters of C. S. Lewis* (1966), edited, with a memoir by W. H. Lewis,* grew out of a very important unpublished biography by his brother, available to read at the Marion E. Wade Center, Wheaton, Illinois, with a copy at Oxford's Bodleian Library. *Letters to an American Lady* (1967), edited by Clyde S. Kilby, is a collection of letters to a woman Lewis never met, Mary Willis Shelburne. The largest collection outside of the *Collected Letters* is *They Stand Together: The Letters of C. S. Lewis to Arthur Greeves (1914-1963)*,* edited by Walter Hooper. Arthur Greeves* was one of Lewis's closest Ulster friends. *Letters to Children* (1985), edited by Lyle W. Dorsett and Marjorie Lamp Mead, contains a foreword by Douglas Gresham,* Lewis's stepson. In 1989 *Letters: C. S. Lewis and Don Giovanni Calabria* was published, edited, and translated by Martin Moynihan. A revised and enlarged edition of the *Letters* edited by W. H. Lewis was brought out in 1988, edited by Walter Hooper and containing some changes to Warnie Lewis's sometimes rather free editing. This is therefore not strictly a replacement for the 1966 volume, which is worth obtaining if possible.

Letters to Malcolm: Chiefly on Prayer (1964) Malcolm is an imaginary friend of C. S. Lewis's to whom he writes twenty-two letters on the theme of prayer and much else, including heaven and the resurrection of the body. In the book Lewis writes as having known Malcolm from undergraduate days. Some have felt that Lewis's theological writings lack an experiential depth (or a shyness of spiritual experience). This last book concerns one of the most experiential subjects of the Christian life, and Lewis handles it with great power. From the moment of his conversion to theism, Lewis was a thoroughgoing supernaturalist, and thus the question of petitionary prayer made in time to a God outside of space-time was a central one to him. He saw it as God's prerogative to change actual events in the light of the prayers of his people.

The letter format allowed Lewis to explore and speculate on prayer in a manner impossible in a more didactic book. Prayer, for Lewis, was necessary for our understanding of our relation to our Father-Creator.

> Now the moment of prayer is for me—or involves for me as its condition—the awareness, the reawakened awareness, that this "real world" and "real self" are very far from being rock-bottom realities. I cannot, in the flesh, leave the stage, either to go behind the scenes or to take my seat in the pit; but I can remember that my apparent self—this clown or hero . . . —under his grease-paint is a real person with an off-stage life. The dramatic person could not tread the stage unless he concealed a real person: unless the real and unknown I existed, I would not even make mistakes about the imagined me. And in prayer this real I struggles to speak, for once, from his real being, and to address, for once, not the other actors, but—what shall I call Him? The Author, for He invented us all? The Producer, for He controls all? Or the Audience, for He watches, and will judge, the performance?

Lewis, Albert (1863-1929) The father of C. S. Lewis and a gifted Belfast Corporation County Solicitor, 1889-1928. When his wife, Flora Lewis,* died of cancer, Albert Lewis was unable to cope with his grief. He sent the nine-year-old C. S. Lewis off to England to boarding school at "Belsen."* Relations between Mr. Lewis and his two sons were often strained. C. S. Lewis portrays his father as having little talent for happiness and as withdrawing into the safe monotony of routine. Biographer A. N. Wilson, however, believes the picture Lewis painted of his father as a "comic character" to be one-sided. The richest heritage he gave to Lewis was, literally, a house full of old books that the gifted boy explored unimpeded. Lewis acknowledges this debt in *Surprised by Joy* and in his preface to *The Allegory of Love** (see: READING OF C. S. LEWIS). Albert Lewis shared an interest in writing with his son and a gift of rhetoric, including recounting "wheezes" (pithy observations often of humorous events). Lewis as a child was taken by Albert and Flora Lewis to worship at nearby St. Mark's, Dundela, on the outskirts of Belfast, wherein today can be seen a stained-glass window placed in memory of their parents by the Lewis brothers. Albert's Irish brogue was a constant source of amusement to his sons—throughout their lives they often referred to him as the "P.B." or "the Pudaita-bird," after the way he pronounced *potato*. Like his wife long before him, Albert Lewis succumbed to cancer (in 1929).

Lewis, Clive Staples (C. S.) Known to his friends as "Jack" (he didn't like Clive Staples), C. S. Lewis was born in the outskirts of Belfast* on November 29, 1898, and he died in his Oxford* home The Kilns* almost sixty-five years later on November 22, 1963. He was equally a scholar and a storyteller. The story of his early life, his conversion from atheism to Christianity, and his awareness of joy* and longing for a fulfillment outside his own self is told in his autobiography *Surprised by Joy** and his allegory *The Pilgrim's Regress.**

His published letters, especially *Letters of C. S. Lewis,** *They Stand Together,** and *Brothers and Friends: The Diaries of Major Warren Hamilton Lewis,** give vivid insights into his life. A selection from his diaries, *All My Road Before Me,** records the years between 1922 and 1927. Jack Lewis was devoted to his brother W. H. "Warnie" Lewis.* The two brothers were brought together by their common interest in creating imaginary worlds as boys, particularly Boxen,* and also by the death of their mother of cancer. Mrs. Flora Lewis* died when Jack was nine. Their father never got over the loss, and relations between father and sons became more and more strained as time went on.

In the year of his mother's ghastly death, Lewis was sent off to Hertfordshire to join his brother at a school dubbed "Belsen."* This title seems no great exaggeration. The brutal headmaster was several years later certified insane. In 1910 Jack was moved first to Campbell College, Belfast, and next year to "Chartres" (Cherbourg House) in Malvern, and later to Malvern College ("Wyvern"), Worcestershire. He was never happy, however, until he was finally sent to a private tutor in Bookham named W. T. Kirkpatrick.*

His brother Warnie wrote in his introduction to *Letters of C. S. Lewis*: "The fact is, he should never have been sent to a public school at all. Already, at 14, his intelligence was such that he would have fitted in better among undergraduates than schoolboys; and by his temperament he was bound to be a misfit, a heretic, an object of suspicion within the collective-minded and standardising Public School system." Characteristically, Jack wrote his first article, "Are Athletes Better Than Scholars?" for a school magazine.

His private tutorage under the Irishman W. T. Kirkpatrick was one of the happiest periods of his life. Not only did he rapidly mature and grow under the stringent rationality of this teacher, but he discovered the beauty of the English countryside and fantasy writers such as William Morris. Full of the discovery of George Macdonald's* *Phantastes*,* Lewis wrote about its power to Arthur Greeves,* his lifelong Ulster friend, in 1915: "Of course it is hopeless for me to try to describe it, but when you have followed the hero Anodos along the little stream of the faery wood, have heard about the terrible ash tree . . . and heard the episode of Cosmo, I know you will agree with me." In *Surprised by Joy*, Lewis describes the effect as "baptising his imagination."

The Great War had broken out, and its shadow loomed over Lewis's peace. Warnie was already on active duty. Lewis was not old enough to enlist until 1917. He spent his nineteenth birthday on the front line. In spring 1918 Lewis was wounded in action and was eventually discharged after a spell in the hospital. During all this time he had been writing poetry and preparing a book of poems, *Spirits in Bondage*,* for publication.

At the front he had lost a billet-mate called "Paddy" Moore. Before his death, according to Warnie Lewis, Lewis had apparently promised Paddy that, should anything happen to him, Lewis would take care of Paddy's mother and sister.

Lewis in fact looked after Mrs. Janie Moore* until her death in 1951, and it is possible that he had an intimate relationship with her up to his conversion to Christian faith, as argued by his biographer, A. N. Wilson. This possibility is also deemed likely by Lewis's biographer George Sayer and by Walter Hooper. Owen Barfield felt the likelihood to be about fifty-fifty. There is no conclusive evidence, however, and Lewis's moral beliefs and Ulster background make the explanatory story of Mrs. Moore being his adoptive mother plausible. Her troublesome personality was more a thorn in the flesh to Warnie, particularly later, than it seemed to be to Jack.

By 1923 Lewis had confirmed his brilliance by gaining a Triple First at Oxford* University (see: "GREATS"). He won a temporary lectureship in philosophy at University College (see: IDEALISM). Then Magdalen College appointed him as a fellow, lecturing and tutoring in English (see: LITERARY CRITIC, LEWIS AS A). He was an Oxford don until 1954, when Cambridge University invited him to the new Chair of Medieval and Renaissance Literature, where he described himself as an "Old Western Man" in his inaugural lecture (see: OLD WEST). C. S. Lewis's pupils included such figures as the critic Kenneth Tynan,* George Sayer,* the poet John Betjeman,* Harry Blamires,* and novelist and poet John Wain.*

In the early Oxford days Professor J. R. R. Tolkien* became one of Jack's lifelong friends. They would criticize one another's poetry, drift into theology and philosophy, pun, or talk English department politics. This deep friendship held great significance for both men. Tolkien found in Lewis an appreciative audience for his burgeoning stories and poems of Middle-earth, a good deal of which was not published until after his death. Without Lewis's encouragement over many years, *The Lord of the Rings* would probably have never appeared in print.

Lewis equally had cause to appreciate Tolkien, whose views on myth* and imagination,* and the relation of both to reality, helped to convince Lewis (who had not long before been a convinced atheist) of the truth of Christianity. Seeing mind to mind on both imagination and the truth of Christianity was the foundation of their remarkable friendship. The Inklings,* the group of literary friends around Lewis, grew out of this rapport between Lewis and Tolkien. A. N. Wilson, in his biography *C. S. Lewis*, remarks that at the very beginning of the association between Lewis and Tolkien: "It must have seemed clear to him at once that Tolkien was a man of literary genius." On Tolkien's side, thinking with sadness in 1929 of his marriage, he wrote: "Friendship with Lewis compensates for much."

Because Tolkien helped to force Lewis to reconsider the claims of Christianity, Jack was first "cornered" by theism and then by biblical Christianity. The movement of Lewis's thinking at this time is vividly captured in his book *Miracles*.* He later confessed: "I never had the experience of looking for God. It was the other way round; He was the hunter (or so it seemed to me) and I was the deer. He stalked me like a redskin, took unerring aim, and fired. And I am very thankful that that is how the first (conscious) meeting occurred. It forearms one against subsequent fears that the whole thing was only wish fulfilment. Something one didn't wish for can hardly be that."

After the war, the American *Time* magazine published a perceptive cover feature on Lewis (September 8, 1947) that was partly responsible for increasing Lewis's appeal in the United States. The article was researched in the later war years and was partly based on an interview with Lewis's friend and fellow Inkling Charles Williams.*

In 1953 Lewis met an American, Helen Joy Davidman Gresham (see: LEWIS, HELEN JOY DAVIDMAN), with whom he had corresponded for some time. She was a poet and novelist who had been converted from atheism and Marxism to Christianity partly through reading Lewis's books. When she was free to remarry and was dying of cancer, Lewis married her. When she died in 1960, Lewis never got over the loss, and his grief was combined with constant worry about his unassuming brother's alcoholism. The last book he saw to press, *Letters to Malcolm: Chiefly on Prayer,** affirmed his hope in heaven.*

Lewis Family Papers When Major Warnie Lewis* moved into The Kilns* (at first on leave from the army, then permanently), he began the enormous task of arranging the family papers (letters, diaries, photographs, and various documents), typing and arranging the material in what ended up being eleven volumes. They are entitled "Memoirs of the Lewis Family: 1850-1930." The volumes were completed in 1935 and bequeathed by Warnie Lewis to the Marion E. Wade Center, Wheaton, Illinois, as a result of his friendship with pioneering Lewis scholar Clyde S. Kilby. The papers include a fragment of Lewis's Ulster novel, never completed, "The Easley Fragment."*

Lewis, Helen Joy Davidman (1915-1960) C. S. Lewis's wife, and subject of his book *A Grief Observed,** written after her death from cancer at the age of forty-five. Joy Davidman was a poet and novelist (see: *ANYA*), and she also published a theological study of the Ten Commandments, *Smoke on the Mountain.* C. S. Lewis's attraction to the American was at first merely intellectual, that of friendship. She was a brilliant Jew on the verge of divorce, with two young sons. Joy had been converted from Marxism to Christianity partly through reading C. S. Lewis.

A short time after making his acquaintance, Joy Davidman came to live in Oxford with her sons. She and Lewis became on close terms. In retrospect he wrote, "Her mind was lithe and quick and muscular as a leopard. Passion, tenderness and pain were all equally unable to disarm it. It scented the first whiff of cant or slush; then sprang, and knocked you over before you knew what was happening." They married in a civil ceremony to give her British nationality in April 1956.

In the autumn of 1956 they learned that Joy had terminal cancer. It was sudden, unexpected news, and Lewis was deeply shocked. Cancer was an old acquaintance. Her two boys were about the same age as the Lewis brothers had been when their mother died; the parallels were uncomfortable. A bedside Christian wedding ceremony took place on March 21, 1957. Joy came home to The Kilns to die.

After prayer for healing, she had a temporary reprieve. By July she was well enough to get out and about. The next year they had a fortnight's holiday in Ireland. The remission was the beginning of the happiest few years of both of their lives. Lewis confessed to his friend Nevill Coghill*: "I never expected to have, in my sixties, the happiness that passed me by in my twenties."

Lewis's brother Warnie points out that the marriage fulfilled "a whole dimension to his nature that had previously been starved and thwarted." It also put an end to a bachelor's doubt that God was an invented substitute for love. "For those few years H. and I feasted on love," he recalled in *A Grief Observed,* "every mode of it—solemn and merry, romantic and realistic, sometimes as dramatic as a thunderstorm, sometimes as comfortable and unemphatic as putting on your soft slippers."

The cancer eventually returned, but the Lewises were able to have a trip to Greece in the spring of the year of her death, a journey much desired by both of them. The story of the happiness that came to Lewis so late in life and his subsequent bitter bereavement has been made into two successful films and a play based around a similar script by William Nicolson, entitled *Shadowlands.* The earliest, for the BBC, is the closest to reality. The dramatic license used in all versions has created much debate, but each is extraordinarily poignant. Many in their audiences have been inspired to read Lewis for the first time.

Lewis, Flora Hamilton (1862-1908) C. S. Lewis's mother was the daughter of the church rector at St. Mark's, Dundela, Belfast, the Lewis family church. Today a stained-glass window in memory of C. S. Lewis's parents can be seen in the church, put there by the Lewis brothers. Flora gained a First Class Honors degree in logic and a Second Class Honors in mathematics at Queen's University, Belfast. Lewis recalled that neither of his parents "had the least taste for that kind of literature to which my allegiance was given the moment I could choose books for myself. Neither had ever listened for the horns of elfland. There was no copy of Keats or Shelley in the house, and the copy of Coleridge was never (to my knowledge) opened. If I am a romantic," he concludes, "my parents bear no responsibility for it." The grim, uncushionable blow of his mother's death from cancer took away all that was stable in nine-year-old Jack's life. His father, unable to cope with his grief, immediately sent him off to a boarding school that Lewis dubbed, feelingly, "Belsen" in *Surprised by Joy.** A dying mother appears in the Narnia* tale *The Magician's Nephew,** but her story has a happy ending.

Lewis, Warren Hamilton "Warnie" (1895-1973) Lewis's only brother, lifelong friend, and member of the Inklings* from its inception. Like his brother, Warren was a gifted writer, producing a number of books on French history. He contributed to *Essays Presented to Charles Williams.** His diaries provide a unique and essential insight into Lewis's life and into meetings of the Inklings. A selection has been published as *Brothers and Friends** (1982), which, inexplicably, was only published in North America.

Warnie Lewis began his military career when he entered the Royal Military Academy shortly before the outbreak of World War I. After the war he served in Sierra Leone and Shanghai before retiring from the army in 1932 with a pension. He joined the unusual household run by his brother and Mrs. Janie Moore* at The Kilns* in Oxford.* This short note cannot do justice to Warnie Lewis's "immeasurable importance" to Jack, an importance that can be seen through his elegantly written diaries. Warnie Lewis devoted himself to the task of editing the Lewis Family Papers* and, after Jack's death, prepared a powerful memoir of his brother, now housed in the Wade Center, Wheaton (with a copy in the Bodleian Library, Oxford). An abridged version of the memoir is published in *Letters of C. S. Lewis.**

***Life of Samuel Johnson,* James Boswell** (1791) This biography resulted from the association of James Boswell, the natural documenter, and Dr. Samuel Johnson, the eighteenth-century man of letters. Lewis listed the book as one of the ten that most influenced his thought and vocational attitude (see: READING OF C. S. LEWIS). A biography perhaps unique in literature, it became at once a classic. In Boswell hero worship and appreciation became an art form. Boswell's documentary brilliance merges with Johnson's towering literary talent. Johnson, like Lewis, was larger than life in personality and in his endlessly active intellect, and he looms large in almost every sentence of this hypnotically admiring book. Boswell seems to forget no detail of speech or manner. As Helen Rex Keller remarks, "Boswell begins with Johnson's first breath (drawn it seems, with difficulty), and will not let him draw a later breath without full commentary."

> We dined at Eight, and saw the noble ruins of the Cathedral. Though it rained, Dr. Johnson examined them with the most patient attention.
>
> Next Sunday, July 31st, I told him I had been at a meeting of the people called Quakers, where I had heard a woman preach.
>
> JOHNSON: "Sir, a woman's preaching is like a dog's walking on his hind legs. It is not done well, but you are surprised to find it done at all."
>
> JOHNSON: "Well, we had a good talk."
> BOSWELL. "Yes, sir; you tossed and gored several persons."
>
> JOHNSON: "A man, indeed, is not genteel when he gets drunk; but most vices may be committed very genteelly: a man may debauch his friend's wife genteelly: he may cheat at cards genteelly."

James Boswell (1740-1795) was a member of Samuel Johnson's London Literary Club, and the two men traveled to Scotland together, their journeys recorded in Boswell's *Journal of the Tour to the Hebrides* (1785). Born in Edinburgh, Boswell studied law, but he soon centered his ambitions on literature and politics. Boswell's long-lost personal papers became public in 1949, and his journals are of particular interest.

Lilygloves In *Prince Caspian,** a chief mole, a talking animal* who helped plant an orchard at Cair Paravel.* At the time of the events recorded in this book, the orchard had run wild for centuries.

Lindsay, David (1878-1945) His *A Voyage to Arcturus* (1920) is today recognized as one of the masterpieces of science fiction, though its first edition sold under 600 copies, making it difficult for Lindsay to sell subsequent work. C. S. Lewis, hearing of the book, had great difficulty in obtaining a copy. When he finally did, it greatly influenced his own science-fiction trilogy and his unfinished book *The Dark Tower.** Writing of *Out of the Silent Planet** in 1944, Lewis responded to an inquiry about influences on his work: "The real father of my planet book is David Lindsay's *A Voyage to Arcturus*, which you also will revel in if you don't yet know it. I had grown up on [H. G.] Wells's stories of that kind: It was Lindsay who first gave me the idea that the 'scientifiction' appeal could be combined with the 'supernatural' appeal. . . . His own spiritual outlook is detestable, almost diabolist, I think, and his style is crude: but he showed me what a bang you could get from mixing these two elements."

Lindsay's "Tormance," in far-off Arcturus, perhaps gets its name from a contraction of *torment* and *romance*. In an essay "On Stories," which appeared in *Essays Presented to Charles Williams*,* Lewis wrote that David Lindsay's "Tormance is a region of the spirit. He is the first writer to discover what 'other planets' are really good for in fiction. No merely physical strangeness or merely spacial distance will realize that idea of otherness which is what we are always trying to grasp in a story about voyaging through space: you must go into another dimension. To construct plausible and moving 'other worlds' you must draw on the only real 'other world' we know, that of the spirit."

David Lindsay's other tales of fantasy were *The Haunted Woman* (1922), *Sphinx* (1923), and *Devil's Tor* (1932). He also wrote a historical novel, *The Adventures of M. de Mailly* (1926). In 1970 a memorial volume appeared, *The Strange Genius of David Lindsay*, including articles by Colin Wilson and E. H. Visiak (who finds parallels between *A Voyage to Arcturus* and Milton's *Paradise Lost*).

The Lion, the Witch and the Wardrobe (1950) This is the first tale of Narnia* that C. S. Lewis wrote. Its inspiration owed something to evacuee children who lodged in Lewis's Oxford* home The Kilns,* and began with a picture that he saw in his head of "a faun carrying an umbrella and parcels in a snowy wood." Four children—Peter, Edmund, Susan, and Lucy Pevensie*—are evacuated from wartime London to stay with Professor Digory Kirke* (who, as a boy, had visited Narnia, as recounted in *The Magician's Nephew**). In one room of his vast house is a bulky wardrobe made out of a tree that grew from a magical Narnian seed. Through this wardrobe the children enter a snowy wood in Narnia's Lantern Waste.* Three of them join forces with the talking animals* who are loyal to Aslan,* the great talking lion, creator of Narnia. Edmund, however, turns traitor and goes over to the White Witch,* who has Narnia in her spell, so that it is always winter and never Christmas. Aslan pays the terrible cost of Edmund's treachery by sacrificing his own life to break the witch's magic. Narnia is freed, Aslan returns to life, the witch is destroyed, and the creatures that she had turned to stone are unpetrified by the lion. See also: NARNIA, HISTORY.

Literae Humaniores See: "GREATS"

Literary critic, C. S. Lewis as a C. S. Lewis was an outstanding literary critic, being invited to the newly created Chair of Medieval and Renaissance Literature at Cambridge University in 1954 as a result of his work in these periods. Prior to that he was for almost thirty years fellow and tutor in English at Magdalen College, Oxford. His main works of literary criticism are *The Allegory of Love: A Study in Medieval Tradition** (1936), *Rehabilitations and Other Essays** (1939), (with E. M. W. Tillyard) *The Personal Heresy: A Controversy** (1939), *A Preface to "Paradise Lost"** (1942), (with Charles Williams) *Arthurian Torso** (1948), *English Literature in the Sixteenth Century, Excluding Drama** (1954), *Reflections on the Psalms** (1958), *Studies in Words** (1960), *An Experiment in Criticism** (1961), *The Discarded Image: An Introduction to Medieval and Renaissance Literature** (1964), *Studies in Medieval and Renaissance Literature* (1966), (edited by Alistair Fowler) *Spenser's Images of Life** (1967), and *Selected Literary Essays* (1969).

Literature is more than mere written language. R. Wellek and A. Warren's definition in *Theory of Literature* is useful: "The term *literature* seems best if we limit it to the art of literature, that is, to imaginative literature. . . . We recognize 'fictionality,' 'invention,' or 'imagination' as the distinguishing trait of literature." Older views of the nature of literature, in nineteenth-century literary criticism for instance, have a wider perspective than this, and thus a larger canon, but did recognize the importance of the aesthetic element in literary works.

What is C. S. Lewis's place in twentieth-century literary criticism? Generally, recent literary theories have had one of three dominant emphases: They have been author-centered, text-centered, or reader-centered. It is worth making a simple thumbnail sketch of these positions to see C. S. Lewis's contribution to criticism and continuing value as a critic more clearly.

Traditionally, criticism has been concerned with what is extrinsic to the literary text—its origin, authorship, original setting, and the like. The critic has needed to know about the activities and thinking of the author. This practice has been described by recent critics as the "intentional fallacy," and part of it by C. S. Lewis as "the personal heresy." Traditional criticism interpreted the meaning of a piece of literature by concentrating on the author and his or her social and cultural world. Questions of origin and authority are central, standing in the stream of Western metaphysics.

In the 1940s and 1950s the so-called New Criticism shifted from an extrinsic to an intrinsic regard for the text. It moved away from authorial intent to an emphasis on the autonomy of the literary work. The

New Criticism was rooted in the thought of T. S. Eliot, I. A. Richards, and William Empson. As a trend, it included several American scholars and F. R. Leavis in Britain.

The trend takes its name from John Crowe Ransom's *The New Criticism* (1942). This school sees the text as self-sufficient, with the author's intention and background unimportant. The literary text is typically perceived as an artifact or "verbal icon." A parallel in the modern novel is John Fowles's (and others') rejection of an all-knowing narrator. The New Criticism requires a close reading of the text and has been deeply influential in English studies.

Another text-centered movement is structuralism. Structuralism is actually rooted in linguistics, but has affected many disciplines, as described by Jean Piaget in his book *Structuralism* (1971). A general theory about human culture, this view sees all aspects of culture as characterized by signs, the meaning of which lie in their interrelatedness. Metaphor is key to all human thought, from the caveman to our present Information Age, being based upon our human ability to recognize similarity in difference. Literature is particularly important to structuralism because its "material" is language itself. Instead of appreciating the originality and genius of an author, the concern of structuralist criticism is with the writer's actual transformations of deep structures or pre-existing meanings.

In contrast, reader-centered theories emphasize the reader's role in creating the meaning of the literary text. Softer views within this camp are interested in the objective interaction between the reader and the text, rather on the analogy of an orchestra performing a musical score. Just as the music lives as it is performed, the text is realized as it is read. There are therefore good and bad readers, ideal readers, competent readers. Feminist or Marxist criticism (or other ideologies) can fall into a reader-centered approach, as can psychoanalytical criticism. This last approach has drawn attention to the "preunderstanding" or worldview of the reader in coming to the text.

An important movement in literary criticism is deconstruction. This movement is part of a wider postmodernist trend seeking the dismantling of all Western metaphysics, including Christian theism. As in the thought of Don Cupitt, "God" is a symbol of human aspirations and has no objective reference—there is no thing or person called God that exists. Deconstruction questions the basis of author-, text-, and reader-centered approaches. It rejects any univocal, unambiguous view of meaning.* Jacques Derrida is a central force behind deconstruction. He links the "myth" of authorial presence in a text with authority. Concepts of authority need to be abandoned. Literary meaning is an "endless labyrinth." He exalts writing over speech, seeing earlier literary critics as speech-centered and thus "logo-centered."

Deconstruction is characteristic of postmodernism. The movement's abandonment of Western metaphysics, particularly theism, is expressed for example by Roland Barthes in his essay "The Death of the Author": "Literature (it would be better from now on to say writing), by refusing to assign a 'secret,' an ultimate meaning, to the text (and to the world as text), liberates what may be called an anti-theological activity, an activity that is truly revolutionary since to refuse to fix meaning is, in the end, to refuse God and his hypostases—reason, science, law." Not only is God dead, as prophesied by the philosopher Nietzsche, but so are the author and ultimately the critic.

In the kind of movements sketched above, literary criticism has become an important part of the shaping of contemporary culture. Can C. S. Lewis's own work in this area still contribute to this momentous debate?

Though Lewis died nearly forty years ago, his literary criticism has much to contribute today. He still offers a sturdy defense of a literary criticism based upon theism and what he would call "Old Western values" (see: OLD WEST). He would see much contemporary criticism as helping the cause of those working for the abolition of mankind, in dismantling transcendent, objective values. More remarkable, he also avoids, in my view, the extremes of reader-, author-, or text-centeredness, while appreciating the importance of all these dimensions of literary meaning.

The critic David Lodge sums up Lewis's position as a historical approach to literature. For him, C. S. Lewis's literary criticism

> shows a remarkable range of interest and expertise, but Lewis was probably best known and admired for his work on medieval literature, especially his masterly book on the literature of Courtly Love, *The Allegory of Love: A Study in Medieval Tradition*. . . . C. S. Lewis in many ways represented the "Oxford" tradition of literary criticism at its best: relaxed, knowledgeable, enthusiastic, conservative. Certainly he stood for principles and practice antithetical to those of the Scrutiny group at Cambridge. . . . It is clear that he regarded the study of literature as primarily a historical one, and its justification as the conservation of the past. "*De Descriptione Temporum*" expresses eloquently, learnedly and wittily this conception of the subject and Lewis's doubts about its viability in the future.

"*De Descriptione Temporum*"* was C. S. Lewis's inaugural lecture at Cambridge. However, Lewis is not simply a literary historian. His historical work had a double purpose—to shed light on the textual meaning (e.g., its iconography) rather than on the author's personality, society, or other extrinsic feature, and to value a historically distant text as a remarkable window into a previous cultural world. That world was the fruit of corporate human imagination and power, containing values that we need to take into account. We need perspectives on the narrow limitations of our own world model of today.

As regards the reader, in his seminal *An Experiment in Criticism*, Lewis attacks the evaluative criticism of F. R. Leavis and others. He rejects their "good" and "bad" literature in favor of "good" and "bad" readers. Good readers attend to and receive the text rather than using it for some end. Literary texts are intended to have readers. Some texts may be too poor to merit the attention of readers. But where a good reader finds nourishment in a text, one can be sure that meaning is captured there—presence, transcendence, authority, power, insight, and understanding.

Much of C. S. Lewis's critical work was on Spenser, Chaucer, the Arthurian tales, Milton, and Dante, as well as on myth,* allegory,* world models, meaning,* story, metaphor, linguistics, and fairy stories. He also wrote key essays on John Bunyan, Jane Austin, Shelley, and William Morris, many of them collected in *Selected Literary Essays*.

Through all his work Lewis advocates and demonstrates the close reading of texts, where readers and critics have a firsthand experience of an author's work. Lewis argues that "we invariably judge a critic by the extent to which he illuminates reading we have already done." Such close reading ought to be in the original languages, if possible. It was important therefore, thought Lewis, for a student and reader of English literature to be acquainted with Anglo-Saxon. Lewis himself was able to read German, French, and Italian, as well as classical languages, and this ability enriched his critical work.

Complementary to this textual concern is a historical engagement. He is always interested in the intellectual and cultural currents of a period. Lewis feels that the extrinsic features of the literary work are essential to consider, such as its worldview, including the model of reality and the universe it embodied, and authorial intention. For him this does not mean that the text is a personal, cultural, or moralistic expression, or simply a quarry for anthropologists, theologians, psychologists, and sociologists. The work is *poiema* as well as *logos*, something made as well as something said. Therefore as a unique entity, it should be taken on its own terms.

He emphasizes the interrelationship of literary works, particularly in what he perceives as a unified period before the rise of the stranglehold of modernism, a period he sees as stretching from ancient pagan times to sometime in the nineteenth century. Literary works illuminate each other, contributing to a symbolic language and iconography. Lewis is not a narrow specialist. He is at ease in a number of disciplines, such as philosophy, classics, and history, but he is usually humble about the extent of his knowledge when he steps out of his professional field, as when he writes popular theology.

Related to this wideness of view is his preoccupation with Christianizing paganism* and with a rehabilitation of premodernist literature and values. For Lewis there is a vast, ancient continuity. So he is not simply rehabilitating the medieval period but the entire premodernist period. He has a strong polemical purpose. Lewis paints the inner world using allegory, symbol, or myth—following the example of the medievals and the earlier ancient Western world. His fiction and literary work are therefore of a piece. He believes that, with skill, contemporary literature can take us into the literature of the Old West, by our recognizing likeness, going from the more familiar to the less. A child, for example, may read *The Voyage of the "Dawn Treader"* and later discover that Homer's *The Odyssey* is familiar.

In his literary criticism Lewis maintains both continuity and discontinuity with the present (he is a premodernist who has a postmodern appeal). He is thus valuable in giving a transcendent perspective on our times. His early rejection of "chronological snobbery" allowed this freedom. His preoccupation with story and metaphor as a condition of all good thinking was fought out in opposition to modernism and its characteristic naturalism. These interests are highly palatable in our postmodernist era. Yet at the same time his work refuses to be reduced to a postmodernist position; he is unashamedly premodernist in his chosen beliefs and tastes. Another (and related) feature of his work that appeals to a postmodernist climate is his hallmark emphasis upon particularity—the distinctiveness that exists in people, places, and books.

To him the symbolic and imaginative are supremely important. They were a significant factor in his move from atheism to Christianity and in his professional life thereafter. He advocates what might be called a symbolic perception of reality. The flair of his criticism is notable: It is elegantly written, with a timeless element. Furthermore, his literary and related criticism fuels his imaginative writing. There are often parallels between his works of criticism and particular fictions. The pattern is established in the inspiration that *The Allegory of Love* gives to the writing of *The Pilgrim's Regress** (1933); his *A Preface to Paradise Lost** (1942) naturally leads to *Perelandra** (1943); *The Abolition of Man** (1943) theoretically treats the themes of *That Hideous Strength** (1945); his many explorations of myth and pre-Christian paganism result in *Till We Have Faces** (1956); and it could perhaps be argued that his consideration of Spenser's *The Faerie Queene* over many years provides a pattern for the imaginative eclecticism yet coherent unity of the Narnian Chronicles (1950-1956).

See also: THEOLOGY, C. S. LEWIS AND; THEOLOGY OF ROMANCE.

FURTHER READING

Tremper Longman, *Literary Approaches to Biblical Interpretation* (1987).

David Lodge, ed., *20th Century Literary Criticism: A Reader* (1972).

Bruce L. Edwards, *A Rhetoric of Reading: C. S. Lewis's Defense of Western Literacy* (1985).

Doris T. Myers, *C. S. Lewis in Context* (1994).

"Little Lea" Leeborough House, Lewis's childhood home from 1905, described in detail in his autobiography *Surprised by Joy.** The house is located in Strandtown on the outskirts of Belfast. When the Lewis family moved there, the house was set in open countryside with an uninterrupted view of Belfast Lough, but now it is in a suburban area. Bernagh,* home of Arthur Greeves,* and Glenmachan,* residence of the Ewarts,* were near neighbors. The "little end room" in the attic area was of particular importance to the young Lewis brothers, providing a haven for writing, reading, and drawing.

Lone Islands A group of islands comprised of Felimath,* Doorn,* and Avra,* visited by the travelers in *The Voyage of the "Dawn Treader."** Ancient King Gale of Narnia* had once rid these islands of a dragon, and they were given to him to be part of Narnia. They lie 400 leagues to the east of that land in the Eastern Ocean. See also: NARNIA—GEOGRAPHY; NARNIA—HISTORY.

Love See: THE FOUR LOVES.

Lucy, Queen See PEVENSIE, PETER, SUSAN, EDMUND, AND LUCY.

Lune, King The jolly father of Cor* (or Shasta*) and Corin,* and king of Archenland* during the Golden Age of Narnia.* He ruled from the strategic castle at Anvard.* Lune features in the famous Narnian tale *The Horse and His Boy.**

M

McCallum, Ronald B. (1898-1973) A member of the Inklings* and fellow of Pembroke College, Oxford,* until 1955, when he was elected Master of Pembroke.

MacDonald, George The Scottish writer George MacDonald (1824-1905) was born in Huntly in rural Aberdeenshire, the son of a weaver. C. S. Lewis regarded his own debt to him as inestimable. Like C. S. Lewis, he lost his mother in boyhood, a fact that touched his thought and writings. His views on the imagination* anticipated those of Lewis and J. R. R. Tolkien,* and inspired G. K. Chesterton.* He was a close friend of Charles Dodgson (Lewis Carroll) and John Ruskin, the art critic. His insights into the subconscious mind predated the rise of modern psychology. Like Lewis and Tolkien, he was a scholar as well as a storyteller. George MacDonald made a memorable appearance in C. S. Lewis's *The Great Divorce*,* for Lewis regarded him as his "master."

MacDonald's sense that all imaginative meaning originates with the Christian Creator became the foundation of C. S. Lewis's thinking and imagining. Two key essays by MacDonald, "The Imagination: Its Functions and Its Culture" (1867) and "The Fantastic Imagination" (1882), remarkably foreshadow Tolkien's famous essay "On Fairy Stories" (1947). Tolkien's views on imagination persuaded C. S. Lewis of the truth of Christianity on a night in 1931. Many years before, Lewis had stumbled across a copy of MacDonald's *Phantastes** (1858), resulting in what he described as a baptism of his imagination. George MacDonald wrote nearly thirty novels, several books of sermons, a number of abiding fantasies for adults and children, short stories, and poetry. His childhood is beautifully captured in his semi-autobiographical *Ranald Bannerman's Boyhood* (1871). He never lost sight of his humble childhood and adolescence, spent living in a cottage so small that he slept in an attic. He was a happy boy, riding, climbing, swimming, and fishing, and reading while lying on the back of his beloved horse. We catch many glimpses of the countryside he knew and loved in his writings.

George MacDonald entered Aberdeen University in 1840 and had a scientific training. For a few years he worked as a tutor in London. Then he entered Highbury Theological College and married. He was called to a church in Arundle, where he fell into disfavor with the deacons, who reduced his small salary to persuade him to leave. Some of the poorer members, however, rallied around with offerings they could ill afford. Then he moved to Manchester for some years, preaching to a small congregation and giving lectures. The rapidly growing family was always on the brink of poverty. Fortunately, the poet Byron's widow, recognizing MacDonald's literary gifts, started to provide financial help. The family moved down to London to live in a house then called The Retreat, near the Thames at Hammersmith, later owned by William Morris.

Many famous writers and artists came to visit the MacDonalds, as well as people who shared a concern for London's desperate and crowded poor. One friend was Charles Dodgson, who let the MacDonald children hear his story, *Alice in Wonderland*. As a result of their enthusiasm, he decided to publish it. One of MacDonald's sons, Greville, remembered calling a cab for the poet Tennyson.

For a time George MacDonald was Professor of Literature at Bedford College, London. Because of continued ill health, the family eventually moved to Italy, where MacDonald and his wife were to remain for the rest of their lives. There were, however, frequent stays in Britain during the warmer months and a long and successful visit to the United States on a lecture tour. One of his last books, *Lilith* (1895), is among his greatest, a fantasy with the same power to move and to change a person's imaginative life as *Phantastes*.

In her book *The Stars and the Stillness*, Kathy Triggs points out the paradox of a leading nineteenth-century writer being virtually forgotten today, and she hazards some reasons for this. We live in a post-Christian world where MacDonald's values are alien. Television and other claims on our time deprive us of the leisure to tackle his lengthy novels. Yet, she points out, we lose out on so much if we neglect to read him. His theological insights are still needed today. He was the master of ageless symbolism in his imaginative work—a fact that captured C. S. Lewis, bringing him face to face with the quality of holiness, though he didn't acknowledge it for many years.

FURTHER READING

Greville MacDonald, *George MacDonald and His Wife* (1924).

C. S. Lewis, *George MacDonald: An Anthology* (1946).

R. N. Hein, *The Harmony Within: The Spiritual Vision of George Macdonald* (1982).

Kathy Triggs, *The Stars and the Stillness: A Portrait of George MacDonald* (1986).

William Raeper, *George MacDonald* (1987).

Michael Phillips, *George MacDonald* (1987).

Macgowan, John (1726-1780) A Baptist minister and author of *Infernal Conference; or Dialogues of Devils*, a forerunner of C. S. Lewis's *The Screwtape Letters*,* though Lewis may never have read it. There are striking similarities of aim. One devil is the uncle of another, and Lewis's preface echoes Macgowan's introduction. John Macgowan wrote several other popular works, including *Death: A Vision* and a life of the biblical character Ruth.

McNeil, Jane Agnes (1889-1959) A close family friend and neighbor of C. S. Lewis's childhood. She was the daughter of the headmaster of Campbell College, briefly attended by Lewis. Both Lewis brothers dedicated books to her, C. S. Lewis's choice being *That Hideous Strength.** Was it a coincidence that a leading character is called Jane?

Mrs. Macready In *The Lion, the Witch and the Wardrobe,** Professor Digory Kirke's* formidable housekeeper in his large country house.

The Magician's Nephew (1955) This tale tells of the creation of Narnia* by Aslan.* It also tells us about the Edwardian childhood of Professor Digory Kirke,* who owned the big country house with the wardrobe in *The Lion, the Witch and the Wardrobe,** and how the London gas lamppost came to be in Narnia at all. Also it speaks of the origin of the White Witch* and explains the arrival of evil in Narnia—showing the evil as older than that world.

Digory and his dying mother were staying with his Uncle Andrew* and Aunt Letty in London, his father being in India. The boy made friends with Polly Plummer,* his neighbor, and the two were tricked into an experiment with magic rings by the uncle, a mad scientist.

At first they found themselves in the dying world of Charn,* blighted by Jadis, the White Witch, whom Digory awakes from a spell, despite warnings from Polly. They are unable to leave her behind as they return to London with the aid of the rings. There Jadis wreaks havoc, until the children are able to whisk her back to The Wood Between the Worlds, but not before she had wrenched off a handle from a lamppost, intending to use it to punish those who opposed her. The trio, along with Frank,* a London cabby, and his horse, and Uncle Andrew, end up in an empty world of Nothing in time to hear Aslan's creation song. At the words and music of the lion's song, mountains, trees, animals, and other creatures come into being to make Narnia and the world of which it is part. The sequence is reminiscent of passages from J. R. R. Tolkien's* *The Silmarillion*, parts of which Lewis was familiar with in unfinished form.

Aslan gives Digory the opportunity of undoing the evil he had brought into Narnia. His task is to find a magic apple, the seed of which would produce a tree to protect the young world from Jadis for many a year. Polly joins him on the adventure, which requires journeying into the mountains of the Western Wild to find a delightful valley. In a garden there on a hilltop grew an apple tree with the magic apples. To help them, the Cabby's horse, Strawberry, renamed Fledge* by Aslan, is transformed into a flying and talking horse to carry them.

Upon the children's return, Aslan allows Digory to bring back an apple from the tree that immediately sprang up from seed. This apple restored his dying mother. C. S. Lewis's own mother, Flora Hamilton Lewis,* died when he was a boy in Edwardian Belfast.

In the fecundity of new growth associated with Narnia's creation, the metal pole brought by the Witch grows into a lamppost in Lantern Waste,* and a great apple tree grows from the core of the magic apple eaten by Mrs. Kirke. Later, after the great tree fell, Digory had it made into a large wardrobe, the very same wardrobe that features in *The Lion, the Witch and the Wardrobe*.

Main Road An allegorical feature of the country depicted on the Mappa Mundi* in *The Pilgrim's Regress.** In the story John* the pilgrim usually strays to the north of the road (the intellectual rather than the visceral part of the world).

Malacandra The name for Mars in Old Solar.* See *OUT OF THE SILENT PLANET*; THE PLANETS.

Maleldil the Young In *Out of the Silent Planet,** the name by which God's son was known in Old Solar,* he who had become incarnate as a rational creature on the Silent Planet, Earth.

Mappa Mundi This map is found inside *The Pilgrim's Regress.** Theologian J. I. Packer describes the world it depicts as "the personal world of wandering and return that the story explores." In his preface to the third edition, Lewis explains the map as a scheme of "the Holy War as I see it." It depicts "the double attack from Hell on the two sides of our nature" (the mind and the physical sensations). Packer points out that the idea of the Holy War, drawn from Bunyan and others, as well as Lewis's war experience, not only informs *The Pilgrim's Regress* but "gives shape and perspective to Lewis's output as a whole." The attack on the soul from north and south represent, in Lewis's words, "equal and opposite evils, each continually strengthened and made plausible by its critique of the other." The Northern people are cold, with "rigid systems whether sceptical or dogmatic, Aristocrats, Stoics, Pharisees, Rigorists, signed and sealed members of highly organized 'Parties.'" The emotional Southerners are the opposite—"boneless souls whose doors stand open day and night to almost every visitant, but always with the readiest welcome for those . . . who offer some sort of intoxication. . . . Every feeling is justified by the mere fact that it is felt: for a Northerner, every feeling on the same ground is suspect."

Both tendencies actually dehumanize us, a thesis he explored in *The Abolition of Man.** To remain human we have no choice but the straight and narrow, the "Main Road"*: "With both the 'North' and the 'South' a man has, I take it, only one concern—to avoid them and hold the Main Road. . . . We were made to be neither cerebral men nor visceral men, but Men." See also: COSMIC WAR.

FURTHER READING

J. I. Packer, "Living Truth for a Dying World: The Message of C. S. Lewis," in Alister McGrath, ed., *The J. I. Packer Collection* (1999).

Mars See: *OUT OF THE SILENT PLANET.*

Marshwiggles In *The Silver Chair*,* long, froglike creatures who are occupied with most of the watery and fishy work in Narnia. The most famous marshwiggle is Puddleglum.*

Master Bowman In *The Voyage of the "Dawn Treader,"** the sailor in the company who shot the dreadful Sea Serpent.

Materialism See: NATURALISM AND SUPERNATURALISM.

Mathew, Gervase (1905-1976) One of the Inklings,* and a contributor to *Essays Presented to Charles Williams.** Educated at Balliol College, Oxford, he joined the Catholic order of Dominicans in 1928 and was ordained a priest in 1934. He lectured in modern history, theology, and English at Oxford and wrote books on Byzantium and medieval England.

Mavramorn In *The Voyage of the "Dawn Treader,"** one of the seven lords for which the voyagers searched. They found him sleeping under a spell on Ramandu's Island.*

Meaning and imagination The question of meaning (both of reality itself and of language) is central in the modern world. It is a key theme running throughout the writings of C. S. Lewis. For him, meaning was intimately tied up both with the role of the imagination* and with the fact that the entire universe is a dependent creation of God. He saw reason as the organ of truth, and imagination as the organ of meaning. Reason and imagination each had their own integrity, an integrity he attempted to respect in his fiction and theoretical writings. He was also concerned with their interrelationship, both within a mature person and in their complementary roles in the pursuit of knowledge. He particularly stressed the dependence of even the most abstract of thinking upon imagination.

C. S. Lewis, like his friend J. R. R. Tolkien,* believed that in some real sense the products of imagination in the arts could be true. Myth* could become fact. In writing fantasies such as The Chronicles of Narnia* and *The Hobbit*, they felt that they were discovering inevitable realities that were not the product of theories of the conscious mind (even though rational control is not relinquished in the making of good fantasy). It was this attitude that prompted both men to create consistent secondary worlds, or subcreations,* such as Middle-earth and Perelandra.* Fiction, for C. S. Lewis, was the making of meaning. It reflects the greater creativity of God when he originated and put together his universe and us.

Meaning is at the core of real things and events. Natural objects are not mere facts. Human beings are not merely personalities. Objects, events, and people are real insofar as they are in relationship to other objects, events, and persons, and ultimately in relationship to God. With persons, this relationship is more than the relationship of an object to God, its creator; human relationships involve personal factors such as choice. The complex web of relationships that is the hallmark of reality confers objects, events, and people with meaning. In themselves, they do not mean: They refer elsewhere for their meaning.

The heart of Lewis's Christian view of meaning is captured by a Dutch Christian philosopher: "Meaning is the mode of being of all that is created. This universal character of referring and expressing, which is proper to our entire created cosmos, stamps created reality as meaning, in accordance with its dependent non-self-sufficient nature. Meaning is the being of all that has been created and the nature even of our selfhood. It has a religious root and a divine origin" (Herman Dooyeweerd).

A similar view seems to have been held by the brilliant thinker Michael Polanyi, at least in equating meaning and being as a consequence of a theistic view of the universe. C. S. Lewis has sometimes been accused of crude rationalism, the belief that reason alone is enough to convince us that A is true and B is false. Lewis, however, saw reason itself in the light of the primacy of meaning (that is, in the light of the reference of all things, events, and people to God). In *Miracles** he points out that when we analyze our thinking as an actual event, two levels are evident. On one level are the physical facts about the actual state of our brain at the time—the natural state of that particular bit of the universe. Our thinking, as an event, is obeying the laws of physics and chemistry and mechanistic principles. The other level is the meaning to which these physical facts point, providing the character of the event that enables it to be called thinking. We always think about something; our thoughts refer to or mean something other than themselves as events.

As a literary critic,* C. S. Lewis also saw literary works in the light of the primacy of meaning. A good literary work takes us into meanings not normally or often perceived by us (or even by its author). These meanings give the work its character, even though the actual literary arrangement of the work, with all the skill that that involves, is a necessary condition for receiving the meanings.

It is on the relationship between concept and meaning, and thought and imagination, that C. S. Lewis makes his most distinctive contribution to our understanding. He has set an agenda that could be fruitful in literary criticism, philosophy, linguistics, and theology. He argues that good imagining is as vital as good thinking, and either is impoverished without the other. C. S. Lewis set out some key ideas, which owed much to his friend Owen Barfield,* in an essay in *Rehabilitations**:

> It must not be supposed that I am in any sense putting forward the imagination as the organ of truth. We are not talking of truth, but of meaning: meaning which is the antecedent condition both of truth and falsehood, whose antithesis is not error but nonsense. . . . For me, reason is the natural organ of truth; but imagination is the organ of meaning. Imagination, producing new metaphors or revivifying old, is not the cause of truth, but its condition. It is, I confess, undeniable that such a view indirectly implies a kind of truth or rightness in the imagination itself . . . the truth we [win] by metaphor [can] not be greater than the truth of the metaphor itself; and . . . all our truth, or all but a few fragments, is won by metaphor. And thence, I confess, it does follow that if our thinking is ever true, then the metaphors by which we think must have been good metaphors. It does follow that if those original equations, between good and light, or evil and dark, between breath and soul and all the others, were from the beginning arbitrary and fanciful—if there is not, in fact, a kind of psycho-physical parallelism (or more) in the universe—then all our thinking is nonsensical. But we cannot, without contradiction, believe it to be nonsensical. And so, admittedly, the view I have taken has metaphysical implications. But so has every view.

There are a number of suggestive ideas here, many of which Lewis developed and refined in later years, leading to his definitive statement about literature, *An Experiment in Criticism.** Some of the basic ideas are as follows. (1) There is a distinction between reason and imagination as regards roles—reason has to do with theoretical truths; imagination has to do with meanings. (2) There are standards of correctness, or norms, for the imagination, held tacitly and universally by human beings. (3) Meaning is a condition of the framing of truth; poor meanings make for poor thoughts. (4) The framing of truths in propositions necessitates the employment of metaphors supplied by the imagination. Language and thought necessarily rely upon metaphor.

One of the most controversial and difficult points here is that meaning is somehow a condition of thought in a manner obviously different from how the physical brain is. A footnote in Barfield's *Poetic Diction* sheds light on this, if "poet" is read as "the imagination": "Logical judgments, by their nature, can only render more explicit some one part of a truth already implicit in their terms. But the poet makes the terms themselves. He does not make judgments, therefore; he only makes them possible—and only he makes them possible." Imagination is the maker of meaning, the definer of terms in a proposition, and as such is a condition of truth.

The place of metaphor in thinking was central to C. S. Lewis's beliefs. In *Miracles* he points out that to speak of anything beyond the perceptions of our five senses, metaphorical expression is required; this is as true in the fields of psychology, economics, philosophy, and politics as it is in the fields of religion and poetry. To speak of super-sensibles, he argues, is inevitably to talk "as if they could be seen or touched or heard (e.g., must talk of 'complexes' and 'repressions' as if desires could really be tied up in bundles or shoved back; of 'growth' and 'development' as if institutions could really grow like trees or unfold like flowers; of energy being 'released' as if it were an animal let out of a cage)."

Meldilorn In *Out of the Silent Planet,** the habitation of the ruling Oyarsa, the great eldil.* Meldilorn is an island on a sapphire lake set within a border of purple forest. It lies in the Marsian handramit,* or lowland. On the island is a broad avenue of monoliths and magnificent trees.

"Mere Christianity" Lewis's preferred name for common ground or "great-tradition" Christian orthodoxy, or "Christianity without water." He discovered the term in the Puritan divine Richard Baxter, who writes in his *Church History of the Government of Bishops* (1680):

> I am a CHRISTIAN, a MEER CHRISTIAN, of no other Religion; and the Church that I am of is the Christian Church, and hath been visible where ever the Christian Religion and Church hath been visible: But must you know what Sect or Party I am of? I am against all Sects and dividing Parties: But if any will call Meer Christians by the name of a Party, because they take up with Meer Christianity, Creed, and Scripture, and will not be of any dividing or contentious Sect, I am of that Party which is so against Parties: If the Name CHRISTIAN be not enough, call me a CATHOLICK CHRISTIAN; not as that word signifieth an hereticating majority of Bishops, but as it signifieth one that hath no Religion, but that which by Christ and the Apostles was left to the Catholick Church, or the Body of Jesus Christ on Earth.

Mere Christianity (1952) One of the most well-known of C. S. Lewis's books, *Mere Christianity* is a revised and enlarged edition of three previous books of talks given on BBC radio, *Broadcast Talks* (called *The Case for Christianity* in the United States) (1942), *Christian Behavior* (1943), and *Beyond Personality* (1944). It is straightforward and lucid, and its contents are captured in its section titles: "Right and Wrong as a Clue to the Meaning of the Universe," "What Christians Believe," "Christian Behavior," and "Beyond Personality: or First Steps in the Doctrine of the Trinity." C. S. Lewis was invited to give popular talks on BBC radio early in 1941, when war had made people generally more thoughtful about ultimate issues. Lewis had to overcome two dislikes—the radio and traveling to London—but his sense of duty won. He regarded England as post-Christian, and he felt that many people were of the opinion that they had rejected Christianity, whereas they had never had it. His feelings about the first set of talks were recorded in a letter. The broadcasts were pre-evangelism "rather than evangelism, an attempt to convince people that there is a moral law, that we disobey it, and that the existence of a Lawgiver is at least very probable, and also (unless you add the Christian doctrine of the Atonement) that this imparts despair rather than comfort." Some years after the BBC talks C. S. Lewis recorded a series for radio that was the basis for his book *The Four Loves*.* They were broadcast only in the United States. These talks are some of the few recordings of Lewis's voice available.

Merlin In *That Hideous Strength*,* the magician from the time of King Arthur who returns to help to save Logres, the true Britain. See: ATLANTIS.

Miracles: A Preliminary Study (1947; revised new edition, 1960) This book, which reveals more than any other C. S. Lewis's view of God* and nature,* was intended for people for whom the question of miracles is real. It is not couched in the specialist language of theology or philosophy, though it has an enormous amount to contribute to both theology and philosophy of religion.

The book was substantially revised and improved after chapter three in the first edition, "The Self-Contradiction of the Naturalist," was criticized by philosopher Elizabeth Anscombe at the Oxford University Socratic Club.* The substance of her critique and Lewis's response is found in the essay "Religion Without Dogma?" in *Undeceptions*.*

The first part of the book, consisting of the first seven chapters, describes two basic attitudes of thought about life, the universe, and everything. The first, which Lewis felt was now habitual in the modern person, he called naturalism.* This materialistic view sees the natural universe as all that is; nature is "the whole show." Nothing else exists. Any reality beyond what can be perceived by the five senses lacks plausibility. The possibility of miracles is ruled out in advance; seeking evidence for a miracle is as silly as looking for Santa Claus.

The second, and opposite, view is supernaturalism, the theistic view that the universe is a dependent creation of God. Time, space, and geometry are all God's creation, and these only exist now because he chose to make them out of nothing. For C. S. Lewis, the naturalist sees nature as a pond of infinite depths made up of nothing but water. The supernaturalist sees nature as a pond with a bottom—mud, earth, rock, and finally the planet itself. The central point is that if naturalism is true, miracles are impossible. If supernaturalism is true, miracles are possible and, indeed, to be expected.

Lewis points out two insurmountable difficulties with naturalism. It undermines the validity of thought itself and, therefore, even the claims of naturalism to be true. It also reduces the "oughtness" of things to "isness." If moral obligation turns out only to be caused naturally, then it is no longer an obligation. We can only then be forced or manipulated into behaving as some other people (the Nazis, for example) wish us to. For C. S. Lewis, both conscience and reason provide an analogy for the way a miracle imposes itself upon the natural order. Both conscience and reason are testimonies to the reality of the supernatural world.

The argument in this part of the book owes much to Arthur Balfour's* *Theism and Humanism,** the Gifford Lectures for 1914, which Lewis greatly admired and felt to be unjustly neglected.

After this preparation, C. S. Lewis proceeds to his main theme, the biblical miracles, particularly the incarnation of Christ. He is particularly concerned with demolishing modern chronological snobbery.* This is the tendency to treat the past as more primitive than the present and as therefore superseded. There are two characteristic ways that this attitude bars itself from the New Testament miracles. One is to see the people of that time as gullible in accepting as miracles events that today would have a natural explanation. The other is to see their imagery as mythological and therefore in need of de- or re-mythologizing in modern terms. The idea of God coming down to earth from up there in heaven is an example. C. S. Lewis's treatment of both modern fallacies is brilliant and helpful. Of particular interest is his treatment of the function of imagery and metaphor in language. He presents some seminal ideas on the relationship between imagination* and thinking, meaning* and truth. Such ideas were at the very foundation of his thinking, scholarship, and fictional work.

See also: THEOLOGY, C. S. LEWIS AND.

Miraz, King In *Prince Caspian,** the prince's wicked uncle who had stolen the throne from King Caspian* the Ninth. Miraz was aided and abetted by Queen Prunaprismia, and he came to a bad end.

Monopods See: DUFFLEPUDS.

Moonwood In *The Last Battle,** a hare with such exceptional hearing that it was told that he could sit by Cauldron Pool under the waterfall and hear what was whispered at Cair Paravel.*

Moore, Mrs. Janie King Askins (1872-1951) The woman adopted by C. S. Lewis, according to Owen Barfield (*The Independent*, March 7, 1994) as a mother in fulfillment of a promise made to her son, a billet-mate of Lewis's killed during the Great War. Alternatively, according to some (see: LEWIS, CLIVE STAPLES), Lewis's lover for some years before his commitment to Christian faith. Mrs. Moore, along with her surviving child Maureen, shared Lewis's household from soon after the war. With typical generosity, Lewis focused on her virtues, praising her hospitality. His brother "Warnie" was less charitable; he could not understand how Lewis put up with her. As far as Warnie was concerned, "Minto," as she was dubbed, was Jack Lewis's thorn in the flesh. He sketched out her life and character in a journal entry a few days after her death for posterity in *Brothers and Friends: The Diaries of Major Warren Hamilton Lewis** (entry, January 17, 1951).

Lewis's own diaries (abridged in *All My Road Before Me**) were most likely written for the benefit of Mrs. Moore, whom he refers to as "D." There is speculation that "D" in the typescript made by Warnie Lewis (in the Lewis Family Papers*) may be transcribed from the Greek letter Delta and may stand for Diotima, a priestess in Plato's *Symposium* who introduces Socrates (in a platonic way, of course) to the meaning of love. Mrs. Moore, as Diotima, may have introduced love to the young Lewis in a less platonic way, the speculation continues.

Owen Barfield was acquainted with Mrs. Moore in the 1920s: "People have argued that Jack had a relationship with her. It's certainly possible, but unlikely to have been long-enduring; she was quite a lot older than him, and not, I should have thought, physically attractive" (*The Independent,* March 7, 1994).

Mother Kirk An allegorical figure representing the Christian church* in *The Pilgrim's Regress.** She represents common-ground Christian faith of the "great tradition" (see: MERE CHRISTIANITY).

"Mountbracken" Lewis's name, in *Surprised by Joy,** for Glenmachan House, home of his mother's cousin, Lady Ewart, and Sir William Quartus Ewart.*

Mount Pire In *The Horse and His Boy,** a mountain in Archenland* created when Fair Olvin fought the two-headed giant, Pire, and turned him into stone. Shasta* uses the twin-peaked mountain as a landmark for finding Archenland.

Muil In *The Voyage of the "Dawn Treader"** the westernmost of the Seven Isles.* It is separated from the isle of Brenn* by a choppy strait.

Mullugutherum In *The Silver Chair,** the Warden of the Marches of Underland.* He was chief of the Earthmen* in the Underworld realm, the Shallow Lands* of the Green Witch.*

Myth C. S. Lewis, like his friend J. R. R. Tolkien,* placed the highest value on the making of myth—or *mythopoeia*—in imaginative fiction and poetry. Some stories are outright myths—as is the story of Cupid and Psyche* retold by Lewis in *Till We Have Faces.** Other stories have what Lewis called a "mythical quality." Examples he gave were the plots of *Dr. Jekyll and Mr. Hyde*, H. G. Wells's *The Door in* *the Wall*, Kafka's *The Castle*, and the conceptions of Gormenghast in Mervyn Peake's *Titus Groan* and of the Ents and Lothlorien in Tolkien's *The Lord of the Rings*. Both Lewis and Tolkien aspired to myth-making in their fictional creations. They had a theology of myth (see: THEOLOGY OF ROMANCE).

Recognizing that the term *myth*, like *Romanticism*, has many loose meanings (including "untrue"), C. S. Lewis tried to pin down its meaning in his *An Experiment in Criticism.** A story that achieves myth has a number of characteristics. (1) It is independent of the form of words used to tell the story. (2) Narrative features such as suspense or surprise play little part in the distinctive pleasure of myth. (3) Our empathy with the characters of the story is at a minimum; we do not imaginatively transport ourselves into their lives. (4) Myth is always fantasy, dealing with the impossible and preternatural. (5) Myth is never comic; though the experience may be joyful or sad, it is always grave. (6) The experience in fact is awe-inspiring, containing a numinous* quality. In defining myth in terms of its effect upon us, Lewis was clear that one person's myth may only be a story to another. A story may give enjoyment to a person without being perceived as myth, even though it is myth. C. S. Lewis regarded the nineteenth-century writer George MacDonald* as one of the greatest masters of myth-making, especially in *Phantastes** (which, Lewis says, "baptized" his imagination long before he became a Christian believer) and *Lilith*.

Myth has had a central place in modern anthropology and also in contemporary theology. At the time of his conversion, C. S. Lewis wrestled with the anthropology of James G. Frazer (1854-1941), as represented in the widely influential *The Golden Bough: A Study in Magic and Religion* (abridged edition, 1922). Later in his life, Lewis made known his disquiet with key ideas of myth propounded in contemporary theology, ideas associated for example with Rudolf Bultmann (1884-1976). Lewis saw serious errors in Frazer's view of myth, and in the understanding of myth in the work of leading biblical critics. Sir James Frazer explored magic and religions throughout the world in the hope of tracing an important part of the evolution of human thought. As a result *The Golden Bough* (originally in thirteen volumes) is truly encyclopedic. In seeking a unified development, Frazer denied the value of asking whether religions were true or false. Christianity had no uniqueness, a theme that is increasingly heard in contemporary theology, through John Hick and others. Frazer helped to lay the foundation for the relativism that is so familiar today. Though at first the similarities between biblical teaching and ancient myths seemed devastating to Christian belief, C. S. Lewis came to the conclusion that they can argue for the truth of Christianity as well as against it.

James Frazer had documented many myths of dying and rising gods throughout the world. As C. S. Lewis grew as a Christian thinker, he continued to reflect on such myths. He argued that "We must not be nervous about 'parallels' and 'pagan Christs': they ought to be there—it would be a stumbling block if they weren't." He explored such "parallel" themes in his powerful "myth retold," *Till We Have Faces*.

At the heart of Christianity, C. S. Lewis believed, is a myth that is also a fact—making the claims of Christianity unique. (See: MYTH BECAME FACT.) But by becoming fact, Lewis points out, it did not cease to be myth or lose the quality of myth. Lewis praised John Milton for retaining the tangible quality of myth in most of *Paradise Lost*, his great epic and one of the most powerful of creedal affirmations in Christian literature. Lewis strived to follow Milton's example in his own fiction.

Rudolf Bultmann is widely considered to be the most significant and influential New Testament scholar of this century. Bultmann's key belief was that "faith must not aspire to an objective basis in dogma or in history on pain of losing its character as faith." Bultmann saw the gospel records as myths, and myths as attempts to portray happenings in the world as having supernatural causes. In the case of Christ's virgin birth, the event could only have occurred with divine intervention into the world of cause and effect. The modern person, Bultmann believes, cannot accept the idea of supernatural causes of events in the world we see. We must strip the Gospels of myths and get to the core of what Christ's followers believed in the first century. They were "objectifying" their beliefs in myths appropriate to their day.

C. S. Lewis's counter to this kind of thinking is found in his apologetical study *Miracles*.* There he argues that a supernaturalist view is not outmoded, but is essential for proper human thinking and intellectual discovery at any time or place. He also addressed modern biblical critics directly on one occasion (see: THEOLOGY, C. S. LEWIS AND). Lewis objected to biblical critics who saw the Gospels as legend or romance rather than a factual, historical record. As a literary critic and avid reader of myth, Lewis felt that the critics had little idea of what myth actually is. In several instances, he found them poor readers of the texts they had pored over, perhaps for years.

Like Bultmann, however, C. S. Lewis did recognize the difficulties modern people have in reading the Gospels. Bultmann's procedure was to "demythologize." Lewis, who wanted as an orthodox "mere Christian" to retain the Gospels as the greatest story but true, chose rather to remythologize central Christian beliefs. He attempted stories that would put over Christian meanings in a modern way, particularly in his Narnia* stories for children (of all ages) and his science-fiction trilogy. Even his historical novel *Till We Have Faces* is fresh and contemporary as a work of art.

Myth Became Fact An important factor in Lewis's conversion to Christianity was his acceptance of J. R. R. Tolkien's* argument (captured in his poem "Mythopoeia") that the biblical Gospels have all the best qualities of pagan myth,* with the unique feature that the events actually happened in documented history. Lewis and Tolkien thus radically differed from views of myth espoused by liberal biblical scholars of the time that divorced myth from history as a matter of definition.

Lewis, like Tolkien, faced ancient tensions. The tension between realism and fantasy is just one such tension, as myth is a form of fantasy. The use of myth and fantasy didn't denote lack of confidence until nowadays. Its use by C. S. Lewis and in J. R. R. Tolkien is a matter of confidence. When Lewis applied the category of myth to the Gospels, he was not displaying uncertainty about historicity. So even though there was an awareness of ancient tensions between myth and realism so far as Lewis was concerned, the tension for him was basically reconciled, despite the fact that the tension is embedded in the very definition of myth. Myth can be defined in terms of the symbolic capture or embodiment of a worldview of a people or culture, thus having an important believed element. Myth can also be defined as untrue, fictional, and merely imaginative. The existence of myth writes large the dilemma that the "lies" of the poet and the fiction writer capture profound realities, realities impossible to capture in any other way. Fiction, poetry, and metaphor, though they are "lies," by necessity have a representational element.

Other forms of the inherent tension of myth are evident. The tension between myth and reason (or *logos*), myth and history, and myth and knowledge, goes back to ancient times. Again, however, it is only in the modern period that this tension has represented a crisis in knowledge. In ancient times, up to what Lewis would have described as the Great Divide (see: OLD WEST) between the Old and post-Christian West, the tension between myth and fact was creative, as it is in the work of Lewis. He has a tangible confidence that the polarity between myth and fact has been reconciled—which reflects a more ancient confidence. Heaven has come down to earth, and our humanity has been taken up to God.

Some tentative examination of the concepts of myth and "fact" is necessary in order to be able to see how Lewis considered their reconciliation justified in the first-century gospel narratives.

What is fact? For many people, the existence of the material world is proved by kicking a stone. But it is generally accepted by less naïve reflection that there is an interpretative dimension to all facts—there may be an intellectual, imaginative, or perceptual element in a fact, or indeed all these elements at a time—even when the stone you kick is real. There is, in other words, a subjective, personal element in objectivity. This is brilliantly pointed out, for example, in Michael Polanyi's book *Personal Knowledge*.

If it is true that myth plays a part in a symbolic perception of reality (which Lewis believed), then there is an inner connection between myth and the real world of sensible things and events.

The symbolic aspect of the factual can be seen in the way Lewis viewed the issues of abstraction and of the truths contained in paganism.* He was fascinated by how theoretical imponderables such as free will and necessity, or prophecy and its human agency, are embodied in a concrete, unified way in imaginative fiction, myth, and even history. Lewis was also characteristically interested, in his book *Miracles,** in the fact that in the actual event of thinking, there is a mind-body unity, even though thought (if it has any validity other than psychological) cannot be reduced to physical causality. Extending Lewis's idea, any human action we make—moving one's hand to paint a picture, talking to communicate, or thinking a rational train of thought—concretely displays a mind-body unity that is baffling or at least resistant to theoretical abstraction. Similarly, in history, as in fiction and myth, ideas almost impossible to grasp abstractly can be perceived concretely in their relationship—such as in the relationship between the divine and human natures of Jesus Christ or the relationship between human responsibility and divine sovereignty (as when Judas betrayed Christ). Lewis (like Tolkien), not surprisingly, was deeply interested in the paradox of prophecy and its fulfillment in real and imagined history.

In his essay "Myth Became Fact," Lewis writes:

> Human intellect is incurably abstract. Pure mathematics is the type of successful thought. Yet the only realities we experience are concrete—this pain, this pleasure, this dog, this man. While we are loving the man, bearing the pain, enjoying the pleasure, we are not intellectually apprehending Pleasure, Pain or Personality. When we begin to do so, on the other hand, the concrete realities sink to the level of mere instances or examples: we are no longer dealing with them, but with that which they exemplify. This is our dilemma—either to taste and not to know or to know and not to taste. . . . "If only my tooth-ache would stop, I could write another chapter about Pain." But once it stops what do I know about pain?
>
> Of this tragic dilemma myth is the partial solution. In the enjoyment of a great myth we come nearest to experiencing as a concrete what can otherwise be understood only as an abstraction.

In the matter of paganism, Tolkien and Lewis explored anticipatory myth—plausible myth that anticipated the *evangelium*, the historic Gospels where myth became fact. *The Silmarillion, The Lord of the Rings*, and Lewis's *Till We Have Faces** are all set in a pagan pre-Christian world where fact is anticipated in unfocused, limited pagan myth.

But the element of fact is not only found in the anticipation of the Gospel. For both men, myth was also tied with a thousand ties to the ordinary world of nature and humble fact. In reviewing his friend's *The*

Lord of the Rings, Lewis describes just how Tolkien's invented mythology is applicable to the primary, real world. Lewis concentrates on the aspect of recovery:

> The value of the myth is that it takes all the things we know and restores to them the rich significance which has been hidden by the veil of familiarity. . . . As long as the story lingers in our mind, the real things are more themselves. This book applies the treatment not only to bread or apple but to good and evil, to our endless perils, our anguish and our joys. By dipping them in myth we see them more clearly. I do not think he could have done it in any other way.

What is a Gospel? Expectations both of author and reader are a vital ingredient in the character of a piece of writing. These expectations shape the writing process and the interpretation of the text by its reader. The nature of the Gospels—and thus the kind of expectations they arouse—has been keenly discussed over the past century and a half—ranging from the view that the Gospels are totally unique in their time to seeing them as part of the genre of Hellenistic biography. The former view concentrates on the content of the Gospels, as if they were naïve collections of oral tradition, whereas the latter view takes very seriously their literary nature and the skilled presence of their distinctive authors in their written text. The approach of Lewis (and Tolkien) to the Gospels is important but unnoticed in biblical scholarship. It combines a view of the uniqueness of the Gospels in terms of their folk context, with a literary and structural understanding in terms of archetype, myth, and symbolic power.

The approach is suggested in C. S. Lewis's essay, "Myth Became fact":

> The heart of Christianity is a myth which is also a fact. The old myth of the Dying God, *without ceasing to be myth*, comes down from the heaven of legend and imagination to the earth of history. It *happens*—at a particular date, in a particular place, followed by definable historical consequences. We pass from a Balder or an Osiris, dying nobly nobody knows when or where, to a historical Person crucified (it is all in order) *under Pontius Pilate*. By becoming fact it does not cease to be myth: that is the miracle. . . . To be truly Christian we must both assent to the historical fact and also receive the myth (fact though it has become) with the same imaginative embrace which we accord to all myths.

It follows from this view that the Gospels would be imaginatively recognized and have an imaginative appeal to both Jewish and Gentile readers. These readers would recognize their symbolic and archetypal patterns. "This is the marriage of heaven and earth," writes C. S. Lewis, "Perfect Myth and Perfect Fact: claiming not only our love and obedience, but also our wonder and delight, addressed to the savage, the child, and the poet in each one of us no less than to the moralist, the scholar, and the philosopher." Lewis was convinced of this view, while still a non-Christian, by his great friend J. R. R. Tolkien, who expounds it in his "Essay on Fairy Stories" and poem "Mythopoeia." He argues that the very historical events of the gospel narratives are shaped by God, the master story-maker, having a structure of the sudden turn from catastrophe to the most satisfying of all happy endings—a structure shared with many of the best human stories. The Gospels, in their divine source, thus penetrate "the seamless web" of human storytelling, clarifying and perfecting the insights that God in his grace has allowed to the human imagination. In the Gospels, Tolkien concludes, "art has been verified."

N

Nain In *Prince Caspian,** King of Archenland* in the dark time of Miraz* of Narnia.*

Narnia See: NARNIA—HISTORY.

Narnia, The Chronicles of Seven tales for children by C. S. Lewis that cover almost half of this century and over two and a half millennia of Narnian years, from its creation to its final days. In chronological order the titles are *The Magician's Nephew,** *The Lion, the Witch and the Wardrobe,** *The Horse and His Boy,** *Prince Caspian,** *The Voyage of the "Dawn Treader,"** *The Silver Chair,** and *The Last Battle.** In reading order, it is preferable to enjoy *The Lion, the Witch and the Wardrobe* first.

Narnia—geography In The Chronicles of Narnia,* Narnia is a small country south of which lies Archenland* and Calormen.* Narnia is inhabited by both talking and dumb beasts and trees, the chief of all its creatures being also its creator, Aslan,* a talking lion. To the far west lies the land of Telmar,* and nearer is the Western Wild—a mountainous region covered with dark forests or with snow and ice. From this region rushes a river that becomes a waterfall under which is Caldron Pool.* From this pool flows the River of Narnia, which runs all the way to the Eastern Ocean.* Lantern Waste* lies to the east of the wilderness.

Narnia's capital is Cair Paravel,* the seat of human kings and queens, located at the mouth of the River of Narnia. The marshwiggles* (found only in Narnia) live to the north of Cair Paravel. More northerly lies the River Shribble, and then the forlorn moorland of Ettinsmoor.* Farther north still is a mountainous region and Harfang,* a stronghold of giants. Near Harfang are the ruins of a once great city, under which lie a number of subterranean lands, including the kingdom of the Green Witch,* destroyed in the time of Prince Rilian,* son of Caspian,* the tenth Telmarine* king.

To Narnia's east lies the vast Eastern Ocean,* in which are many islands, and finally the Silver Sea and the World's End, where lies Aslan's Country.* In the geography of Narnia, it is likely that Lewis has captured something of the Ulster that he loved from childhood, particularly County Down.

Narnia is also the name of a small Italian town mentioned by Livy.

Rev. Cosslet Quinn, a former rector of St. Mark's, Dundela, recalls vividly the Ulster side of Lewis: "I still remember from one occasion when I met C. S. Lewis, seeing the flash in his eyes as he spoke of the 2,000-year-old epic of Cuchulain, and what it ought to mean for an Ulsterman."

Professor Frank Kastor of Witchita State University is one scholar who finds parallels between the geography and landscapes of Narnia and those of the Ulster that Lewis knew as a boy. Kastor adds his comments in brackets to a quotation from *The Magician's Nephew.**

> All Narnia, many-colored with lawns and rocks and heather and different sorts of trees, lay spread out below them; the river winding through it like a ribbon of quicksilver [THE LAGAN]. They could already see over the tops of the low hills which lay northward on their right [HILLS OF ANTRIM]; beyond those hills, a great moorland sloped gently up and up to the horizon. On their left [southward] the mountains were much higher [MOUNTAINS OF MOURNE], but every now and then there was a gap when you could see, between steep pine woods, a glimpse of the southern lands that lay beyond them [NOW THE REPUBLIC OF IRELAND] looking blue and far away.

Professor Kastor adds that their destination is the garden with the magic apple tree. This garden lies west of Narnia at the end of the blue lake [LOUGH NEAGH], in the mountains of the Western Wild [NORTHWESTERN IRELAND]. See also: NARNIA, HISTORY.

Narnia—history. Because the time of earth is different from that of Narnia, the children who are drawn into Narnia on a number of occasions find themselves at various parts of its history. Thus, although The Chronicles of Narnia* cover only about fifty years of our history (from the beginning to the mid-twentieth century), we get a picture of the entire history of Narnia from its creation to its unmaking and the new creation of all worlds, including Narnia and England.

Narnia's creation is recounted in *The Magician's Nephew.** Digory Kirke* and Polly Plummer,* after entering the old and dying world of Charn* through a pool in the Wood Between the Worlds,* find their way by accident into a land of Nothing. Here, gradually, Narnia is created before their eyes by the song of Aslan.* Unfortunately Digory brings evil into that perfect world in the form of Jadis,* destroyer of Charn,* whom he had previously awakened in that world. Jadis goes off to the fringes of Narnia, but she reappears in later ages as the White Witch* who puts a spell over Narnia, a spell of winter but never Christmas. The arrival of the four Pevensie* children through the wardrobe (told in *The Lion, the Witch and the Wardrobe**) coincides with the return of Aslan and the beginning of the end of her curse. Aslan's death on behalf of Edmund Pevensie and return to life by a deeper law than the one by which the witch operates her magic leads to her defeat and death. Narnia's Golden Age follows.

With the return of the children to their world, Narnia slowly falls into disorder. The Telmarines,* led by Caspian* the First, occupy the land and silence the talking beasts and trees. "Old Narnia" only survives under cover as Aslan's remnant keep faith alive that he will return. Prince Caspian* (his story is told in the book of that name), brought up by his wicked Uncle Miraz* and Aunt Prunaprismia,* who have deposed his father Caspian the Ninth, learns of the myth of Old Narnia and longs for it to be true. He escapes a plot to kill him and joins forces with the Old Narnians. In the nick of time, help comes from the four Pevensie children drawn back into Narnia.

Caspian becomes Caspian the Tenth after adventures at sea recounted in *The Voyage of the "Dawn Treader."** His son, Prince Rilian,* is kidnapped and held in servitude in an underworld for ten years by a witch of the line of Jadis. She plots to take over Narnia using him as a puppet king. As told in the chronicle of *The Silver Chair*,* he is rescued by two cousins of the Pevensie children, Eustace Scrubb* and Jill Pole,* who are brought into Narnia for this task.

After many ages the last King of Narnia, Tirian,* and indeed Narnia itself are threatened by a devilish plot that uses a counterfeit Aslan and links up with the Calormene* forces (who are a constant threat to Narnia's security). This is Narnia's darkest hour. As told in *The Last Battle,** Tirian prays for help from the sons and daughters of Adam, and Aslan brings Eustace and Jill to his aid. Aslan himself finally intervenes and dissolves the whole world. This turns out to be a beginning rather than an end, as the new Narnia is revealed. See also: NARNIA—GEOGRAPHY.

FURTHER READING

Walter Hooper, *Past Watchful Dragons* (1980).
Martha C. Sammons, *A Guide Through Narnia* (1979).
Paul F. Ford, *Companion to Narnia* (1994).

Narrative Poems (1969) C. S. Lewis wrote both lyrical and narrative verse, and he originally hoped to make his name as a poet. This volume contains four stories, including *Dymer*,* *Launcelot, The Nameless Isle*, and *The Queen of Drum*—about the escape of a queen from a dictator into Fairy Land. See also: POEMS.

Narrowhaven In *The Voyage of the "Dawn Treader"** a town on the island of Doorn* ruled by Gumpas.* See also: LONE ISLANDS.

Naturalism and supernaturalism Naturalism is the term Lewis uses in his book *Miracles: A Preliminary Study** for the view that nature* is "the whole show," with nothing outside nature existing. He contrasts naturalism with its opposite, supernaturalism—the theistic view that nature is contingent. God has created it, but he did not have to create it. He could have created other natures or not created at all. God is complete irrespective of whether or not he created a real nature outside of himself.

Two things need to be said about Lewis's formulation of nature and supernature. One is that he is representing an orthodox Judeo-Christian position, a position that many believe was an essential presupposition for the rise of modern science. The other is that Lewis's view can be formulated in other terms and, no doubt, in more sophisticated and precise philosophical language. C. S. Lewis was deliberately popularizing. In the process, his thinking (especially as embodied in *Miracles*) is more timeless than a full-fledged philosophical study. He was careful to call *Miracles* a "preliminary study." Nevertheless, after his encounter with philosopher Elizabeth Anscombe* at a meeting of the Oxford University Socratic Club,* he greatly improved his case for the later paperback edition of *Miracles*.

C. S. Lewis's fundamental distinction between nature and supernature has, surprisingly, been criticized by some evangelicals who seem to take a position difficult to separate from deism. Two key elements of this criticism are as follows: One is a dislike of Lewis's metaphors of "interruption" and "violation" of nature by the supernatural. The critics point out that God's creation in every aspect, natural and spiritual, reveals the mark of his personal hand. The other is a rejection of Lewis's analysis of the causation of thinking, in its link to the brain as a mechanism. Lewis's opponents are happy for the brain as a mechanism to have a complete causal story in terms of the laws of physics and chemistry. Thought and human consciousness have a complementary story, perceived by the dimension of faith and ourselves as responsible observers. Thus Lewis's central argument of the self-contradiction of naturalism is undermined.

This criticism, however, ignores the underlying force of Lewis's attack on naturalism, and also is un-self-critical, by failing to realize the popular character of Lewis's study and apologetic. A number of Christian thinkers have worked on the question of causality on various hierarchical levels, such as the physical and chemical, the biological, and the historical. They have also wrestled with the logical relationship between causal levels—a necessity for any complementarian approach. This work, particularly by Michael Polanyi (who spoke several times to the Oxford University Socratic Club) and Herman Dooyeweerd, strengthens Lewis's approach, and indeed the traditional theistic position for which he stood. C. S. Lewis's own essay "Transposition" is powerfully suggestive of such an approach. C. S. Lewis's views both of naturalism and of the self-contradiction of the naturalist are seminal for contemporary Christian apologetics. "Naturalism" can be extended as a concept to any view that makes an aspect of the created world into a God-substitute, or idol. This aspect is therefore made transcendent and creates an inner tension, a contradiction, in the resulting humanistic system. This internal contradiction is capable of structural analysis and exposure. A brilliant use of such "transcendental criticism" is made by Dooyeweerd in his *A New Critique of Theoretical Thought* (1935-1936).

Lewis's key metaphors, describing the supernatural as invading or interfering with nature, do not imply a dualism in God's created world. Lewis was not a Platonist, though Plato* was a rich source for his imagination. Lewis uses such metaphors in the context of a nature that is fallen, and hence abnormal. He believed in a real historical Fall by disobedient mankind that affected the whole of nature, even though nature still reveals God himself. Unless one is an atheist or a deist, it is difficult to see why such metaphors are objectionable. Supernature, like nature, is marked by both good and evil as a result of primeval disobedience by mankind and some angels. C. S. Lewis's case would perhaps have been more elegant if he had introduced more the biblical concept of the cultural mandate, where mankind is commanded in Genesis to order and name the natural world. The whole human cultural process rearranges nature; it transcends the laws of physics and chemistry. Lewis could therefore have extended his analogy between supernatural acts and thinking to include culture (of which thinking is but a part). Such a broader canvas, however, might not have interested him because of his distrust of overblown systems.

Nature

> "In our world," said Eustace, "a star is a huge ball of flaming gas."
>
> "Even in your world, my son," replied the old man, "that is not what a star is but only what it is made of."
>
> THE VOYAGE OF THE "DAWN TREADER"

Like his friend Owen Barfield,* C. S. Lewis believed that, as Ransom* remarked to Merlin in *That Hideous Strength*,* "the soul has gone out of wood and water." The world's history is one of mankind's separation from God* on the one hand and from nature on the other. This view led to Lewis's opposition to scientism* (but not true science). Our separation from nature came from our wish to exalt ourselves and thus to belittle all else. Christians, Lewis believed, should recognize God's continued activity in the fecundity of natural things such as trees, grass, flowers, and shrubs. J. R. R. Tolkien,* Lewis's other great friend, also held this view.

In his atheistic mid-teens C. S. Lewis cared mainly about gods, heroes, and an ideal world of beauty. Many years later he eventually, and reluctantly, accepted a Christian universe. He soon realized the implications of commitment to this "real universe, the divine, magical, terrifying and ecstatic reality in which we all live." What fixed the reality of the natural world forever was the incarnation of God* himself as a fully human being in a fully real human body. Christ's resurrection meant that he retains this human body forever. The environment of his resurrected body, and those of his followers in the future, could be called a new nature, though believers, Lewis included, prefer to call this environment "heaven."* C. S. Lewis was once interviewed by *Time* magazine (September 8, 1947). They wondered if his life at Oxford, a life of writing, walking, teaching, and reading, was monotonous. Lewis's reply baffled them: "I like monotony."

It is upon the humble and common things of life that Lewis's wonderlands of the imagination are based, "the quiet fullness of ordinary nature." He also saw the ordinary (he learned this from George MacDonald*) as the basis of spirituality. In a letter he wrote, "The familiar is in itself ground for affection. And it is good, because any natural help towards our spiritual duty of loving is good and God seems to build our higher loves round our merely natural impulses—sex, maternity, kinship, old acquaintances." Conversely, as he demonstrated vividly in his *The Screwtape Letters*,* the small things are likely to play more part in the damnation of a person than great acts such as murder or betrayal. Because of the link between ordinary reality and imaginative creation, Lewis found himself as much on the defensive about fantasy as about his lifestyle. A common charge was that literary fantasy is escapism. In his book *Of Other Worlds*, Lewis says of *The Wind in the Willows* (the popular children's story by Kenneth Graham): "The happiness which it presents to us is in fact full of the simplest and most attainable things—food, sleep, exercise, friendship, the face of nature, even (in a sense) religion." Such fantasy is the opposite of escapism. It deepens the reality of the real world for us—the terror as well as the beauty.

In making such comments and holding fervently to such beliefs, C. S. Lewis was in fact struggling with a most important problem for the Christian in the modern world. The difficulty is to be contented with reality as it is given to us by God without denying that it is abnormal because of the fall of mankind at the beginning of recorded history. Such contentment is by no means synonymous with conservatism in ideas and politics—so called Cosmic Toryism. Lewis himself did not defend the status quo, carefully dissociated himself from the political Right, and even strongly believed that soon the time will come when a Christian in the Civil Service will have a problem about furthering tyranny. In the wartime he urged RAF personnel to face the consequences of refusing to bomb civilian targets. In his satirical science-fiction story, *That Hideous Strength*,* the devil's party are officials! His open Christian position made him unpopular with many in the Oxford* establishment.

For C. S. Lewis, the importance of reality lies in how it impinges upon the individual person. No one can experience the humanist's "happiness of the greatest number." Furthermore, what is unbearably painful to one person can be borne by another. Lewis himself clearly felt life deeply. He does not seem to be exaggerating when he once wrote in a letter early in 1956, "It seems to me that one can hardly say anything either bad enough or good enough about life." In his "myth retold," *Till We Have Faces,** he goes a long way toward achieving both at once. C. S. Lewis saw Christianity as carrying the stamp of this same reality upon it. He wrote in 1953, "Christianity is . . . hard and tender at the same time. It's the blend that does it; neither quality would be any good without the other."

Closely linked to Lewis's zest for ordinary reality, for nature, was his attention to the details of life and experience. This power of observation added detail after detail of exuberant creation to his imaginative writings. He was very aware of nature, seasons, weather, atmosphere, and, of course, animals. In fact, he delighted to put animal characters into his books. In Narnia* many of the animals can speak. In Perelandra* the harmony between the new humans of Venus and its native animals beautifully evokes mankind's unfallen state. In *Out of the Silent Planet,** Lewis brilliantly manages to create talking animals* that are acceptable to adult readers. The "proper" bear in *That Hideous Strength,** called Mr. Bultitude,* was based upon an actual bear in Whipsnade Zoo. The threat to Mr. Bultitude by the sinister N.I.C.E.* illustrates Lewis's hatred of vivisection.

C. S. Lewis's letters are also full of references to animals. In a letter to an American lady he recounted, "We were talking about cats and dogs the other day and decided that both have consciences but the dog, being an honest, humble person, always has a bad one, but the cat is a Pharisee and always has a good one. When he sits and stares you out of countenance he is thanking God that he is not as these dogs, or these humans, or even as these other cats!"

Nature, said C. S. Lewis, has the air of a good thing that has been spoiled. It is not only spoiled in and of itself, but also in our human relationship to it. One way this disfiguring comes about is in our way of seeing the natural world. Lewis vividly illustrated this in his short story "The Shoddy Lands." Here he takes us into the mind of a self-centered young woman who lacks a real perception of nature, and thus of life. A similar impoverished view of reality in its full meaning is expressed in Lewis's disturbing picture of hell in *The Great Divorce.** He may have been influenced by his friend Charles Williams,* who portrayed hell and its inroads in our present world as the absence of meaning.*

The natural world of God's creation imposes a fundamental limit to the human imagination. We cannot, like God, create *ex nihilo*, out of nothing. We can only rearrange elements that God has already made, which are already brimful of his meanings. Mankind's proper mode of imaginative making is what J. R. R. Tolkien dubbed subcreation.* C. S. Lewis believed that evil—whether from human beings or demons—always results in the disruption or even the destruction of nature. In *The Lion, the Witch and the Wardrobe,** the White Witch* kept Narnia* in perpetual winter. In both *The Last Battle** and *That*

Hideous Strength, places of natural beauty are despoiled for the sake of economic exploitation, expansion, and so-called progress. In 1947 C. S. Lewis wrote, "The evil reality of lawless applied science . . . is actually reducing large tracts of Nature to disorder and sterility at this very moment."

Because he normally wrote in a popular manner, Lewis didn't always distinguish between nature as it was originally intended to be from nature as it is now. In his more technical studies, *The Problem of Pain** and *Miracles*,* he goes deeper into the meaning of nature as God's creation. In *Miracles* he contrasts this Christian view with what he calls "naturalism,"* the belief that nature is all that is. He could have used the term *materialism*, except that the term *matter* is even harder to pin down than *nature*. In his book *Studies in Words*,* he devotes a long section to the word *nature* and its family of words: *phusis* (from which the term *physics* is derived) and *kind*. More detail is given on the meaning of the idea of nature in other scholarly works of his, particularly *The Allegory of Love** and *The Discarded Image*.* He expounds on a biblical view of nature in *Reflections on the Psalms** and in *Miracles*.* Ultimately, there was for C. S. Lewis an inevitable connection between nature and joy,* as in nature heaven* itself is foreshadowed:

> The settled happiness and security which we all desire, God withholds from us by the very nature of the world: but joy, pleasure, and merriment, He has scattered broadcast. We are never safe, but we have plenty of fun, and some ecstasy. It is not hard to see why. The security we crave would teach us to rest our hearts in this world and pose an obstacle to our return to God: a few moments of happy love, a landscape, a symphony, a merry meeting with our friends, a bathe or a football match, have no such tendency. Our Father refreshes us on the journey with some pleasant inns, but will not encourage us to mistake them for home. (*The Problem of Pain*, chapter 7)

Nat Whilk Anglo-Saxon for "I know not whom," used by C. S. Lewis as a pseudonym, usually in the form of the initials N. W. In the first edition of *A Grief Observed** he called himself N. W. Clerk. Clerk is Middle English for "scholar." Playing on his pseudonym, Lewis quotes the medieval authority Natvilcius in *Perelandra** regarding eldila.*

New psychology Perhaps the most dominant feature of the intellectual world of the 1920s was what Lewis and his colleagues tended to dub "the new psychology," stemming particularly from the work of Sigmund Freud. This trend had a devastating impact that exists in various forms to this day. One Cambridge literary critic responsible for disseminating such psychological insights was the influential I. A. Richards (1893-1979). He radically reformulated the criteria and techniques for evaluating literature, particularly in *Principles of Literary Criticism* (1924) and *Practical Criticism, A Study of Literary*

Judgment (1929). Like Freud, Richards is ultimately a naturalist (see: NATURALISM). He reduces values (such as beauty) to what was empirically (i.e., measurably) available to the reader. Values in literature are merely a capacity to satisfy the feelings and desires of readers. The language of literature is emotive, rather than describing an objective state of affairs in the real world.

I. A. Richards stimulated a more precise debate into how a work of literature creates meaning than had been common under the sway of idealism.* Owen Barfield* took up a similar task in *Poetic Diction* (1928) from a very different nonpsychological perspective, more in tune with the older philology.

The "new psychology," exemplified in I. A. Richards's approach, created a distrust of the Romanticism* that had so marked the nineteenth century. That suspicion was reinforced by bitter memories of the First World War. Lewis was, as he says, affected by this distrust, forcing him to rethink the whole basis of Romanticism and literary fantasy.

Lewis addresses the question of wish fulfillment and fantasy as daydream in his *An Experiment in Criticism** and in his essay "Psychoanalysis and Literary Criticism" (reprinted in *Selected Literary Essays**). In the latter he gives close attention to several of Freud's lectures on psychoanalysis. Lewis points out that humanity is interested in many other matters than sex. He finds Carl Gustav Jung (1875-1961) of far more relevance to literary study than Freud; Jung has "a much more civil and humane interpretation of myth and imagery," especially in his theory of archetypes. See also: "CHRISTINA DREAMS."

N.I.C.E. In C. S. Lewis's science-fiction tale *That Hideous Strength*,* the N.I.C.E. is the National Institute for Co-ordinated Experiments, set up at Belbury,* near Edgestow,* by a group of corrupt scientists seeking to remake the human race. They wish to purge it of traditional values of freedom and dignity. These individuals represent the most satanic inner ring* in history. One N.I.C.E. member, Filostrato, reveals what he considers to be its inner purpose to Mark Studdock*: "This Institute . . . is for something better than housing and vaccinations and faster trains and curing people of cancer. It is for the conquest of death. . . . It is to bring out of that cocoon of organic life which sheltered the babyhood of mind the New Man, the man who will not die, the artificial man, free from Nature. Nature is the ladder we have climbed up by, now we kick her away." The appliance of science in technology is allowed to have a totalitarian rule; science is distorted into technocracy. In the process, new demons take possession. They are in fact the old demons using a new strategy. This time the domination of the whole human race appears to be within their grasp. The N.I.C.E. represents all that C. S. Lewis was attacking in his powerful essay *The Abolition of Man*.*

Nikabrik, the dwarf One of the Old Narnians in the tale *Prince Caspian,** but he was highly cynical. He prefers the old, "realistic" magic of the witches and turns against Aslan.*

North A key region of the symbolic landscape of *The Pilgrim's Regress** depicted in the Mappa Mundi.* It represents the intellectual domain of the human soul and arid intellectualism.

Numinor See: ATLANTIS.

Numinous An all-pervasive sense of the other is focused in a quality of the numinous, a basic human experience charted by the German thinker Rudolf Otto in his book *The Idea of the Holy** (1923), which deeply influenced Lewis. The primary numinous experience involves a sense of dependence upon what stands wholly other to mankind. This otherness (or otherworldliness) is unapproachable and awesome. But it has a fascination. The experience of the numinous is captured better by suggestion and allusion than by a theoretical analysis.

Many realities captured in imaginative fiction could be described as having some quality of the numinous. C. S. Lewis realized this, incorporating the idea into his apologetic for the Christian view of suffering, *The Problem of Pain,** and he cited an event from Kenneth Graham's fantasy for children, *The Wind in the Willows*, to illustrate it. The final part of *The Voyage of the "Dawn Treader"** particularly embodies the numinous, as the travelers approach Aslan's Country* across the Last Sea (chapters 15, 16).

Where the numinous is captured, its appeal is firstly to the imagination,* which also senses it most accurately. It belongs to the area of meaning* that we cannot easily conceptualize. C. S. Lewis found the numinous when he read George MacDonald's *Phantastes,** describing the effect in *Surprised by Joy** as baptizing his imagination. It was years later that he was able to reconcile this experience with his thinking.

O

Octesian In *The Voyage of the "Dawn Treader"** one of the seven Telmarine* lords sought by the young King Caspian* and his voyagers. Octesian had become the dragon found dying by Edmund Pevensie* on Dragon Island.*

Of Other Worlds (1966) A posthumous collection of Lewis's short fiction and essays and brief pieces on narrative fiction edited by Walter Hooper. The collection was expanded in a 1982 publication entitled *Of This and Other Worlds.*

Old Solar In C. S. Lewis's science-fiction trilogy, the universal language of rational beings, including eldila,* beyond the orbit of the moon and before the fall of mankind and the effects of the Tower of Babel. Earth (or Thulcandra—the silent planet) is unique in having a diversity of languages. Lewis invented a considerable Old Solar vocabulary in providing names and word-forms throughout the stories. The idea of inventing languages in fantasy owes much to J. R. R. Tolkien,* Lewis's friend, who created several languages, including elvish, in which he even wrote lyrics.

Old West Lewis famously defended what he called the Old West in his inaugural lecture upon taking the Chair of Medieval and Renaissance Literature at the University of Cambridge in 1954, a seat his old friend J. R. R. Tolkien* helped him gain. Tolkien was an elector of the newly-established Chair, along with F. P. Wilson and Basil Willey. Tolkien described Lewis as "the precise man for the job."

Joy Davidman,* who was later to become Lewis's wife, described the lecture to a fellow American in a letter as:

> brilliant, intellectually exciting, unexpected, and funny as hell—as you can imagine. The hall was crowded, and there were so many capped and gowned dons in the front rows that they looked like a rookery. Instead of talking in the usual professorial way about the continuity of culture, the value of traditions, etc., he announced that "Old Western Culture," as he called it, was practically dead, leaving only a few scattered survivors like himself. . . . How that man loves being in a minority, even a lost-cause minority! Athanasius *contra mundum,* or Don Quixote against the windmills. . . . He talked blandly of "post-Christian Europe," which I thought rather previous of him. I sometimes

> wonder what he would do if Christianity really did triumph everywhere; I suppose he would have to invent a new heresy. (In a letter to Chad Walsh of December 23, 1954.)

A couple of brief quotations from the lecture will give the flavor:

> Roughly speaking we may say that whereas all history was for our ancestors divided into two periods, the pre-Christian and the Christian, and two only, for us it falls into three—the pre-Christian, the Christian, and what may reasonably be called the post-Christian. . . . I am considering them simply as cultural changes. When I do that, it appears to me that the second change is even more radical than the first. Christians and pagans had much more in common with each other than either has with a post-Christian.

> Between Jane Austen and us, but not between her and Shakespeare, Chaucer, Alfred, Virgil, Homer, or the Pharaohs, comes the birth of the machines . . . this is parallel to the great changes by which we divide epochs of pre-history. This is on a level with the change from stone to bronze, or from a pastoral to an agricultural economy. It alters man's place in nature. (From "*De Descriptione Temporum,*" 1955)

Tolkien, along with their mutual friend Owen Barfield,* was responsible for helping along the process that led Lewis to become aware of a dramatic shift from the Old to the Modernist West, a shift that made the change from Medieval to Renaissance culture insignificant by comparison. Barfield's great achievement was to rid Lewis of his earlier "chronological snobbery,"* an abiding vice of the modern world. Tolkien, in turn, was responsible for pointing out to Lewis that the values of pre-Christian paganism* were not merely of aesthetic interest, but were life and death matters reflecting an objective state of affairs.

As a result of Tolkien's arguments, C. S. Lewis came to the conclusion that similarities between Christian teaching and ancient myth* can argue for the truth of Christianity as well as against it. At the heart of Christianity, C. S. Lewis came to believe, is a myth that became fact*—making the claims of Christianity unique.

Tolkien's tales in their own manner embody antimodernist themes as powerfully as any stories written by Lewis, disclosing his Old Western values. Antimodernism can be seen clearly, for instance, in Tolkien's treatment of the related themes of possession and power, themes central to his work. Tolkien explores power in relation to possession. Possession is a unifying theme, from the desire of Morgoth to have God's power of creation to the temptation of wielding the One Ring. The wrong use of power is often expressed in Tolkien in magic, the mechanical and the technological. Morgoth, Sauron, and Saruman experiment with genetic engineering, and they use or encourage the use of machines. Tolkien contrasts magic with art, typified in the elves, who have no desire for domination.

Similarly Lewis, like the sociologist/theologian Jacques Ellul, saw a machine attitude, or technocracy, as the modern form of magic, seeking to dominate and possess nature, rather than to husband her. The magical power—the instinct to possess at any cost—of modern technocracy is recognized not only by Tolkien and Lewis (as in his science-fiction novel *That Hideous Strength**). Lord Zuckerman, in *Apocalypse Now?* (p. 25), commented about the nuclear arms race: "It is he, the technician, not the commander in the field, who is at the heart of the arms race, who starts the process of formulating a so-called military nuclear need. . . . They have become the alchemists of our times, working in secret ways which cannot be divulged, casting spells which embrace us all."

In our time, modernism increasingly seems to be collapsing in on itself like a stellar black hole. The antimodernism of Lewis and Tolkien is now acceptable to an extent that would have astonished them. It is not really surprising that the popularity of their writings is greater than ever. The current phase of postmodernism is difficult to characterize, but, like premodernism, is identified in relation to what Lewis called the "hideous strength" of modernism. It is interesting that even back in 1954, Lewis defined the Old West by placing it in contrast to modernism. The Great Divide lay, he believed, somewhere in the nineteenth century. It was as much a sociological and cultural divide as a shift in ideas. However, with the recent rise of a new paganism, Lewis would almost certainly caution against assuming that this is the same as the pre-Christian paganism he loved and explored. The new paganism we are experiencing today is on our side of the Great Divide, not on the other side, the side of the Old West. Lewis found values in pre-Christian paganism that prefigured the Christian values that he championed. Lewis warned, in his inaugural Cambridge lecture:

> Christians and pagans had much more in common with each other than either has with a post-Christian. The gap between those who worship different gods is not so wide as that between those who worship and those who do not. . . . A post-Christian man is not a pagan; you might as well think that a married woman recovers her virginity by divorce. The post-Christian is cut off from the Christian past and therefore doubly from the pagan past.

The continuing popularity of Lewis's premodernism—his sustained rejection of modernism in favor of Old Western values—suggests the existence of a continuity between the Old West and now, despite the Great Divide. It indicates a strong though small stream that has never been eradicated, despite Lewis's fears.

The affinity over Old Western values between Lewis and Tolkien allowed Lewis to partly fictionalize his friend as Elwin Ransom* in *Out of the Silent Planet** and *Perelandra.** These values are embodied in the portrayal of Ransom, both positively and negatively. Positively they are displayed in Ransom's perception, which is premodernist and essentially medieval. Lewis, like Tolkien, loved the Renaissance and medieval cosmos, its imaginative model of reality, and it is this world-picture that is smuggled into the minds of modern readers as they enjoy Lewis's story. In deep space, en route to Malacandra in a spacecraft, Ransom finds himself unexpectedly feeling well, despite the ordeal of his kidnapping:

> He lay for hours in contemplation of the skylight. The Earth's disk was nowhere to be seen; the stars, thick as daisies on an uncut lawn, reigned perpetually, with no cloud, no moon, no sunrise to dispute their sway. There were planets of unbelievable majesty, and constellations undreamed of: there were celestial sapphires, rubies, emeralds and pinpricks of burning gold; far out on the left of the picture hung a comet, tiny and remote: and between all and behind all, far more emphatic and palpable than it showed on Earth, the undimensioned, enigmatic blackness. The lights trembled: they seemed to grow brighter as he looked. Stretched naked on his bed, a second Danaë, he found it night by night more difficult to disbelieve in old astrology: almost he felt, wholly he imagined, "sweet influence" pouring or even stabbing into his surrendered body. (From chapter 5)

Negatively, Ransom's premodernist values are expressed in contrast to the attitudes of Professor Edward Weston,* a scientist who represents all that Lewis dislikes about the modernist world. (Note that Lewis is not against science or scientists, but the cult of science, or scientism,* found in modernism.) Weston is the person responsible for kidnapping Ransom, an act he considers completely justifiable. He has disdain for all values of the Old West. His guiding value is the survival of mankind at any cost.

Orual The queen of Glome* in *Till We Have Faces,** and narrator of that story, in which she recounts her life. The physical ugliness of her face (but not her voice) presents a major theme of the novel, shaping many of the events. She is the half-sister of Psyche* and sister of Redival.* See: *TILL WE HAVE FACES.*

Otherness Lewis valued otherness—or otherworldliness. Great stories, he believed, take us outside of the prison of our own selves and our presuppositions about reality. Insofar as stories reflect the divine maker in doing this, they help us face the ultimate Other—God himself, distinct as creator from all else, including ourselves. The very well of fantasy and imaginative invention is every person's direct knowledge of the other. Lewis writes: "To construct plausible and moving 'other worlds,' you must draw on the only real 'other world' we know, that of the spirit." See also: NUMINOUS.

***Out of the Silent Plane*t** (1938) The first volume of C. S. Lewis's science-fiction trilogy. Dr. Elwin Ransom,* a Tolkien*-like philologist don from Cambridge University, is kidnapped while on a walking holiday in the midlands and taken to Malacandra* (Mars) by Devine* and Weston,* the latter a famous physicist and materialist (see: NATURALISM AND SUPERNATURALISM). They are under a misapprehension that the unseen ruler of Malacandra wants a human sacrifice—a fantasy created by their dark minds.

After escaping his captors, Ransom is at first terrified and disoriented by the red planet and its diversity of terrain and inhabitants—various forms of rational life related in a harmonious hierarchy. The inhabitants—sorns* (or, more properly, seroni), hrossa,* and pfifltriggi*—turn out to be civilized and amiable. Ransom, as a linguist, is soon able to pick up the rudiments of their language, Old Solar.* Because of their expectations about the mental level and sensibility of the Malacandrians, however, Weston and Devine only achieve a toehold in the language—leading at times to hilarious effects.

They cannot see the comic contrast between English and the alien language form, which is unable to disguise true meaning.* Weston addresses the Oyarsa* or ruler of Malacandra in the arrogant language of his "scientific" religion of survival, and Ransom interprets for him. Only in translation the effect is not what Weston intended:

> "She—," began Weston.
>
> "I'm sorry," interrupted Ransom, "but I've forgotten who she is."
>
> "Life, of course," snapped Weston. "She has ruthlessly broken down all obstacles and liquidated all failures and today in her highest form—civilized man—and in me as her representative, she presses forward to that interplanetary leap which will, perhaps, place her forever beyond the reach of death."
>
> "He says," resumed Ransom, "that these animals learned to do many difficult things, except those who could not; and those ones died and the other animals did not pity them. And he says the best animal now is the kind of man who makes the big huts and carries the heavy weights and does all the other things I told you about; and he is one of these and he says that if the others all knew what he was doing they would be pleased. He says that if he could kill you all and bring our people to live in Malacandra, then they might be able to go on living here after something had gone wrong with our world. And then if something went wrong with Malacandra they might go and kill all the hnau in another world. And then another—and so they would never die out."

Who or what is this Oyarsa that Weston addressed? In *Out of the Silent Planet* C. S. Lewis imaginatively recreates the medieval picture of the cosmos he later set out in his book *The Discarded Image.** In Deep Heaven the planets are guided by spiritual intelligences, or Oyarsa, who, with the exception of the one concerned with Earth, are obedient to Maleldil the Young,* their mysterious master. Our planet is the Silent Planet, Thulcandra,* because it is cut off from the courtesy and order of Deep Heaven by a primeval disobedience.

C. S. Lewis was angry at the science fiction of his time, which invariably portrayed extraterrestrial beings as evil, as the enemies of mankind. The medieval picture was exactly the reverse, and this appealed to C. S. Lewis. His reversal of the trend of science fiction had a profound impact that has lasted to this day. Half humorously, Lewis complained in a letter in 1939: "You will be both grieved and amused to hear that out of about 60 reviews only two showed any knowledge that my idea of the fall of the Bent One was anything but an invention of my own . . . any amount of theology can now be smuggled into people's minds under the cover of romance without their knowing it." This sort of response to *Out of the Silent Planet* was one of the things that made C. S. Lewis realize that he might have something to offer in theological and ethical writing on a broad front.

In her study *Voyages to the Moon* (1948), Marjorie Hope Nicolson paid this tribute:

> *Out of the Silent Planet* is to me the most beautiful of all cosmic voyages and in some ways the most moving. . . . As C. S. Lewis, the Christian apologist, has added something to the long tradition, so C. S. Lewis, the scholar-poet, has achieved an effect in *Out of the Silent Planet* different from anything in the past. Earlier writers have created new worlds from legend, from mythology, from fairy tale. Mr. Lewis has created myth itself, myth woven of desire and aspirations deep-seated in some, at least, of the human race. . . . As I journey with him into worlds at once familiar and strange, I experience, as did Ransom, "a sensation not of following an adventure but of enacting a myth."

Oxford City and county town of Oxfordshire, England. It was C. S. Lewis's home from immediately after the Great War until his death in 1963. Oxford is located at the meeting of the rivers Thames and Cherwell, about fifty miles northwest of London. Its importance as early as the tenth century is evident from its mention in the Anglo-Saxon Chronicle for 912.

Before the First World War Oxford was known as a university city and market town. Then printing was its only major industry. Between the wars, however, the Oxford motor industry grew rapidly.

University teaching has been carried on at Oxford since the early years of the twelfth century, perhaps as a result of students migrating from Paris. The university's fame quickly grew, until by the fourteenth century it rivaled any in Europe.

University College, where C. S. Lewis was an undergraduate, is its oldest college, founded in 1249. Erasmus lectured at Oxford, and Grocyn, Colet, and More were some of its great scholars in the fifteenth and sixteenth centuries. Other Oxford scholars besides C. S. Lewis who entered wonderland were Charles Dodgson (Lewis Carroll) and J. R. R. Tolkien.*

C. S. Lewis taught philosophy for one year at University College during the absence of its tutor. Then in 1925 he was elected fellow and tutor in English Language and Literature at Magdalen College. He remained there until his appointment to the Chair of Medieval and Renaissance Literature at Cambridge in 1954. During most of C. S. Lewis's life in Oxford, he lived at The Kilns,* on the outskirts of Oxford, at Headington. Originally the house was isolated, but it is now surrounded by a housing estate, where a street is named after him.

Oxford University Socratic Club (1941-1972) A club set up by Miss Stella Aldwinckle to discuss questions about the Christian faith raised by atheists, agnostics, and those disillusioned about religion. C. S. Lewis accepted her invitation to be its first president, a position he held until 1954, when he went to Cambridge. Its committee scoured the pages of *Who's Who* to find intelligent atheists who had the time or the zeal to come and present their creed. Leading Christian thinkers also were main speakers. C. S. Lewis himself took this position on eleven occasions. As president, Lewis usually was expected to provide a rejoinder to the speaker. Lead speakers included Charles Williams,* D. M. MacKinnon, Austin Farrer,* J. Z. Young, C. E. M. Joad, P. D. Medawar, H. H. Price, C. H. Waddington, A. J. Ayer, J. D. Bernal, A. G. N. Flew, J. Bronowski, Basil Mitchell, R. M. Hare, A. Rendle Short, I. T. Ramsey, Iris Murdock, Gilbert Ryle, Michael Polanyi, J. L. Austin, H. J. Blackham, Michael Dummett, E. Evans-Pritchard, Dorothy L. Sayers,* and other outstanding thinkers from different academic disciplines.

Oyarsa See: ELDILA.

P

Pagus A region in *The Pilgrim's Regress** just south of the Main Road,* depicted on the Mappa Mundi.* The city of Aphroditopolis lies within it.

Paganism and mysticism in Lewis In one of his Latin letters* C. S. Lewis speculates that some modern people may need to be brought to pre-Christian pagan insights in preparation for more adequately receiving the Gospel. He writes:

> For my part I believe we ought to work not only at spreading the Gospel (that certainly) but also at a certain preparation for the Gospel. It is necessary to recall many to the law of nature *before* we talk about God. For Christ promises forgiveness of sins: but what is that to those who, since they do not know the law of nature, do not know that they have sinned? Who will take medicine unless he knows he is in the grip of disease? Moral relativity is the enemy we have to overcome before we tackle Atheism. I would almost dare to say, "First let us make the younger generation good pagans and afterwards let us make them Christians." (*Letters: C. S. Lewis and Don Giovanni Calabria,* p. 89)

C. S. Lewis explored pre-Christian paganism,* the idea of what he called the *anima naturaliter Christiana*. This, for him, was a kind of natural theology. It seems that in his apparently foolish preoccupation with myth* and fantasy, a Christian voice was in preparation that would still speak at the beginning of a new millennium to the wider world. Lewis's success as a contemporary Christian writer reveals that Christian faith can strike a deep chord in the world today. The literary critic George Watson points out that Lewis's literary critical works (see: LITERARY CRITIC, C. S. LEWIS AS A) largely belong to the age of modernism, and he was a lifelong antimodernist. Paradoxically, Watson remarks, Lewis's "mingling of formalism and fantasy—a critical and analytical interest in the forms that fantasy takes—was something which, when he died in 1963, was on the point of becoming fashionable."

Lewis's exploration of paganism depends upon a distinction between Christian and theistic (or pagan) mysticism. Theistic mysticism (most notably in the form of Neoplatonism, as shaped by Plotinus) had a profound effect on the medieval West and also on Islam.

Christian mysticism (for example, Christian Platonism) has to struggle to be consonant with orthodox theology.

Lewis's mysticism results in a vision that affects all his life, thought, and experience. One could therefore start almost anywhere in expounding his mysticism, not just in a theme such as preoccupation with the numinous.* Here is an example from Lewis's characteristic literary criticism. He speaks of the humble act of reading a book, which in his vision becomes sacramental. In *An Experiment in Criticism,** he points out that good reading has something in common with love, moral action, and the growth of knowledge. Like all these, it involves a surrender, in this case by the reader to the work being read. A good reader is concerned less with altering his or her opinion than in entering fully into the opinions and worlds of others.

> In reading great literature I become a thousand men and yet remain myself. Like the night sky in the Greek poem, I see with a myriad eyes, but it is still I who see. Here, as in worship, in love, in moral action, and in knowing, I transcend myself; and am never more myself than when I do.

Christian mysticism has to reckon with the Word of God, the *Logos*. The prologue of John's Gospel, which sets the Word at the beginning of creation, is becoming more obviously relevant to our contemporary culture, where mysticism and spirituality are more acceptable than they were under modernism. According to Scripture, God is not in principle ineffable, but the Word. His lordship of the Word extends over all possible human experience and every part of the universe. Even in the visual, relating to dreams and visions, there is a parallel with language. There is a visual language that covers, for instance, the apocalyptic visions of Ezekiel, Daniel, and the book of Revelation. Here there is visual inter-reference, as when John draws on Daniel and Ezekiel in describing the vision of the glorified Christ. In creation also, as presented to our senses, there is a coherent visual language, as celebrated in one of Lewis's favorite biblical poems, Psalm 19. It is entirely in keeping that, in the context of gnostic mystery religions, St. Paul declares: "Behold I *tell* you a mystery" (1 Corinthians 15:51, emphasis mine). In Christian mysticism, mystery is relative. It is our knowledge that is incomplete—the vastness of reality is not a mystery to the Lord who is the Word. Its vastness and riches are not beyond the Word, condemned to silence.

For Lewis (as he learned from his friend Tolkien* particularly) all pagan insights are unfinished and incomplete, anticipating the greatest story, God's "spell," or the Gospel. As a Christian mystic, what he did was grapple with pagan insights, exploring how far the pagan imagination could go without the light of Scripture, God's special revelation (see: THE BIBLE). In grappling with and affirming pagan insights, his attitude belongs to the thought patterns of the Middle Ages, to a premodernist world.

Tolkien's invented world of Middle-earth (as narrated in his *The Lord of the Rings*, *The Silmarillion*, etc.) in general is replete with Christian heroes, and yet it is a pagan world. Ultimately, grace successfully spiritualizes nature. Tolkien's treatment of paganism has the same potency that he found in *Beowulf*, an Old English poem in which its Christian author explored the pagan past. The potency is there also in Lewis's own great exploration of pre-Christian paganism, *Till We Have Faces.** This novel strikingly reveals the imaginative and theological affinity between the two friends.

Princess Psyche* is prepared to die for the sake of the people of a barbaric country. The story is told through the eyes of Queen Orual* of Glome.* The gods, she claims, have misrepresented the story. They had turned her deep love for Psyche into jealousy. Orual, however, undergoes a devastating change of perception. She discovers how her affection for Psyche had in fact become poisoned by possessiveness. Psyche in her turn glimpses the true God himself. She sees his beauty and acknowledges his legitimate demand for a perfect sacrifice. Thus Lewis endorses insights of paganism.

For Lewis, imagination* is the organ of meaning, not truth. Imagination perceives reality. In a sense, reality *is* meaning (see: MEANING AND IMAGINATION), in being a dependent creation of God, referring away from itself to him as its source and meaning.

Mr. Papworth C. S. Lewis's black curly-haired mongrel, mainly a terrier. He was also known as Tykes, Baron Papworth, and Pat. He died in 1937.

Parliament of owls In *The Silver Chair,** a meeting of owls. Jill Pole* and Eustace Scrubb* are carried to it on the back of Glimfeather.* Lewis is probably playing with the title of Chaucer's *The Parliament of Fowls*.

Pavender A beautiful rainbow-colored fish found in Narnia* that provides an excellent meal.

Passarids In *Prince Caspian,** a house of lords under Caspian* the Ninth. When the usurper Miraz* took over, they were sent to their death to fight giants to the north of Narnia.*

Pattertwig In *Prince Caspian,** a magnificent talking red squirrel, the size of a terrier. He is a loyal Old Narnian met by the runaway Caspian.*

Paxford, Frederick (1898-1979) Handyman and gardener at The Kilns,* Fred Paxford was employed by Lewis and Mrs. Moore* in 1930 and remained there until Lewis's death. In his diary Warnie Lewis* records his irritation with Paxford, but Lewis found his gloomy manner amusing, modeling Puddleglum,* the marshwiggle, upon him.

Peepicheek In *Prince Caspian,** one of Reepicheep's* band of talking mice, designated as his successor.

Penelope, Sister (1890-1977) A friend of C. S. Lewis's of the Anglican Community of St. Mary the Virgin at Wantage. He corresponded extensively with her, some of which is preserved in *Letters of C. S. Lewis.* Perelandra** is dedicated to Sister Penelope and her colleagues: "To some ladies at Wantage." There is a story that in one translation this dedication reads: "To some wanton ladies."

Perelandra (Voyage to Venus) (1943) This, the second volume of Lewis's science-fiction trilogy, is set on the planet Perelandra (Venus), a paradisal, oceanic world of floating islands as well as fixed lands. Dr. Elwin Ransom* is transported there to rebuff the attacks of the forces of evil incarnate in the human form of his old enemy, Weston.* Perelandra, Ransom discovers, has its own green-fleshed equivalent of Adam and Eve. The setting is visionary and beautifully realized. The unfallen ecology of Perelandra, which includes the communion between the Green Lady* and her husband and the animal and fish life of the planet, is intended to contrast with the havoc of sin upon our world. Perelandra presents a forceful and inspiring image of perfection, where natural and spiritual are one.

P

While the Second World War rages, Ransom is taken in a casket to Perelandra by the great Oyarsa,* or unseen ruler of Malacandra* (Mars), with whom he had become acquainted in his previous adventure in space. He is away for a whole year. On his return he recounts what happened to his friends C. S. Lewis and Dr. "Humphrey" Havard,* an account that forms the basis of Lewis's book.

After dropping through the Venusian atmosphere, Ransom found himself in a

> delicious coolness. . . . He was riding the foamless swell of an ocean, fresh and cool after the fierce temperatures of Heaven, but warm by earthly standards—as warm as a shallow bay with sandy bottom in a subtropical climate. As he rushed smoothly up the great convex hillside of the next wave he got a mouthful of the water. It was hardly at all flavoured with salt; it was drinkable—like fresh water and only, by an infinitesimal degree, less insipid. Though he had not been aware of thirst till now, his drink gave him a quite astonishing pleasure. It was almost like meeting Pleasure itself for the first time.

He was in fact in paradise, brilliantly evoked by Lewis's descriptions.

One fascinating feature of Perelandra is its floating islands that follow the contours of the sea, with hills becoming valleys in a constant metamorphosis. Many of the dramatic events of the story take place on the islands. In contrast are the fixed lands, upon which the newly created green humans of the planet are as yet forbidden to dwell. This command forms the basis of a reenactment of the temptation of Eve. There are differences, however, not least as a result of the sacrifice of Maleldil the Young* on Thulcandra* (Earth). Ransom plays a key part, much to his surprise, in frustrating the devilish plans of the bent Oyarsa of earth to corrupt the unspoiled world. On one of the floating islands Ransom encounters the beautiful Green Lady and her constant animal companions, including a small dragon with scales of red gold. She was "green like the beautifully colored green beetle in an English garden." She was like "a goddess carved apparently out of green stone, yet alive." As Ransom often found happening, what was myth* in our world could be fact in others. When she started laughing uncontrollably at his strange appearance, he realized that she was fully human.

An unwelcome visitor in a conventional spacecraft arrived in the form of Professor Weston,* who lost no time in engaging the Green Lady in complex and subtle arguments, designed to wear down her resistance to the temptation to disobey the command not to live on the fixed lands. Ransom intervenes with counterargument but, unlike the possessed scientist, suffers the disadvantage of needing to sleep from sheer exhaustion. Eventually Ransom realizes, to his dismay, that he must engage Weston in a physical fight to the death. Weston, given over to Satan, is now an "Un-man." In the bitter struggle, Ransom receives an unhealable wound to his heel.

The story climaxes in a vision of the "Great Dance" of the universe, in which all patterns of human and other life interweave. "Then, at the very zenith of complexity, complexity was eaten up and faded, as a thin white cloud fades into the hard blue burning of the sky, and a simplicity beyond all comprehension, ancient and young as spring, illimitable, pellucid, drew him with cords of infinite desire into its own stillness." As so often in C. S. Lewis's writings, the theme of joy* is embodied.

The arguments over the nature of obedience and goodness and evil were pursued further by Lewis in his brilliant study, *The Problem of Pain,** published three years earlier. They relate also to Lewis's views on warfare—why he found it impossible to be a pacifist. He continued his exploration of evil in *That Hideous Strength,** set several years later.

Just as *That Hideous Strength* is paralleled by his study *The Abolition of Man,** *Perelandra* is complemented by *A Preface to Paradise Lost.** The latter is Lewis's analysis of John Milton's great epic poem, dealing with the fall of mankind and key themes such as hierarchy. Perelandra portrays the imaginative splendor of Milton's themes in a way designed to bewitch the modern reader, bypassing our prejudice against the past—what Lewis dubbed our "chronological snobbery."*

Peridan In *The Horse and His Boy,** one of the lords and advisors of Queen Susan* and King Edmund* in Tashbaan.* Later he leads a charge in battle against the army of Rabadash* the Calormene.*

The Personal Heresy: A Controversy (1939) Jointly authored with E. M. W. Tillyard, a Cambridge literary critic. C. S. Lewis contributed chapters I, III, and V, and a concluding Note, and Tillyard contributed chapters II, IV, and VI, giving an opposing point of view.

C. S. Lewis argues against the view that poetry provides biographical information about the poet and that it is necessary to know about the poet to understand the poem. He focuses on the intrinsic character of a work of literature, rather than on extrinsic factors. In reading a poem, we look through the poet, rather than at him or her. We see with his or her eyes. We can only see if we do not dwell on the particulars of his or her consciousness. Rather, we indwell them as we attend to a new level of meaning.* The poet's consciousness is a condition of our knowledge, not the knowledge itself.

Lewis's analysis bears remarkable similarities to the insights of Michael Polanyi, who was concerned with the structure of consciousness and the way we participate in knowledge.

This passage from *The Personal Heresy* is characteristic: "Let it be granted that I do approach the poet; at least I do it by sharing his consciousness, not by studying it. I look with his eyes, not at him. . . . To see things as the poet sees them I must share his consciousness and not attend to it; I must look where he looks and not turn round to face him; I must make of him not a spectacle but a pair of spectacles: in fine, as Professor Alexander would say, I must enjoy him and not contemplate him."

C. S. Lewis's position here has implications for all the arts (as his late work, *An Experiment in Criticism*,* makes clear). As I understand it, he is saying that art takes us into meanings not normally perceived by us, meanings perceivable only through the actual arrangement of the artwork. We are reaching meanings that were not accessible to us before the making of the artwork, but that are now available to both the artist and the reader, viewer, or audience. C. S. Lewis claimed, "If we mean something, we do not mean alone." His Christian view of the world was that it was full of meaning rather than meaningless (or strictly absurd). An artistic arrangement *means* as part of that world. It follows that artistic value has the value that any part of the world has; but its *special* value for us is that our sense of meaning, our perception, is enlarged. We see with larger eyes than merely our own. Lewis would reiterate the poet Shelley's view, in his brilliant *Defence of Poetry*, that imagination allows us to see quantities as qualities and to perceive what we know. See also: LITERARY CRITIC, C. S. LEWIS AS A.

Peter, High King See PEVENSIE, PETER, SUSAN, EDMUND, AND LUCY.

Pevensie, Peter, Susan, Edmund, and Lucy The four brothers and sisters, evacuees from wartime London, who enter Narnia* in *The Lion, the Witch and the Wardrobe** and become kings and queens there. Peter, as eldest, is the High King during Narnia's Golden Age (echoes of the biblical St. Peter). Edmund had for a time been traitor, but he had repented and been restored by the sacrifice of Aslan* on the Stone Table.* The children return again to Narnia as told in *Prince Caspian.** After that, however, only the two youngest, Edmund and Lucy, are allowed to return, with their cousin Eustace Scrubb,* in the tale of *The Voyage of the "Dawn Treader."** While they are enjoying this adventure, Peter is being tutored for an exam by Professor Kirke,* and Susan has gone to America with her parents for Mr. Pevensie's lecture tour.

The Pevensie children, with the exception of Susan, who is no longer a friend of Narnia, return to Narnia after a train crash in the apocalyptic final story, *The Last Battle.** Lucy is often the favorite character with young readers of The Chronicles of Narnia.* As Martha C. Sammons puts it: "Lucy is one of the most clearly depicted characters in all the Narnia books. . . . Lucy seems to be spiritually closer to Aslan than anyone else, and they seem to share a special relationship of love!" Lucy's response to Aslan,* such as hugging him, is one of the secrets of the lion's success as an imaginative creation. C. S. Lewis achieves a figure of authority, the creator and true sovereign of Narnia, who is eminently approachable by the innocent and good. Those also, like Edmund and later Eustace, who approach him in fear and repentance find a friend like no other.

Pfifltriggi In *Out of the Silent Planet,** one of three intelligent kinds of beings on Malacandra.* These froglike creatures were the crafts people and engineers of the planet. They were expert in digging Malacandra's abundant gold and making artistic objects from it. They also recorded the history and mythology of their planet on the monoliths at Meldilorn.*

Phantastes This is one of ten books Lewis listed as particularly influencing his thinking and vocational attitude (see: READING OF C. S. LEWIS). *Phantastes* was George MacDonald's first prose work of fiction. According to his son and biographer, Greville MacDonald, none of his other writings "has exceeded it in imaginative insight and power of expression. To me it rings with the dominant chord of his life's purpose and work."

It begins:

> I awoke one morning with the usual perplexity of mind which accompanies the return of consciousness. As I lay and looked through the eastern window of my room, a faint streak of peach-color, dividing a cloud that just rose above the low swell of the horizon, announced the approach of the sun. As my thoughts, which a deep and apparently dreamless sleep had dissolved, began again to assume crystalline forms, the strange events of the foregoing night presented themselves anew to my wondering consciousness.

Anodos, the narrator, then recounts how his bedroom metamorphoses into a woodland scene. He continues:

> After washing as well as I could in the clear stream, I rose and looked around me. The tree under which I seemed to have lain all night was one of the advanced guard of a dense forest, towards which the rivulet ran. Faint traces of a footpath, much overgrown with grass and moss, and with here and there a pimpernel even, were discernible along the right bank. "This," thought I, "must surely be the path into Fairy Land, which the lady of last night promised I should so soon find." I crossed the rivulet, and accompanied it, keeping the footpath on its right bank, until it led me, as I expected, into the wood.

Anodos, whose name means "aimless" or "pathless," has many encounters and adventures, the narrative unfolding with a dreamlike logic rather than following the normal pattern of a story. The effect is to convey a mood and new emotional experience that instantly captivated Lewis. He first read the book when studying under W. T. Kirkpatrick.* At that time the teenager was an atheist. He remembers:

> I did not yet know (and I was long in learning) the name of the new quality, the bright shadow, that rested on the travels of Anodos. I do now. It was Holiness. For the first time the song of the sirens sounded like the voice of my mother or my nurse. . . . I saw the bright shadow coming out of the book into the real world and resting there, transforming all common things and yet itself unchanged. Or, more accurately, I saw the common things drawn into the bright shadow. . . . That night my imagination was, in a sense, baptized; the rest of me, not unnaturally, took longer. (*Surprised by Joy*, chapter XI)

Phars In *Till We Have Faces*,* a kingdom neighboring Glome.* After the marriage of king Trunia* of Phars with princess Redival* of Glome, the two countries enter an alliance, forcing Essur,* to the west of Phars, to stay at peace with the two kingdoms.

Phoenix In *The Magician's Nephew*,* a bird larger than an eagle, sitting in a tree in the center of Aslan's* garden. The phoenix is a traditional symbol of rebirth and immortality because of its resurrection from the ashes.

The Pilgrim's Regress: An Allegorical Apology for Christianity, Reason and Romanticism (1933; new edition, 1943) C. S. Lewis was researching the method of allegorical storytelling for his study *The Allegory of Love** when he wrote this book. In fictional and more general form, it covers the ground of his later account of his life up to his conversion, *Surprised by Joy*.* He wrote it during a fortnight's holiday in Ireland.

Twenty years after writing *The Pilgrim's Regress*, Lewis admitted in a letter to a woman: "I don't wonder that you got fogged in *The Pilgrim's Regress*. It was my first religious book, and I didn't then know how to make things easy. I was not even trying to very much, because in those days never dreamed I would become a 'popular author.'"

The Pilgrim's Regress is an intellectual early-twentieth-century version of John Bunyan's great allegory. Instead of Christian, the central figure is John,* loosely based on C. S. Lewis himself. As in *The Pilgrim's Progress*, the quest can be mapped. Indeed, Lewis provides his reader with a Mappa Mundi,* in which the human soul is divided into north and south, the north representing arid intellectualism and the south emotional excess. A straight road passes between them. Needless to say, John's route strays far off the straight and narrow. Like the young Lewis, he tends toward intellectual rather than sensual follies. The story gives a vivid picture of Lewis's intellectual climate of the 1920s and early 1930s.

John's way is a regress rather than a progress, because he in fact is going away rather than toward the beautiful Island* that he seeks. The Island is Lewis's equivalent to the Celestial City of Bunyan. When he gains the knowledge of how to achieve his Island, through Mother Kirk,* he has to retrace his steps.

Born in Puritania,* John early was taught to fear the Landlord of the country. From the first moment, however, that he glimpsed the Island in a vision, he was gripped with an intense longing to find it. John's quest for the Island is a fine embodiment of the theme of joy* that is so central in Lewis's autobiography *Surprised by Joy*. The quest helps John to avoid the various snares and dangers he encounters.

On his journey he comes across characters such as Mr. Enlightenment from the city of Claptrap, Mr. Vertue, who becomes John's companion, and Media Halfways, from the city of Thrill. Later John is imprisoned by the Spirit of the Age and rescued by the tall, blue-clad figure of Reason. She teaches him many things and directs him back to the Main Road.

Upon finding the road abruptly cut off by a vast canyon, John at first refuses the help of Mother Kirk, and he has many adventures as he looks for a way down first to the north and then to the south of the main road. After becoming lost and calling for help, John is aided first by the hermit History and then Reason once more. He finds Vertue in the presence of Mother Kirk, and both follow her guidance and reach the other side of the canyon. From here John can see the sea and his Island. The two are given a guide to lead them back across the world, for the Island in fact is the other side of the mountains near Puritania, not an Island at all. John's idea of the Landlord has turned out to be false, and the home of the Landlord in those mountains is to be John's as well.

In Lewis's new edition of *The Pilgrim's Regress,* he provided a detailed foreword and notes to the chapters to help his readers with the obscurer points of the allegory. It is best to enjoy the book as a story and not be too concerned with the meaning of every allusion. Read as a quest for joy, and in parallel with *Surprised by Joy*, it yields its main meanings. Clyde S. Kilby's study *Images of Salvation in the Fiction of C. S. Lewis* (1978) provides help with interpretation of the allegory, including its frequent classical references. See also: CHEST.

Pittencream In *The Voyage of the "Dawn Treader"** the sailor left behind at Ramandu's Island,* who eventually went to live in Calormen.*

The planets In the science-fiction trilogy (*Out of the Silent Planet,* Perelandra,** and *That Hideous Strength**) the true names of the planets are revealed. These names are in the tongue of Old Solar,* spoken before the fall of mankind and beyond the moon's orbit.

The sun is properly called Arbol; Mercury is Viritrilbia; Venus, Perelandra; Earth, Tellus or Thulcandra (the Silent Planet); Mars, Malacandra; Jupiter, Glundandra; and Saturn, Lurga. Handra in Old Solar means "world."

Plato A Greek philosopher born about 427 B.C. in Athens, who was much admired by C. S. Lewis. Plato was a founding father of idealism* in philosophy. His work provided much imaginative inspiration for C. S. Lewis, though Lewis was not a Platonist as such (see: PAGANISM AND MYSTICISM). Some forms of Platonism were deeply influential during the medieval period, which was C. S. Lewis's great love and which was the object of much of his scholarship. Different aspects of Plato's thought have been emphasized at different periods of Western history, such as his view of existence or his theory of how we know truth. Belief in the immortality of the soul, as held by C. S. Lewis and the Christian tradition, is not in itself Platonism, nor is imaginative use of the Platonic idea of this world as a copy of a more real one. In his essay "Transposition"* C. S. Lewis gives a Christian nondualistic account of the relationship between spiritual and natural reality (see also: NATURE). Lewis provides a remarkable reworking of Plato's Myth of the Cave in *The Silver Chair,** beautifully providing a Christian apologetic in answer to the modern claim that God is a projection of the human being. See also: GOD; THEOLOGY OF ROMANCE.

Platonism See: PLATO.

Plummer, Polly Digory Kirke's* next-door friend in Edwardian London, who is drawn with him into other worlds and eventually into Narnia* in *The Magician's Nephew.**

Poems (1964) This volume contains most of C. S. Lewis's lyrical verse, with the exception of the early cycle of poems titled *Spirits in Bondage.** They reveal a great variety of themes, including "Narnian Suite," which is in two parts—"a march for strings, kettledrums, and sixty-three dwarfs" and a "march for drum, trumpet, and twenty-one giants." See also: *COLLECTED POEMS; NARRATIVE POEMS.*

***Poetic Diction,* Owen Barfield** (1928) Owen Barfield* believed that, corresponding to stellar and biological evolution, there has been an evolution of consciousness. The evolution of consciousness is reflected precisely in changes in language and perception, from a primitive unity of consciousness, now lost, to a future achievement of a greater human consciousness.

Barfield's concept inspired Lewis, especially as it was translated into highly original insights into the nature of poetic language. These insights were embodied in *Poetic Diction*, which concerns the nature of poetic language and a theory of an ancient semantic unity.

Poetic Diction offers a theory of knowledge as well as a theory of poetry. At its heart is a philosophy of language. Barfield's view is that "the individual imagination is the medium of all knowledge from perception upward" (p. 22). The poetic impulse is linked to individual freedom: "the act of the imagination is the individual mind exercizing its sovereign unity" (p. 22). The alternative, argues Barfield, is to see knowledge as power, to "mistake efficiency for meaning," leading to a relish for compulsion.

Knowledge as power is contrasted with knowledge by *participation* (a key word in Barfield). One kind of knowledge "consists of seeing what happens and getting used to it," and the other involves "consciously participating in what is" (p. 24). The proper activity of the imagination is "concrete thinking"—this is "the perception of resemblance, the demand for unity" (the influence of Samuel Taylor Coleridge can be seen here). There is therefore a poetic element in all meaningful language. Lewis elaborates this same point about the poetic condition of meaning in thought in "Bluspels and Flalansferes" in *Selected Literary Essays*, and in the chapter "Horrid Red Things" in *Miracles**—a chapter that tries to capture the core of Barfield's ideas in *Poetic Diction.*

Pole, Jill A fellow sufferer of Eustace Scrubb's* at Experiment House,* who is taken into Narnia with him on two occasions to help in time of need. The stories are told in *The Silver Chair** and *The Last Battle.**

Prayer See: LETTERS TO MALCOLM.

Preface to Paradise Lost, A (1942) *Paradise Lost* is John Milton's great epic, and C. S. Lewis believed that most recent Milton scholarship had hindered rather than helped a proper reading of the poem. Following the lead of his friend Charles Williams's* short preface to an edition of Milton's poetical works, Lewis attempted "mainly 'to hinder hindrances' to the appreciation of *Paradise Lost.*" He defended the epic form of literature that Milton chose to use, arguing that it had a right to exist, as does ritual, splendor, and joy* itself. Lewis argued that he differed from the critics of Milton not over the nature of his poetry, but over the nature of mankind and even of joy itself. Qualities that he (and Milton) regard as virtues, the critics blame him for. Lewis complains: "It reminds us of Aristotle's question—if water itself sticks in a man's throat, what will you give him to wash it down with? If a man blames port wine for being strong and sweet, or a woman's arms for being white and smooth and round, or the sun for shining, or sleep because it puts thought away, how can we answer him?" See also: LITERARY CRITIC, LEWIS AS A.

***Prelude, The,* William Wordsworth** (1850) Lewis listed this as one of the ten foremost books influencing his thinking and vocational attitude (see: READING OF C. S. LEWIS). It was composed by William Wordsworth (1770-1850), the English Romantic poet. *The Prelude, or, Growth of a Poet's Mind* was written by 1805, but it was not published until 1850. It was intended to be preliminary to an autobiographical work, "The Recluse," which was never finished. A philosophical poem, it articulated Wordsworth's view of humanity, of nature, and of society. In *The Prelude* the poet gave an account of his intellectual, imaginative, and emotional development under the influences of education, nature, and society.

Lewis's autobiography *Surprised by Joy** was originally attempted in poetic form and abandoned, and it is likely that *The Prelude* was in his mind as a genre model. In his autobiography Lewis traces the symbiotic themes of his intellectual and imaginative development, always set against a strong moral concern. Like *Surprised by Joy,** Wordsworth's *The Prelude* contains friends, books, experiences, and places that shaped the teller.

Preston, Marjorie In *The Voyage of the "Dawn Treader"** a friend of Lucy Pevensie.* Lucy overhears Marjorie talking about her to another girl through a spell in the book belonging to Coriakin,* the magician.

Prince Caspian (1951) A year after their first adventure in Narnia,* the four Pevensie* children are drawn back to help Caspian,* the true heir to the throne. Caspian's life is in danger from the tyrant Miraz,* who holds control over Narnia. Miraz has suppressed the Old Narnians who remained loyal to the ancient memory of Aslan* and Narnia's long-ago Golden Age, when the children had been kings and queens at Cair Paravel.* This story reveals much about the history of Narnia, the rule of humans over the talking animals,* and the Telmarines* who had stumbled into Narnia long before from our world. See also: NARNIA, HISTORY

Problem of Pain, The (1940) C. S. Lewis's purpose in writing this book was to "solve the intellectual problem raised by suffering." He had never felt himself qualified "for the far-higher task of teaching fortitude and patience." In this respect, he said that he had nothing to offer his readers "except my conviction that when pain is to be borne, a little courage helps more than much knowledge, a little human sympathy more than much courage, and the least tincture of the love of God more than all." Years later he was able to offer more. After his wife, Joy Davidman,* died, he recorded his reactions and reflections in *A Grief Observed.**

For such a small book, Lewis ranged far and wide, discussing God's control over all human events, including suffering, the goodness of God,* human wickedness, the fall of mankind, human pain, hell, animal pain, and heaven.* He took up similar themes in imaginative form in his science-fiction story *Perelandra.** Austin Farrer* comments that Lewis presents "a world haunted by the supernatural, a conscience haunted by the moral absolute, a history haunted by the divine claim of Christ."

The Problem of Pain, like *Miracles*,* is among the best of C. S. Lewis's theological writings and a key text in the philosophy of religion. It contains fine passages on heaven, joy,* hell, and the sense of the numinous* that is present in so much of Lewis's fiction. The book argues from the starting point of God's relationship to the universe that he has made, and is uncompromising in its supernaturalism.* *The Problem of Pain* also reveals Lewis's position when he was an atheist and why he found such a position untenable later.

The Dutch title of the book is *God's Megaphone*, taken from Lewis's memorable claim: "God whispers to us in our pleasures, speaks in our conscience, but shouts in our pains: it is His megaphone to rouse a deaf world."

Prunaprismia In *Prince Caspian*,* the red-haired wife of Caspian's* uncle, the usurper Miraz.*

Psyche A character whose name means the soul, from Apuleius's *The Golden Ass,** upon which C. S. Lewis based his character of the same name in his novel *Till We Have Faces.** In Apuleius's story, Psyche is so beautiful that Venus becomes jealous of her. Cupid, sent by Venus to make Psyche fall in love with an ugly creature, himself falls in love with her. After bringing her to a palace, he only visited her in the dark and forbade her to see his face. Out of jealousy, Psyche's sisters told her that her lover was a monster who would devour her. She took a lamp one night and looked at Cupid's face, but a drop of oil awoke him. In anger the god left her. Psyche sought her lover throughout the world. Venus set her various impossible tasks, all of which she accomplished except the last, when curiosity made her open a deadly casket from the underworld. At last, however, she was allowed to marry Cupid.

In *Till We Have Faces,** C. S. Lewis essentially follows the classical myth, but he retells it through the narration of Orual,* Psyche's sister, who seeks to defend her actions to the gods as being the result of deep love for Psyche, not of jealousy.

Psyche's palace In *Till We Have Faces,** the palace of the god of the Gray Mountains* in which Princess Psyche* dwelt after her marriage. It couldn't normally be seen by mortal eyes, though Orual* glimpsed it in the swirling mist. As a child, Psyche had dreamed of living in a gold and amber castle married to the "greatest king of all." When Orual glimpsed the palace, she saw "wall within wall, pillar and arch and architrave, acres of it, a labyrinthine beauty." It was like no house she had ever seen. Pinnacles and buttresses seemed to be springing up. They were unimaginably tall and slender, looking as if stone were shooting out into branch and flower.

Psychology See: NEW PSYCHOLOGY.

Puddleglum, the marshwiggle In *The Silver Chair,** the companion of Jill Pole* and Eustace Scrubb* in their quest for the lost Prince Rilian.* Puddleglum is one of C. S. Lewis's most memorable Narnian creations, delightfully pessimistic, though never cynical or disloyal to Aslan.* He is tall and angular, with webbed hands and feet, as befits a marshy existence. His character owed something to Lewis's gardener at The Kilns, Fred Paxford.*

Puritania The region in *The Pilgrim's Regress** in which John* is brought up, beside the Eastern Mountains* to which he eventually returns. Though the work was not intended as a portrait of his native Ulster, there are echoes of his childhood in the speech-patterns of John's mother and father, the cook, the steward, and Uncle George, and the book was composed during a holiday to Northern Ireland.

Puzzle, the ass A simple donkey duped by Shift,* the ape, into dressing in a lion skin and pretending to be Aslan* in *The Last Battle.**

Q

The quest The quest often takes the form of a journey in symbolic literature. In fiction such as Lewis's, life and experience have the character of a journey, and this character can be intensified by art. The Christian possibilities of the quest have been explored by Thomas Malory (in *Morte d'Arthur*), by John Bunyan (in *The Pilgrim's Progress*), as well as by J. R. R. Tolkien* and Lewis—to name a few writers.

The quest motif is a hallmark of Lewis's writings, both fiction and nonfiction. *The Magician's Nephew** records Digory's double quest for the magic apple and to save his dying mother; *The Voyage of the "Dawn Treader"** also concerns a double quest, to find the lost lords and to discover Aslan's Country; *Perelandra** features a quest to save the humans of a new world; *The Pilgrim's Regress** documents John's quest for the Island of his vision; in parallel, Lewis's autobiography *Surprised by Joy** tells of his personal quest for an elusive joy; and *Till We Have Faces** is a tale of Psyche's* quest for her lost lover and Queen Orual's* search for the truth about her sister's story about a palace in the mists and a god who loves her.

R

Rabadash, Prince Also called "The Ridiculous." In *The Horse and His Boy*,* the vain Calormene* prince who, after being rejected by Queen Susan,* attempts to conquer Archenland* and Narnia* during the reign of High King Peter* and the other children. After the battle at Anvard* he is left dangling from a wall hook. Later Aslan* temporarily turns him into a donkey.

Ram the Great According to *The Horse and His Boy*,* the popular Narnian tale, he becomes King of Archenland.* He is the son of Cor* and Aravis.*

Ramandu In *The Voyage of the "Dawn Treader"** a retired star, resplendent in silver clothes, who lives near Aslan's Table on World's End Island* far across the Eastern Ocean.* The voyagers in the *Dawn Treader* encountered him on their way toward Aslan's Country.* King Caspian* later married Ramandu's daughter.

Ramandu is undergoing renewal until he once more can return to the stars. The stars of Narnia and its world are not made up of flaming gas but of glimmering people with silver clothes and hair. Ramandu had been brought down to World's End Island when old and fading. The birds each day would bring him a fire berry from the valleys of the sun. These berries were restoring him.

Ramandu's daughter In *The Voyage of the "Dawn Treader"** the travelers met Ramandu* and his daughter on World's End Island.* Later King Caspian* married her. In the adventure of *The Silver Chair** we learn that one day many years later, while she was sleeping, she was slain by the Green Witch* in the form of a green serpent. It was while Prince Rilian* was seeking revenge for his mother's murder that he was bewitched by the Green Witch.

Ransom, Dr. Elwin (1898?-) Hero of C. S. Lewis's science-fiction trilogy, later renamed the Fisher King, and partially modeled on J. R. R. Tolkien* and Owen Barfield.* He was a philologist of Cambridge University. Much like C. S. Lewis, he was a bachelor, had a war wound, and was a "sedentary scholar." One of his publications was *Dialect and Semantics*. Swimming was the only sport he excelled in (a skill that proved useful in watery Perelandra*). Ransom was also an anti-vivisectionist. He combined intellectual and heroic qualities, though he tended to put himself down. Clyde S. Kilby pointed out that Ransom speaks like Lewis himself.

In *Out of the Silent Planet,** Ransom was kidnapped to the planet Malacandra* (Mars), enabling him to learn Old Solar,* the Great Tongue, and discover the nature of life outside of quarantined planet Earth. On his return he spent three months in the hospital recuperating. (It may have been in this period that Lewis described him, in *The Dark Tower,** as a pale man with gray, distressed-looking eyes.) In *Perelandra** he was transported by the Oyarsa* or ruler of Mars to the planet Venus (Perelandra) to foil a satanic plot against a new Adam and Eve in that paradisal world. Here he suffered his debilitating wound to the heel.

In *That Hideous Strength** Ransom was revealed as the latest in the succession of Pendragons of Logres, withdrawn from Cambridge to secretly run a community at St. Anne's.* This community, what was left of Logres, the true Britain, was pitted against the demonic forces of the N.I.C.E.* He may have found The Manor at St. Anne's on one of his walking tours—he originally had a country cottage in Worchester [*sic*]. After the routing of the N.I.C.E., Ransom was permitted the rare honor of returning forever to Perelandra, the Third Heaven, to dwell with King Arthur* and others in Aphallin.*

Elwin Ransom was tall, slightly built, golden-haired, but a little round-shouldered and weak-eyed, age about thirty-five to forty in the late 1930s when the events of *Out of the Silent Planet* took place. He didn't have much dress sense and at first sight might have been mistaken for a doctor or schoolmaster. His only relation was a married sister in India.

Lewis tells us that "Ransom" was not (or was no longer?) his real name, though he was told by the Oyarsa that his name literally meant "ransom." Lewis had known Dr. Ransom slightly before the events of the first science-fiction tale, corresponding with him on literary and philological subjects, though at that time they seldom met. They became firm friends when Ransom had the idea of asking Lewis to cast his adventures in fictional form. Lewis regarded him as sane, wholesome, and honest. We may speculate that some of their conversations and correspondence resemble the themes of C. S. Lewis's book *Studies in Words.**

When Ransom returned from Perelandra after his second planetary adventure, Lewis found him glowing with health, rounded with muscle, wearing a golden beard (which he retained), and seeming ten years younger. This process of rejuvenation continued in the story *That Hideous Strength*, where he at first appeared to Jane Studdock* to be a boy of twenty, until she noticed his strength and his full beard. She was reminded of her mental picture of King Arthur or Solomon.

Reading of C. S. Lewis According to the eminent literary critic William Empson, Lewis was "the best read man of his generation, one who read everything and remembered everything he read." Lewis had a bookish background, spending long, silent hours in the library. What emerged from this background is a richness of thought, imagination, and writing that has influenced literary criticism, science fiction, children's literature, literary approaches to the Bible, and Christian apologetics throughout the West. As well as influencing millions of readers of his books, Lewis acknowledged an enormous debt to his own wide reading.

From childhood onward, Lewis read voraciously and eclectically. He typically defended the value of "low-brow" reading such as Rider Haggard and John Buchan. This bookishness and eclecticism is an important characteristic of Lewis throughout his life and is reflected in his diaries and letters. The "house full of books" Lewis was indebted to is, he writes in *Surprised by Joy*,* "almost a major character in my story."

Lewis's capacity for endless reading made him a natural library dweller from his undergraduate studies onward. Oxford's Bodleian Library has a central place in Lewis's life, work, and affection, as this extract from a letter to his father on March 31, 1928 shows:

> I spend all my mornings in the Bodleian. . . . If only one could smoke and if only there were upholstered chairs, this would be one of the most delightful places in the world.

The literary critic Helen Gardner noticed his reading habits in the Bodleian in later years with admiration:

> One sometimes feels that the word "unreadable" had no meaning for him. To sit opposite him in Duke Humphrey when he was moving steadily through some huge double-columned folio in his reading for his Oxford history was to have an object lesson in what concentration meant. He seemed to create a wall of stillness around him.

As well as using the Bodleian, Lewis accumulated over the years a considerable personal library, over 2,000 volumes, which are now housed in the Marion E. Wade Collection at Wheaton College, Illinois, United States. He frequently moved until becoming established at The Kilns in 1930, and thereafter his books were divided between his home and his college rooms. Even then shelf space was always insufficient.

Lewis's interest from the beginning, and increasingly so, was in the books of an older period even larger than but including medieval times. For Lewis, all books before the period of modernism, spanning the millennia at least since the ancient Greeks, had important values in common, and thus interrelated in a constantly stimulating way. It was reading, even more so than intellectual debate and friendship (though he hungered for the latter), that fed his mind and imagination and kept him mentally alive. He saw the world through texts, as part of a symbolic perception of reality. Thus, while experiencing the horrors of trench warfare, he reflected: "This is War. This is what Homer wrote about."

What were some of the texts that helped to provide an intellectual framework for Lewis the scholar and writer? Near the end of his life, Lewis responded to a question from *The Christian Century*: "What books did the most to shape your vocational attitude and your philosophy of life?" This was his list:

*Phantastes,** by George MacDonald
*The Everlasting Man,** by G. K. Chesterton
*The Aeneid,** by Virgil
*The Temple,** by George Herbert
*The Prelude,** by William Wordsworth
*The Idea of the Holy,** by Rudolf Otto
*The Consolation of Philosophy,** by Boethius
*Life of Samuel Johnson,** by James Boswell
*Descent into Hell,** by Charles Williams
*Theism and Humanism,** by Arthur James Balfour

This group of books reflects Lewis's wide interests. There are two works of prose fantasy, three of poetry (two of them in narrative), one biography, and the remaining four books philosophical theology. Lewis described MacDonald's *Phantastes* as "baptizing his imagination" long before he accepted the claims of Christ, in its account of Anodos's journeys in Fairy Land. Charles Williams's horror fantasy *Descent into Hell* traces a process of damnation to which Lewis felt professional scholars are particularly prone, which he seems to have taken as a moral warning to himself. Virgil's *The Aeneid* is an epic poem about the founding of Rome by its Trojan hero, Aeneas, one of the greatest Latin literary works. Virgil's work epitomizes the adopting of the classical past by Christian Europe in the Middle Ages. *The Temple, Sacred Poems and Private Ejaculations* is a collection of some 160 of Herbert's devotional poems, published for the first time shortly after his death. *The Prelude, or, Growth of a Poet's Mind* is a confessional quasi-religious narrative poem in praise of the poetic imagination by Wordsworth, his greatest work. From another poem Lewis took Wordsworth's phrase "surprised by joy" for his own autobiography, which he started composing in verse, perhaps modeled on *The Prelude*. Lewis was a great admirer of Dr. Johnson, resembling him in the sharpness of his wit. Johnson comes alive in James Boswell's *Life*. Warren Lewis, looking over his uneven diary, laments that he did not "Boswellise" his brother.

The earliest theology listed by Lewis, Boethius's *The Consolation of Philosophy,* Christianized the wisdom of classical paganism and provided a model for philosophy for a thousand years. No other book in the medieval period was more widely read. One-time British Prime Minister Arthur James Balfour wrote up *Theism and Humanism* from the first of his two Gifford Lecture series for the University of Glasgow. He was concerned with the way naturalistic humanism impoverished reality, in contrast to theism. Rudolf Otto's *The Idea of the Holy* is a study of the sacred that deeply influenced Lewis's understanding of the numinous* and similar experiences of otherness such as "joy."*

G. K. Chesterton was a formative influence on Lewis. The book that Lewis picks out for his Top Ten, *The Everlasting Man*, is typical of Chesterton's apologetics and characteristically highlights the persuasive power of the Gospels. It was the nature of the Gospels in combining history with the quality of great story that was pivotal in Lewis's conversion from naturalism* to Christianity. Lewis remarks in *Surprised by Joy* that in reading *The Everlasting Man* he saw for the first time "the whole Christian outline of history set out in a form that seemed to me to make sense."

Particularly in his letters Lewis frequently refers to other books that made their mark on him. He writes about much of his favorite reading in literary essays (e.g., on Bunyan, Jane Austen, William Morris, Edmund Spenser). Some of his favorite authors, like Charles Williams* and Tolkien,* belonged to the Inklings.*

Recognition See: UNDECEPTION AND RECOGNITION.

Recovery An important feature of fantasy exploited by Lewis is restoration or recovery, which brings a healing of the wounds caused when we act through the blindness of sin. Lewis rejected what he saw as the restless quest of the modern world to be original. Indeed, meaning was to be discovered in God's created world, not somehow to be created by mankind. In this discovery imagination* working through fantasy was an effective aid.

G. K. Chesterton, in his book *Orthodoxy*, speaks of the way that children normally do not tire of familiar experience. In this sense they share in God's energy and vitality; he never tires of telling the sun to rise each morning. The child's attitude, in fact, is a true view of things, and dipping into the world of story can restore such a sense of freshness. Lewis explains that the child "does not despise real woods because he has read of enchanted woods: the reading makes all real woods a little enchanted." Similarly, Lewis's friend J. R. R. Tolkien* believed that fairy tales help us to make such a recovery—they bring healing—and "in that sense only a taste for them may make us, or keep us, childish."

Lewis was convinced that through story the real world becomes a more magical place, full of meaning. We see its pattern and color in a fresh way. The recovery of a true view of things applies both to individual things such as hills and stones, and to the cosmic—the depths of space and time itself. For in subcreation,* as Tolkien taught him to believe, there is a "survey" of space and time. Reality is captured in miniature. Through subcreative stories—the type to which The

Chronicles of Narnia* and his science fiction belong—a renewed view of reality in all its dimensions is given, including the homely, the spiritual, the physical, the moral.

Redival In *Till We Have Faces,** the frivolous golden-haired sister of Orual* and half-sister of Psyche.* When Orual becomes queen of Glome,* she marries Redival off to Trunia* of the neighboring kingdom of Phars,* to improve their alliance. Redival's son Daaran becomes heir of Glome's throne on the unmarried Orual's death.

Reepicheep, the mouse A brave and decorous talking mouse of Narnia* who journeys to Aslan's Country* in *The Voyage of the "Dawn Treader."** Mice were granted the privilege of becoming talking animals* after gnawing through Aslan's* cords in *The Lion, the Witch and the Wardrobe.** Reepicheep, the chief of the mice, is around two feet in height, wears a long crimson feather on his head, and carries a long, sharp sword. In *Prince Caspian** he is badly wounded, and his proud tail is severed. Lucy* is able to heal his tail, and Aslan restores his pride.

Reflections on the Psalms (1958) C. S. Lewis disliked the view that the Bible is only literature and should be read as such. If the Bible is taken for what it is, those parts of it that are literature can be properly received in this way. The Psalms are an important literary part of the Bible, and Lewis felt that he had something he could say about them as a layperson and literary critic. The Psalms, he considered, are great poetry, and some, such as Psalms 18 and 19, are perfect poems. Unless the psalms are read as poetry, "we shall miss what is in them and think we see what is not." Lewis's book is particularly good at bringing out how the Hebrews had an appetite and longing for God,* how they appreciated his Law (which they saw as rooted into nature* as the very structure of reality), and how they viewed nature. There are three key chapters that deal with the inspiration of Scripture and "second meanings" within it.

See also: THEOLOGY, C. S. LEWIS AND; THE BIBLE, C. S. LEWIS AND; LITERARY CRITIC, C. S. LEWIS AS A.

Rehabilitations and Other Essays (1939) In his preface, C. S. Lewis tells us that all the pieces in this collection are written in defense of things that he loves that have been the objects of attack. The first two essays defend great Romantic poets such as Shelley and William Morris against "popular hatred or neglect of Romanticism." The third and fourth defend the present (1939) Oxford English syllabus. The fifth supports the reading of many popular books that had, he believed, greatly increased his power of enjoying more serious literature as well as what is called "real life." The sixth essay champions Anglo-Saxon poetry. The contents are as follows.

"Shelley, Dryden, and Mr. Eliot" A reasoned and powerful defense of Shelley's greatness as a poet, even judged by classical criteria. C. S. Lewis's deep sympathy for the unbeliever is strikingly evident.

"William Morris" This essay is of particular interest for a study of C. S. Lewis's fiction, for he owed a debt to William Morris.

"The Idea of an 'English School'" This piece is of historical interest, because C. S. Lewis, along with J. R. R. Tolkien,* helped to shape the Oxford University English syllabus for many years.

"Our English Syllabus" C. S. Lewis reveals his thoughts on the purpose of education.*

"High and Low Brows" This defense of some popular reading as being acceptable as "good literature" anticipates the ideas that reached mature form in C. S. Lewis's *An Experiment in Criticism.**

"The Alliterative Meter" Along with this defense of an Anglo-Saxon and Old Norse meter, C. S. Lewis includes an example of his own poem employing it, "The Planets." In *Narrative Poems,** a longer example is included, "The Nameless Isle."

"Bluspels and Flalansferes: a Semantic Nightmare" This is a seminal essay on the relationship between thinking and imagining, truth and meaning,* metaphor and concept.

"Variation in Shakespeare and Others" An essay on Shakespeare's poetic method. He saw Shakespeare's greatness as having "combined two species of excellence . . . the imaginative splendor of the highest type of lyric and the realistic presentation of human life and character."

"Christianity and Literature"* An early attempt by C. S. Lewis to relate his faith to literature.

See also: LITERARY CRITIC, C. S. LEWIS AS A.

Restimar In *The Voyage of the "Dawn Treader"** he was one of the seven Telmarine* lords of Caspian* the Ninth. The usurper Miraz* had sent them away to search for new lands across the vast Eastern Ocean.* Restimar was found by the voyagers turned to gold in a bewitched pool on Deathwater Island.*

Revilian In *The Voyage of the "Dawn Treader"** he was one of the seven Telmarine* lords of Caspian* the Ninth. The usurper Miraz* had sent them away to search for new lands across the vast Eastern Ocean.* The travelers discovered him sleeping at Aslan's Table on World's End Island,* along with two other lords, Argoz* and Mavramorn.*

Rhince Drinian's* ship's mate in the tale of *The Voyage of the "Dawn Treader."**

Rhindon In *The Lion, the Witch and the Wardrobe,** the name of the sword given to Peter Pevensie* by Father Christmas.

Rhoop In *The Voyage of the "Dawn Treader"** he was one of the seven Telmarine* lords of Caspian* the Ninth. The usurper Miraz* had sent them away to search for new lands across the vast Eastern Ocean.* He was discovered trapped on the nightmarish Dark Island.* Later in the voyage he was granted restful sleep at Aslan's Table* on World's End Island.*

Rilian, Prince The son of Caspian* the Tenth (formerly Prince Caspian). The Green Witch* kidnapped Rilian for ten years. The tale of his daring rescue by Eustace Scrubb,* Jill Pole,* and Puddleglum,* the marshwiggle,* is told in *The Silver Chair.**

Rishda In *The Last Battle,** a Calormene* captain who assists Shift, the ape,* and Ginger the Cat* against King Tirian.* His fate is to be carried away by the demon god of Calormen,* Tash.*

Romance, theology of See: THEOLOGY OF ROMANCE.

Romanticism C. S. Lewis wished for the word *romantic* to be banned, as it now had so many usages as to be virtually useless. He failed to find another term, however, to characterize the central preoccupation he shared with his friends J. R. R. Tolkien* and Charles Williams,* or kindred spirits such as G. K. Chesterton* and his mentor George MacDonald.*

He tells us in his preface to the third edition of *The Pilgrim's Regress** that, when he wrote that book in the early 1930s, he used *romanticism* to mean the special experience of inconsolable longing, or joy.* He certainly was not in revolt against reason or classicism, which romanticism is sometimes taken to mean. He was not a subjectivist, seeing art as the expression of its maker's soul.

In English literature, the Romantic Movement is often taken to begin with the publication of *Lyrical Ballads* in 1798 by Wordsworth and Coleridge. The movement was part of a wide reaction against deism and a mechanistic view of nature and mankind. Romanticism gave rise to the Gothic genre and its offspring, Mary Shelley's remarkable *Frankenstein* (1818)—and thus to the beginning of science fiction. The movement also created a vogue for historical romance, as in the novels of Sir Walter Scott. In Germany Romanticism was connected with the rise of modernist theology, in reaction to rationalism. George MacDonald's rejection of his native Calvinism was part of the same trend.

The subjective link between different aspects of romanticism, as far as C. S. Lewis was concerned, is a preoccupation with the imagination* and creative fantasy. This linking thread can be seen in all the main influences upon C. S. Lewis. Indeed, a brief outline of these influences is the best way of characterizing the romanticism of C. S. Lewis. "Romantic" influences upon him can, for convenience, be divided into four areas: (1) ancient mythologies; (2) older writers; (3) nineteenth-century authors; and (4) contemporary sources. These influences are mentioned by C. S. Lewis, or they come through friends and acquaintances such as J. R. R. Tolkien, Charles Williams, Dorothy L. Sayers,* or from his mentor George MacDonald.

(1) Ancient mythology. Old Norse mythology affects some features of Lewis's Narnia* stories and deeply influenced J. R. R. Tolkien's fantasies. Lewis drew more upon classical mythology, most notably in *Till We Have Faces** and in characters such as Mr. Tumnus* in Narnia. Lewis mentions his great love of Irish mythology. Welsh and British mythology—especially "The matter of Britain" and Merlin (see: ATLANTIS)—are found in *That Hideous Strength*.* Lewis believed that, scattered among pagan myths, there are certain "good stories" that prefigure Christian truth (see: PAGANISM AND MYSTICISM). They anticipate and give form to adequate vehicles of truth.

(2) Older writers. The main sources seem to be Boethius (see: *THE CONSOLATION OF PHILOSOPHY*), Spenser, Malory, Bunyan, and Milton, whose influence on *Perelandra** is marked. Milton is probably an important root of the science-fiction genre, of which, according to Brian Aldiss, C. S. Lewis is an important part. John Bunyan and earlier medieval allegorists deeply influenced C. S. Lewis also. Edmund Spenser was one of Lewis's favorite authors.

(3) Nineteenth-century writers. Most important of writers from this period was George MacDonald. MacDonald in turn confesses a debt to the German Romanticism of Novalis and others. C. S. Lewis's concept of joy* or *Sehnsucht* is found in German Romanticism. C. S. Lewis points out that William Morris (1834-1896) influenced his work. While an undergraduate at Oxford,* C. S. Lewis gave a paper on Morris to The Martlets, a university society. Here he compared Morris to Homer and Thomas Malory, but, the minute book records, "the general sense of the Society was that too high a position had been claimed" for the writer. Lewis later wrote (the piece can be found in *Selected Literary Essays*) that Morris "seems to retire far from the real world and to build a world out of his wishes; but when he has finished the result stands out as a picture of experience ineluctably true."

(4) Contemporary writers. A number of influences on his work are mentioned by C. S. Lewis, including James Stephens, G. K. Chesterton* (his thought, not so much his fiction), E. R. Eddison, and David Lindsay.* He also discusses the ideas of Rudolf Otto on the numinous* (see: *THE IDEA OF THE HOLY*) in *The Problem of Pain*,* and seeks to embody that quality in his fantasies, for example in Aslan's Country.*

Both C. S. Lewis and J. R. R. Tolkien considered E. R. Eddison (1882-1945) an important writer, and he was much discussed by the Inklings.* Tolkien disliked his invented names; he felt that they lacked color and conviction. Eddison's geography of his imaginary three kingdoms—Rerek, Meszria, and Fingiswold—bears a superficial resemblance to the geography of Tolkien's Middle-earth. Eddison was appreciated for his attempts at subcreation.*

The Inklings themselves influenced C. S. Lewis, particularly Tolkien, Charles Williams, and Owen Barfield.*

See also: THEOLOGY OF ROMANCE; LITERARY CRITIC, C. S. LEWIS AS A; MYTH; MEANING AND IMAGINATION.

Roonwit In *The Last Battle,** a great and golden-bearded centaur. He reads of danger in the stars over Narnia* and warns King Tirian.* He is slain by a Calormene* arrow.

For readers interested in learning more of centaurs, Robert Siegal's story *Alpha Centuri* is worth reading. Centaurs originate in Greek mythology. The upper half of their bodies is human; the remainder is composed of the body and legs of a horse.

Rumblebuffin In *The Lion, the Witch and the Wardrobe,** the giant who assists in the fight against the White Witch.* In attempting to borrow a handkerchief from Lucy,* he picked her up by mistake. The giant was a member of the respected Buffin family, a family not very clever but old and with traditions.

Rush River In *Prince Caspian** we are told that it joins the Great River* at Beruna.* See also: NARNIA: GEOGRAPHY.

Rynelf In *The Voyage of the "Dawn Treader"** a sailor on the galleon.

S

St. Anne's The country house in *That Hideous Strength** in which Dr. Elwin Ransom* formed a community in opposition to the sinister N.I.C.E.* The group represented the spiritual Britain (Logres), the remnant of Atlantis.*

St. Mark's, Dundela The Church of Ireland (Episcopal) place of worship attended by the Lewis family in Jack's Ulster childhood. Dundela is on the outskirts of Belfast and the church only a short walk from "Little Lea."* Lewis was baptized here on January 29, 1899, and confirmed on December 6, 1914. Lewis's grandfather, Thomas Hamilton (1826-1905), was St. Mark's first rector. In 1932 the Lewis brothers gave a stained-glass window to the church in memory of Albert and Flora Lewis,* their parents. The traditional symbol of St. Mark is the lion, which is also the title of the church magazine; so it is fitting that Aslan* of Narnia* is a lion.

Salamander In *The Silver Chair*,* salamanders dwell in Bism* in the great fire-river. They are witty and eloquent small dragons.

Sallowpad In *The Horse and His Boy*,* an old, wise raven who is advisor to King Edmund* and Queen Lucy.*

Sayer, George (1914-) A pupil and friend of C. S. Lewis who in 1988 published a major biography of his one-time tutor, *Jack: C. S. Lewis and His Times*. Lewis sometimes stayed in Sayer's home in Malvern. George Sayer was head of the English Department at Malvern College from 1949 to 1974. When Sayer first met his tutor, he was told by J. R. R. Tolkien,* "You'll never get to the bottom of him." Sayer's biography particularly dwells on Lewis's early life, his early poetry, his relationship with Mrs. Janie Moore,* his life as a university lecturer, and his domestic life.

Sayers, Dorothy Leigh (1893-1957) Dorothy L. Sayers, best known for her detective stories about Lord Peter Wimsey, was a friend of C. S. Lewis and later met his wife, Joy Davidman.* Sayers also was acquainted with Charles Williams* and contributed to *Essays Presented to Charles Williams*,* the posthumous tribute from the Inklings.* Her robust, popular theological writings such as *The Mind of the Maker*

(1942) reveal a sharp and brilliant mind which, like those of Lewis and G. K. Chesterton,* delighted in dogma and orthodoxy. Her series of BBC radio plays, *The Man Born to Be King*, was immensely popular in wartime Britain. Toward the end of her life she discovered Dante's *The Divine Comedy* and translated it into fresh, contemporary English (a task completed after her death by Barbara Reynolds).

C. S. Lewis wrote a panegyric to Dorothy L. Sayers that was read at her memorial service, concluding, "let us thank the Author who invented her."

Scientism Science is one of the most significant communal endeavors of mankind, the historical origins of which lie in the Judeo-Christian idea of the Two Books, the Word of God and the Book of Nature, from a single Author. Scientism is the idolatry of science, where it becomes the sole authority, the model, and arbiter of truth, as under modernism. Lewis attacks scientism particularly in his science-fiction trilogy. Professor Weston* embodies all that Lewis dislikes in the attitude of scientism. Its inevitable consequence, technocracy—the tyranny of technique, the subjugation of nature* by technology—is satirized by Lewis in *That Hideous Strength,** where it is epitomized in the N.I.C.E.* Under technocracy, he tried to demonstrate, scientific technology becomes the characteristically modern form of magic, truth by power. Lewis sought to rehabilitate an older view of nature in order to help his contemporaries become aware of the grotesque shortcomings of scientism. Such a rehabilitation can be seen in his exposition of the medieval model of the cosmos, *The Discarded Image**; in the world of Narnia*; in the figure of Merlin* in *That Hideous Strength*;* and in the philologist-hero Dr. Elwin Ransom* who later becomes the Fisher King of Arthurian legend.

Screwtape In *The Screwtape Letters** and its brief sequel *Screwtape Proposes a Toast,** an eminent Under-Secretary to the High Command of Hell, and uncle of the junior tempter Wormwood.* Lewis deliberately gives Screwtape a certain twisted eminence, in his belief that greater beings are capable of greater evil. Interestingly, Screwtape admits hell's lack of power against its Enemy, but continues to trust optimistically in its bureaucracy. Screwtape ceased to be a practicing tempter in the latter half of the nineteenth century, when he was rewarded with an administrative post.

The Screwtape Letters (1942) The most direct of several books about devilry that C. S. Lewis wrote and, of all his books, the one he found most unpleasant to compose. It gave him, he says, a sort of spiritual cramp because of the inverse perspective of hell that it employs. The book is a comic, satirical look at perhaps the most serious subject possible, damnation. The letters first appeared in a religious journal called *The Guardian*. One reader, a country clergyman, wrote in to cancel his subscription on the grounds that "much of the advice given in these letters seemed to him not only erroneous but positively diabolical."

The Screwtape Letters consists of letters of advice and warning from a senior devil prominent in the lowerarchy of hell to his nephew Wormwood, a trainee tempter. Wormwood, fresh from the Tempters' Training College, has been assigned a young man. His task is to secure his damnation. Unfortunately for Wormwood, his client becomes a Christian. Screwtape passes on a number of useful suggestions for reclaiming the young man. These come both from his centuries of experience and from information from Hell's Intelligence Department. Screwtape is also in touch with other tempters assigned to the patient's friends, acquaintances, and relations. Wormwood particularly sees great possibilities in the person of the young man's mother, who is very trying. The young man successfully avoids the pull of the inner ring* of a smart set of people. Wormwood faces hell when, first, his patient falls in love with a Christian girl, and, secondly, when he fails to keep the young man out of the danger of death, and he is killed in an air raid, forever out of hell's clutches. Screwtape's only consolation lies in devouring his incompetent nephew.

The Screwtape Letters is one of C. S. Lewis's most popular books. The author's view of a personal devil comes over clearly, despite the satirical genre that he employs. Though considered by Lewis not to be among the best of his books, it stands in a long line of books concerned with angels, demons, heaven,* and hell, such as Dante's *Divine Comedy*, Milton's *Paradise Lost*, and John Macgowan's* *Dialogues of Devils*. The novels of C. S. Lewis's pupil Harry Blamires,* including *Highway to Heaven*, continue the same tradition.

Screwtape Proposes a Toast (1965) A collection of literary and theological pieces, including several reprinted from *Transposition and Other Addresses** and *They Asked for a Paper.** It contains "Screwtape Proposes a Toast," "The Inner Ring,"* "Is Theology Poetry?," "Transposition,"* "On Obstinacy in Belief," "The Weight of Glory," "Good Work and Good Works," and "A Slip of the Tongue." See also: *THE SCREWTAPE LETTERS*.

Scrubb, Eustace A cousin of the Pevensie* children, he is drawn into Narnia,* along with Lucy and Edmund, in *The Voyage of the "Dawn Treader."** He returns to Narnia on two other occasions with Jill Pole,* a school friend, as recounted in *The Silver Chair** and *The Last Battle.** When we first meet him, he is self-centered and spoiled by the modern education he is receiving at Experiment House.* His adventures with the travelers on the *Dawn Treader* give him a wider view of life, particularly after his experience of turning into a dragon* on Dragon Island.* This experience and his undragoning by Aslan* provide a powerful image of sin, repentance, and Christian salvation. But unlike his cousins, Eustace is never a monarch in Narnia.

Sea girl In *The Voyage of the "Dawn Treader"** a girl seen herding fish by Lucy* as the ship passed over the clear waters of the Last Sea before Aslan's Country.* She and Lucy became friends simply by seeing each other, even though their worlds could never touch. See also: SEA PEOPLE.

Sea people In *The Voyage of the "Dawn Treader"** undersea people seen by Lucy* as the ship passed over the clear waters of the Last Sea before Aslan's Country.* They rode sea horses, wore no clothes, and had bodies the color of old ivory, with dark purple hair. Their beautiful submarine land was made up of mountains, hills, forests, and parkland. The sea people enjoyed hunting and used small fierce fish the way falcons are used in our world.

Sea Serpent In *The Voyage of the "Dawn Treader"** this creature attacks the ship after the travelers have visited Burnt Island.*

Mr. Sensible An allegorical figure in *The Pilgrim's Regress** representing cultured worldliness.

Seven Isles A group of seven small islands a few days' sailing from the coast of Narnia,* described in *The Voyage of the "Dawn Treader."** Muil is the westernmost island, separated from Brenn by a choppy stretch of water. On Brenn the town of Redhaven provides supplies for shipping in the area.

Seven lords Telmarine* lords of Caspian* the Ninth. The usurper Miraz* had sent them away to search for new lands in the Eastern Ocean* during his reign, as recounted in *Prince Caspian.** In its sequel, the tale of *The Voyage of the "Dawn Treader,"** Caspian seeks the seven missing lords. The seven are Argoz,* Bern,* Mavramorn,* Octesian,* Restimar,* Revilian,* and Rhoop.*

***Severe Mercy, A,* Sheldon Vanauken** (1977) This is an account of love, courtship, marriage, and grief in which C. S. Lewis played an important pastoral part, mainly through letters to its author, Sheldon Vanauken. The American movingly records his romance with Jean Davis, whom he calls "Davy," their conversion, and her subsequent early death. A key discovery of the young couple's is that God's love is stronger than their own deeply romantic love of each other. The "shining barrier" they had erected around their love was invaded by Christ, who replaced each other as the center of their lives. At Oxford, where they studied, C. S. Lewis and Christian friends influenced their conversion. Thereafter Lewis is both mentor and friend.

After Davy's death, though Sheldon is in America, Lewis stays close to his suffering by letter. Vanauken's book is particularly important to those for whom C. S. Lewis inspires a sacramental view of Christian faith. Such a view is exemplified well in Leanne Payne's study *Real*

Presence: The Holy Spirit in the Works of C. S. Lewis (1979, 1988, British edition 1989). See also: IDEALISM, C. S. LEWIS AND.

Shadowbrute See: GOD OF THE GRAY MOUNTAINS.

Shadow Lands In *The Last Battle,** the name given to this world by Aslan* to mark its contrast to the real, new world of Aslan's Country.* In this contrast Lewis makes powerful use of Plato,* particularly his famous Myth of the Cave.

Shallow Lands See: UNDERLAND.

Shasta See: COR.

Shift, the ape In *The Last Battle,** a Narnian* talking animal* who deceives many loyal beasts and trees into believing that Aslan* has returned and that Puzzle, the ass,* draped in an ill-fitting lion skin, is he. Shift's treachery knows no boundaries, and he forms an alliance with Narnia's traditional enemy, Calormen.*

S

Shribble River In *The Silver Chair,** a river flowing from east to west near Ettinsmoor.*

Silent Planet, The See: THE PLANETS.

Silver Chair, The (1953) This Narnia* story is a sequel to *The Voyage of the "Dawn Treader."** It concerns Eustace Scrubb* and another pupil, Jill Pole,* of Experiment House,* a "modern school." They are brought to Narnia by Aslan* to search for the long-lost Prince Rilian,* son of Caspian* the Tenth, the Caspian of the previous adventure, now in his old age. Their search takes them into the wild lands north of Narnia and eventually into a realm under the earth called Underland.* The two children are accompanied by one of C. S. Lewis's most memorable creations, Puddleglum,* the marshwiggle.* They encounter and destroy the Green Witch,* murderer of Rilian's mother. Before that, they narrowly escape being eaten by the giants of the city of Harfang,* for whom man is a delicacy, and even marshwiggle is in their cookbook.

Silver Sea The reach of ocean covered with lilylike white flowers found by the travelers in *The Voyage of the "Dawn Treader."** As they penetrated the dazzlingly bright sea, the voyagers discovered its waters becoming gradually more shallow as they approached World's End. It was necessary to leave the *Dawn Treader* and use a rowboat instead. Beyond World's End lay Aslan's Country.*

Slubgob In *The Screwtape Letters,** Dr. Slubgob is principal of the Tempters' Training College* of hell.

Slumtrimpet The tempter assigned to the fiancée of Wormwood's* charge in *The Screwtape Letters.**

Smith, Sarah One of the inhabitants of heaven, the Solid People,* who travel to its hinterlands to meet bus trippers from hell in the dream story *The Great Divorce.** One tripper, a dwarf named Frank,* was Sarah's husband in Golder's Green, London, in the previous life. There is a magnificent procession in Sarah's honor that is observed by Lewis, who has accompanied the trippers, and the solid spirit of George MacDonald,* his mentor. The encounter between Sarah Smith and Frank, which fails to persuade Frank to stay, leads Lewis to ask some searching questions of MacDonald.

Socratic Club See: OXFORD UNIVERSITY SOCRATIC CLUB.

Solid People The inhabitants of heaven* in *The Great Divorce** whose reality contrasts with the insubstantiality of the bus trippers from hell. Lewis was particularly drawn to the biblical image of "the weight of glory," the title of a published sermon of his. He felt that there was a correspondence between particularity in people, places, and things and substance. See: NATURE; GOD.

Sopespian In *Prince Caspian,** a lord of the usurper King Miraz,* who turns traitor and plans his death.

Sorlois In *The Magician's Nephew,** a city of the long-dead world of Charn.*

Sorn Sorns (or, properly, seroni) are one of three intelligent kinds of beings living on the planet Malacandra.* As befits their nature as the planet's intelligentsia, they had long, thin legs, top-heavy bodies, and thin faces with long, drooping noses and mouths. They were three times as tall as the earthman Elwin Ransom.* Sorns had scientific interests, including cosmology and astronomy, and enjoyed metaphysical speculation. Ransom found, in response to their eager probing, that his knowledge of earth geography, history, and science was extremely sketchy.

South A key region in the symbolic landscape of *The Pilgrim's Regress,** depicted on the Mappa Mundi.* It represents the emotional and visceral side of the human soul (see: CHEST).

Spear-head In *The Voyage of the "Dawn Treader"** Narnia's* north star, brighter than our own pole star.

Spenser's Images of Life (1967) C. S. Lewis's longest piece of literary criticism, as opposed to literary history. It is based upon his Cambridge lectures on Edmund Spenser's great poem *The Faerie Queene*. He intended to turn his material into a book, but he did not live to do so. Lewis's holograph notes were expanded and edited into this book by his friend Alistair Fowler of Brasenose College, Oxford. Fowler comments: "The best I hope for is that some may agree with me that if Lewis himself had lived to write the book, it might have stood out among his works as a critical new departure. Here I am not thinking of the iconographical interpretations (although these have their interest) so much as of the adumbration of a manner of approach to fiction not suitable for textual analysis."

C. S. Lewis approaches *The Faerie Queene* as a splendid and majestic pageant of the universe and nature* that celebrates God,* in Lewis's own phrase, as "the glad creator." He argues that if the poem is to be fully enjoyed and understood by the modern reader, conventional views of epic and allegory* need to be modified. He suggests in his introduction: "We should expect, then, from Spenser's poem, a simple fairy-tale pleasure sophisticated by polyphonic technique, a simple 'moral' sophisticated by a learned iconography. Moreover, we should expect to find all of these reacting on one another, to produce a work very different from what we are used to." Lewis considers *The Faerie Queene* to be perhaps the most difficult poem in English, above the demand of great literature for both a simple and a sophisticated response. His final chapter analyzes the story of King Arthur in the poem. See also: LITERARY CRITIC, C. S. LEWIS AS A.

Spirit of the Age An allegorical figure in *The Pilgrim's Regress** portrayed as a giant who imprisons John,* the modern pilgrim.

Spirits in Bondage: A Cycle of Lyrics (1919) Written while C. S. Lewis was an atheist and when he had a strong ambition to be a poet, this collection of poetry was published under the pseudonym of Clive Hamilton (Hamilton was his mother's maiden name and his brother's middle name). According to Lewis, the poems are "mainly strung around the idea . . . that nature is wholly diabolical and malevolent and that God, if he exists, is outside of and in opposition to the cosmic arrangements." The volume has similarities of outlook with his early, long narrative poem *Dymer.** See also: *NARRATIVE POEMS*; *COLLECTED POEMS; POEMS.*

Stable Hill In *The Last Battle,** there is a stable in which Shift* keeps Puzzle,* the ass, as the donkey pretends to be Aslan.* Later Tash,* the Calormene* demon god, enters the stable, followed by Aslan himself. When the great lion takes the stable over, its inside turns out to be larger than its outside.

Sterk In *That Hideous Strength,** a town between Stratford and Edgestow* on the railway line to London. In *Out of the Silent Planet,** the deserted country home of Professor Weston* lay on the far side of the hills a good four miles from Sterk. Elwin Ransom* came across

Weston's home while on a walking tour heading for Sterk. The town had industrial areas beyond it, in contrast to the featureless, desolate countryside in which Ransom was kidnapped.

Stevens, Courtenay ("Tom") (1905-1976) A member of the Inklings* and fellow and tutor in Ancient History at Magdalen College, Oxford,* from 1934. He acquired the nickname "Tom Brown Stevens" while a schoolboy at Winchester.

Stone knife This was used by the White Witch* to slay Aslan,* as recounted in *The Lion, the Witch and the Wardrobe.** Later in the history of Narnia,* the travelers discover it kept by Ramandu* at Aslan's Table in *The Voyage of the "Dawn Treader."**

Stone Table In *The Lion, the Witch and the Wardrobe,** a table of ancient magic upon which Aslan,* the great lion, is slain by the White Witch.* The table is split forever when he returns to life. It is a slab of gray stone supported by four upright stones, obviously ancient and covered with engraved lines and figures. A mound called Aslan's How* is eventually built over it and plays a significant part in the actions recorded in *Prince Caspian.**

Strawberry In *The Magician's Nephew,** the horse of London cabby, Frank,* who is turned into a talking and flying horse by Aslan* and renamed Fledge.*

Studdock, Jane In *That Hideous Strength,** the wife of Mark Studdock.* Like Damaris Tighe in Charles Williams's much-admired novel *The Place of the Lion,** Jane is a postgraduate student. Six months after her marriage, alone during the day in their tiny flat, she is experiencing a crisis over the meaning of romantic love* even while she works on John Donne's love poetry.

As a child, Jane had given up any belief in the supernatural along with Santa Claus. She is, however, gifted with unwelcomed second sight, by which the devilish activities of the N.I.C.E.* are opened to her. She is the innocent agent who alone can reveal the hidden whereabouts of the sleeping Merlin,* in a trance since the Dark Ages. As such, she is sought both by the N.I.C.E. and the opposing forces of humanity led by Dr. Elwin Ransom.*

As Jane is slowly drawn into the community surrounding Ransom, there is no violation of her personhood, unlike what happens to her husband, Mark, as he moves closer to the inner ring* of the N.I.C.E. at Belbury.* Gradually her sense of reality and her commitment to the marriage of love return until she is able to receive back again the undeceived and restored Mark (see: UNDECEPTION AND RECOGNITION).

Studdock, Mark Gainsby In *That Hideous Strength,** a junior fellow of Bracton College* of the midland university of Edgestow.* His subject is sociology. Six months before the story opens, he married Jane,* a postgraduate student of English literature. Mark is drawn into involvement with the sinister N.I.C.E.,* whose headquarters are within a few miles at Belbury.* There his very soul is endangered by the lure of the N.I.C.E.'s "inner ring" of members. We learn that the temptation of the inner ring* has beset Mark throughout his young life.

With dauntless self-honesty, C. S. Lewis modeled Mark on aspects of himself as a new lecturer at Magdalen College, Oxford.* Mark finds himself constantly denying his spontaneous like and dislike of people in order to go deeper into Belbury's inner circle. In fact, naturally he disliked all the core people.

Jane, his wife, provided his connection with reality. Whenever he thought about her, she was a mirror. He imagined her disliking his heavy drinking at Belbury. She would be scathing about its leading lights. He knew that she wouldn't fit in there, despite efforts to persuade him to get her to join Belbury. Her real self would be a living criticism of all that the N.I.C.E. stood for. From Jane's point of view, she considered Mark a person easily taken in. He liked to be liked, which opened him to manipulation.

According to the story's narrator, revealed as Lewis himself, Mark's mind held virtually no remnant of noble thought, either Christian or pagan. He hadn't had either a properly scientific or a classical education,* merely a modern one. He had bypassed the disciplines of abstract thought and of the traditions of civilization, the "literatures of freedom and dignity." These deficiencies made him a man of straw. He had done well in academic subjects that required no exact knowledge, being good at essays and general papers. He had typically once written an article on vagrancy though he had no knowledge of the tramp's life of the roads.

Mark experienced "undeception"* after being falsely arrested for the murder of Hingest, a fellow of Bracton disillusioned after a brief flirtation with the N.I.C.E. Painful self-knowledge suddenly enlightened Studdock. He saw himself as always drawn towards odious inner rings, even at school losing his only real friend in his efforts to get into an unpleasant society called Grip. Later he had left behind his undergraduate friends such as Arthur Denniston.* In this new state of being undeceived, his public self or face fell off, leaving himself as the person responsible for all his follies. Jane was the only real person he had left, and he had nearly discarded her for the N.I.C.E. and the sinister forces behind it.

Mark's undeception is part of the story of his faltering steps towards Christian conversion. At Belbury Mark was Wither's* pupil for initiation into the satanic inner circle. At the point when he was expected to despoil a figure of a crucified man, he suddenly realized for the first time that there might be something in Christianity. Whereas his wife, Jane, had abandoned belief in Christianity along with Father Christmas, Mark had never believed.

Studies in Words (1960; 1967) C. S. Lewis became Professor of Renaissance and Medieval Literature at Cambridge University in 1954, setting the pattern of his work with his inaugural address, "*De Descriptione Temporum.*"* His book *Studies in Words*, enlarged for the second edition after his death, is based on lectures he gave at Cambridge and is mainly addressed to undergraduates studying literature. He warns in his preface that the book is not an essay in linguistics; his purpose is merely lexical and historical. His approach, however, differs greatly from that of a dictionary, with a number of advantages. His studies provide an aid to more accurate reading, and the words studied are selected for the light they shed on ideas and sentiments. The history of ideas, Lewis believed, is intimately recorded in the shifts of meaning* in words. There is value in considering the relationship between words in a family of meaning, rather than considering words and their roots individually.

The modern reader's natural tendency is to assume that he or she knows the meaning of words in old texts. Lewis confesses that he early cultivated the habit of following up the slightest "semantic discomfort" he felt with a word, a habit that became second nature. Any such discomfort roused him, like a terrier, to the game of discovering the history of thought and sentiment that underlies the semantic biography of a word. His friend Owen Barfield* displayed a similar instinct. See also: LITERARY CRITIC, LEWIS AS A.

Subcreation Subcreation is a concept developed by C. S. Lewis's friend J. R. R. Tolkien,* one that deeply influenced Lewis. The idea is expressed in Tolkien's contribution to *Essays Presented to Charles Williams.**

Tolkien believed that the art of true fantasy or fairy-tale writing is subcreation—creating another or secondary world with such skill that it has an "inner consistency of reality." This inner consistency is so potent that it compels secondary belief or primary belief (the belief we give to the primary or real world) on the part of the reader. Tolkien calls the skills to compel these two degrees of belief "fantasy" and "enchantment" respectively.

A clue to the concept of subcreation lies in the fact that the word *fairy*, or more properly *faery*, etymologically means "the realm or state where faeries have their being." A faery tale is not thus a story that simply concerns faery beings. They are in some sense otherworldly, having a geography and history surrounding them. Tolkien's key idea is that faery, the realm or state where faeries have their being, contains a whole cosmos, a microcosm. It contains the moon, the sun, the sky, trees and mountains, rivers, water and stones, as well as dragons, trolls, elves, dwarfs, goblins, elves, talking animals,* and even a moral person when he or she is enchanted (through giving primary belief to that other world). Faery is subcreation rather than either mimetic representation or allegorical interpretation of the "beauties and terrors of the world."

Subcreation comes, said Tolkien, as a result of a twofold urge in human beings: (1) the wish to survey the depths of space and time, and (2) the urge to communicate with living beasts other than mankind, to escape from hunger, poverty, death, and to end the separation between mankind and nature. Just as the reason wishes for a unified theory to cover all phenomena in the universe, the imagination* also constantly seeks a unity of meaning* appropriate to itself.

Tolkien took the idea of subcreation much further than C. S. Lewis, disliking the lack of genuine subcreation in Lewis's Chronicles of Narnia,* which he regarded (relatedly) as too allegorical. Tolkien's concept of subcreation is the most distinctive feature of his view of art. Though he saw it in terms of inventive fantasy, the applicability might well prove to be wider. Secondary worlds can take many forms. The philosopher Nicholas Wolterstorff sees "world-projection" as one of the universal and most important features of art, particularly fiction. World-projection has large-scale metaphorical power. Wolterstorff claims: "by way of fictionally projecting his distinct world the fictioneer may make a claim, true or false as the case may be, about our actual world." Its metaphorical quality deepens or indeed modifies our perception of the meaning of reality.

Sunless Sea In *The Silver Chair,** the sea crossed by Eustace Scrubb,* Jill Pole,* and Puddleglum* in order to reach Underland* in their quest for the lost Prince Rilian.*

Supernatural, Supernaturalism See: NATURALISM AND SUPERNATURALISM.

Surprised by Joy: The Shape of My Early Life (1955) This book is C. S. Lewis's autobiography up to his conversion to Christianity at the age of thirty-one. "Joy"* is a technical term used by C. S. Lewis to help to define a distinct tone of feeling he discovered in early childhood. The experience stayed with him on and off throughout his adolescence and early manhood. This inconsolable longing contradicted the atheism and materialism that his intellect embraced. In first theism and then Christianity both his intellect and his imagination were fulfilled. A key moment in his journey to faith was the discovery of George MacDonald's* *Phantastes.**

Prior to that reconciliation Lewis portrays the "two hemispheres" of his mind in turbulent conflict: "On the one side a many-islanded sea of poetry and myth; on the other a glib and shallow 'rationalism.' Nearly all that I loved I believed to be imaginary; nearly all that I believed to be real I thought grim and meaningless."

In writing Lewis may have had in mind as a genre model William Wordsworth's powerful autobiographical poem *The Prelude.** See also: LEWIS, C. S.

Susan, Queen See PEVENSIE, PETER, SUSAN, EDMUND, AND LUCY.

Swanwhite In *The Last Battle,** a queen of such beauty that if she looked into any pool, her reflected face shone out for a year and a day afterwards just like a star in the night sky. She lived in Narnia* before the days of the ascendancy of the White Witch,* who brought perpetual winter to the land.

Symbolism C. S. Lewis belongs to the tradition of romanticism,* but with important differences, one being his belief that the imagination* is not the organ of truth. As with the Romantics, but not to the extent of his friend J. R. R. Tolkien's* fantasy, symbols play an integrating part in his fiction. His symbolism helps to make his work a lamp as well as a mirror—depicting reality but also illuminating it. In this *Encyclopedia* a number of his characteristic symbols or symbolic themes are included, such as angels,* cosmic war,* joy,* the Mappa Mundi,* recovery and healing,* north* and south,* the numinous,* and the quest.*

The geography and history of Narnia* are also symbolic, enriching the stories scattered across Narnian history. Further enrichment is obtained from invented beings such as Puddleglum,* the marshwiggle.* There are also the powerful symbolic landscapes of Malacandra* and Perelandra,* inhabited with creatures such as the sorns,* pfifltriggi,* and eldila.*

The process of invention that Tolkien called subcreation* allows the imagination to employ both subconscious and conscious resources of the mind. This is particularly so with regard to language, which is intimately connected to the whole self, and not just to theoretical thought. Subcreation allows powerful archetypes to became an effective part of an artwork. This helps to account for the universal appeal of deeply imaginative writing like Lewis's.

Archetypes are recurrent symbols, plot structures, and character types that make up much of the material of literature. In symbolic literature like Lewis's, the archetypes are focused and definite, but so-called realistic fiction is also replete with hidden archetypes. Lewis takes many archetypes from the Bible* (such as the End of the World in *The Last Battle**), which Northrope Frye called "a grammar of literary archetypes," and Leland Ryken described as "the great repository of archetypes in Western literature."

T

Talapal In *Till We Have Faces,** the name for Ungit* (or Aphrodite) used in the kingdom of Essur.*

***Tale of Squirrel Nutkin, The,* Beatrix Potter** (1903) This tale belongs to the nursery tradition of talking-animal* stories, a genre that inspired the child Lewis's *Boxen.* Squirrel Nutkin* provided Lewis with his second glimpse of joy* (the first being a flowering currant bush), as recounted in his autobiography *Surprised by Joy.**

Talking animals C. S. Lewis was constantly fascinated by the gap between humanity and the subhumanity of beasts. The title of his Narnian* tale *The Horse and His Boy** tells it all. The pronoun *his* bridges the gap between animal and human; the boy, Shasta* (Cor*), belongs as much to the talking Narnian horse, Bree,* as Bree belongs to Shasta. Lewis's fascination with this gap is evident also in his description of the warm inner life of the bear, Mr. Bultitude,* in *That Hideous Strength** and in his magnificent concept of Narnia as a land of talking beasts created by the great talking lion, Aslan.* Talking animals are normally found only in children's books such as *The Wind in the Willows* by Kenneth Graham, a book much admired and quoted by C. S. Lewis. In his science-fiction tale *Out of the Silent Planet,** however, Lewis smuggles in talking animals that are palatable to its adult readers. Most notably this is the case with the hrossa* who, though personal beings, also retain the qualities of animals.

C. S. Lewis regarded the invention of talking beasts as a feature of what his friend J. R. R. Tolkien* called "subcreation."* Lewis once wrote: "We do not want merely to see beauty . . . we want something else which can hardly be put into words—to be united with the beauty we see, to pass into it, to receive it into ourselves, to bathe in it, to become part of it. That is why we have peopled air and earth and water with gods and goddesses and nymphs and elves." And, we could add, with the talking beasts of Narnia and Malacandra.* See also: NATURE.

Tao, The Lewis's adopted name for The Way, values and virtues held universally and based on nature* as structured by a divine creator. Lewis's most eloquent defense of the objectivity of values and virtues is his essay *The Abolition of Man,** the themes of which are treated fictionally in *That Hideous Strength.** Lewis believed that a cosmic war* is raging between goodness and evil, and he memorably depicted the battle for the human soul in the allegorical Mappa Mundi* found in his *The Pilgrim's Regress.** Lewis also sketches The Tao in his case for Christian belief, *Mere Christianity.**

Tarin In the novel *Till We Have Faces,** a young officer of the king's guard at the royal palace in Glome.* After the king discovers that he has been flirting with Redival,* his daughter, Tarin is castrated and sold as a slave in Ringal. This was one of King Trom's* many mistakes, as Tarin's father sought revenge. Tarin became great in the south and east of Glome and later visited Queen Orual.* From him Orual learned of her selfish neglect of Redival, a factor that helps in the queen's painful undeception.*

Tash The demon god of Calormen,* who appears in terrifying form in the story of *The Last Battle.** It had a head of a bird and four arms. The Calormene nobility considered itself descended from Tash. As part of the deception in the last days of Narnia* and Calormen, "new theologians" led by Shift* syncretized Tash and Aslan* into a mixture they called "Tashlan."

Tashbaan The capital of Calormen, named after the country's deity, Tash.* See: CALORMEN.

Telmar, Land of Lying to the far west of Narnia,* Telmar was populated by pirates who accidentally stumbled into the region from our world. See also: TELMARINES.

Telmarines Descendents of pirates who accidentally stumbled into the land of Telmar* after entering a magical cave in a South Sea island. They became a proud and fierce nation. After a famine the Telmarines, led by King Caspian* the First, crossed the Western Mountains and conquered the peaceful land of Narnia,* long after the reign of High King Peter and the other Pevensie* children. They silenced the talking animals* and trees, drove away dwarfs and fauns, and even tried to cover up the memory of such things. Prince Caspian learns of the "Old Narnia," as it is then called, as recounted in the book *Prince Caspian.** See also: NARNIA, HISTORY.

Tempters' Training College In *The Screwtape Letters** and its brief sequel *Screwtape Proposes a Toast,** the college where junior devils learn their skills in damning human beings or in attempting to reclaim those who have gone over to the Enemy. After graduation, novices appear to have practical experience under the guidance of an experienced devil. Wormwood* is a recent graduate, advised by letter by his eminent Uncle Screwtape.* Every year the Tempters' Training College holds a dinner. One year Screwtape was the quest of honor, and his speech is recorded in *Screwtape Proposes a Toast*. The college's principal is Dr. Slubgob.*

Tegner's *Drapa* A poem by Esaias Tegner, translated by Longfellow, that provided the young Lewis's third recalled glimpse of joy* when it spoke of the death of Balder.*

***Temple, Sacred Poems and Private Ejaculations, The,* George Herbert** (1633) A collection of 160 poems first published shortly after the death of George Herbert (1593-1633). Herbert ministered in the Church of England, obtaining the living of Bemerton in Wiltshire in 1630. He was an outstanding poet from an age of great writers, a fame he never knew. It was when he realized he was dying of tuberculosis that he sent the collection of poems in manuscript form to his friend Nicholas Ferrar to judge whether to burn them or to publish them. Herbert's notable poems include "The Church Porch," a doctrinal poem, and "The Altar" and "Easter Wings," pattern poems where the lines form the shape of the subject. Isaak Walton's biography of Herbert appeared in 1670.

Lewis listed *The Temple* as one of the ten books that most influenced his thinking and vocational attitude (see: READING OF C. S. LEWIS). He remarked about George Herbert in *Surprised by Joy:* "Here was a man who seemed to me to excel all the authors I had ever read in conveying the very quality of life as we actually live it from moment to moment."

Here is a typical poem of great beauty from *The Temple*:

Love

Love bade me welcome; yet my soul drew back,
Guilty of dust and sin.
But quick-eyed Love, observing me grow slack
From my first entrance in,
Drew nearer to me, sweetly questioning
If I lacked anything.

"A guest," I answered "worthy to be here":
Love said, "You shall be he."
"I, the unkind, ungrateful? Ah, my dear,
I cannot look on Thee."
Love took my hand, and smiling did reply,
"Who made the eyes but I?"

"Truth, Lord; but I have marred them: let my shame
Go where it doth deserve."
"And know you not," says Love, "who bore the blame?"
"My dear, then I will serve."
"You must sit down," says Love, "and taste my meat."
So I did sit and eat.

Terebinthia An island visited by the travelers in the tale of *The Voyage of the "Dawn Treader."** It lay off the coast of Narnia,* beyond Galma.* The island, a haunt of pirates, had been plagued by a terrible disease, and its main town was in quarantine. In *The Silver Chair,** King Caspian* seeks Aslan* there.

That Hideous Strength (1945); abridged paperback version (1955) The final volume of the science-fiction trilogy, which began with *Out of the Silent Planet** and *Perelandra* (Voyage to Venus)*. The third book continues C. S. Lewis's presentation of the problem of good and evil.* In this "modern fairy tale for grownups," Dr. Elwin Ransom* stays on earth. The setting is the small midland university town of Edgestow* just after the war. The "progressive element" among the fellows of Bracton College* engineer the sale of a piece of property called Bragdon Wood* to the N.I.C.E.,* the National Institute for Co-ordinated Experiments. According to Arthurian legend, the magician Merlin lay secretly in a trance within the wood, his "sleeping" body preserved from aging.

The N.I.C.E. was a sinister, totalitarian organization of technocrats—scientists given over to the pragmatic use of technology for social and individual control. Deeply involved in the institute was Dick Devine,* now Lord Feverstone. Ransom first encountered Devine before the war as the kidnapper, along with Professor Weston,* who took him off to Mars.

Mark Studdock,* a fellow in sociology at Bracton, is duped into working for the N.I.C.E., whereas his wife, Jane,* a research student, finds herself helping the other side, led by Ransom, now revealed as the great Pendragon of Logres. Her gift of second sight helps to locate Merlin and to provide vital intelligence. Merlin's ancient magic, linked into the power of the eldila* of Deep Heaven,* overcomes the evil of the N.I.C.E. In a satirical climax, Merlin revives the curse of Babel, confused speech, as a fitting judgment on people who have despised ordinary humanity.

This book, as a sequel to the previous stories set on other planets, brings matters "down to earth." This change of setting reveals the influence of Lewis's friend Charles Williams. The story is set on Thulcandra,* the Silent Planet Earth, so called because Earth is cut off by evil from the beatific language and worlds of Deep Heaven. In another sense, matters are brought "down to earth" because Lewis takes pains in characterizing the marriage and personalities of Mark and Jane Studdock. In the style of Charles Williams,* the supernatural world impinges upon the everyday world of ordinary people. There are other Williams-like touches also. Jane, like Damaris in *The Place of the Lion*, is engaged upon literary research. More notably, C. S. Lewis makes use of the mythical geography of Logres, the Arthurian matter that is the focus of Williams's unfinished cycle of poems.

As Lewis makes clear in his preface, his story illustrates the point that he made in one of his most forceful studies of ethics, *The Abolition of Man** (1943). The point is that a world that rejects objective principles of right and wrong, beauty and ugliness, also rejects what constitutes mankind's very nature and creates an unhumanity. The new society projected by the N.I.C.E. is the corruption of the Un-man* of Perelandra writ large.

As a study of evil, *That Hideous Strength* shows how wickedness sows the seeds of its own destruction. Professor Weston's forays into space with evil intent had allowed the ending of an ancient prohibition. This restriction provided that no inhabitants of Deep Heaven would ever come to the quarantined planet Earth until the very end of things. Now that bent mankind had tried to contaminate unfallen worlds such as Mars and Venus, however, the eldila of Deep Heaven could unleash their good powers through a suitable human agent—Merlin.

The novel has been criticized for being over-complex in structure. It has, for example, an uneasy mixture of satire and serious study of damnation, a mixture that worked in *The Screwtape Letters*.* Nevertheless, it is one of Lewis's fictions that makes the most impact upon its reader, revealing a power to portray ordinary human beings in a "realistic" setting. It is plausible as an anti-utopian parable of our times, such as Aldous Huxley's *Brave New World* (1932) and George Orwell's *1984* (1949). Furthermore, it was a necessary preparation for probably his best novel, *Till We Have Faces*.*

***Theism and Humanism,* Arthur James Balfour** (1915) This is one of ten books that Lewis claimed particularly shaped his thinking and vocational attitude (see READING OF C. S. LEWIS). Balfour* was a brilliant British prime minister who authored several works of philosophy. This book was based upon the prestigious Gifford Lectures given at the University of Glasgow in 1913-14. Balfour fervently believed, and argued in this book, that God, personal and infinite, was the origin of what was "most assured in knowledge, all that is, or seems, most beautiful in art or nature, and all that is, or seems, most noble in morality" (pp. 18-19). God must be central in a system of belief. Like Descartes, he saw God as the guarantor of knowledge. Indeed, wrote Balfour, God is

> the condition of scientific knowledge. If He is excluded from the causal series which produces beliefs, the cognitive series which justifies them is corrupted at the root. And it is only in a theistic setting that beauty can retain its deepest meaning, and love its brightest lustre, so these great truths of aesthetics and ethics are but half-truths, isolated and imperfect, unless we add to them a third. We must hold that reason and the works of reason have their source in God; that from Him they draw their inspiration; and that if they repudiate their origin, by this very act they proclaim their own insufficiency (p. 274).

Such ideas anticipate Lewis's arguments in the early chapters of *Miracles*,* particularly chapter 3, and elsewhere.

An earlier work, *Philosophic Doubt* (1879), was read appreciatively by Andrew Seth (later known as Professor Pringle-Pattison), who invited the young Balfour to address his philosophy class at Edinburgh University. The second half of the Gifford Lectures, delayed by the onset of war, was published as *Theism and Thought* in 1923. A lecture given in Oxford in 1909, "Beauty: and the Criticism of Beauty," contains insights that anticipate Lewis's thinking on aesthetics, in for instance *An Experiment in Criticism*.* Balfour asks: "Why should we be impatient because we can give no account of the characteristics common to all that is beautiful, when we can give no account of the characteristics common to all that is lovable?" He concludes: "Let us, then, be content, since we can do no better, that our admirations should be even as our loves" (*Essays Speculative and Political*). Like Lewis he distrusts the aesthete's distinction between high and low art.

Balfour had the astonishing ability to lecture, whether on philosophy or a political issue, virtually without notes. He would simply jot down several bare headings on the back of a long envelope. Such a method could sustain him for an hour-long, closely argued discourse. See also: IDEALISM AND C. S. LEWIS.

Theology, C. S. Lewis and C. S. Lewis, by profession, was a literary critic who also had philosophical interests. Anything that he wrote on theology, such as *Miracles*, *The Problem of Pain*, *Reflections on the Psalms*, or *Mere Christianity*, he regarded as the offerings of a layperson. Some of his opinions he presented explicitly as speculation. He tried to set forward an orthodox theology, what Francis Schaeffer called the historic Christian position, and he called this position "mere Christianity."* A few of the views he held (such as on the inspiration of Scripture), evangelicals could not be entirely happy with. However, many of his views were searingly painful to a liberal Christian—such as his supernaturalism;* his literal belief in heaven,* hell, and the devil; and his unflinching emphasis on the demands of truth. (He had no concept of a merely religious truth separate from reason and historical fact.) His many years as an atheist gave him a deep sympathy for the unbeliever's position.

An important contribution Lewis made to theology was on the nature of language and how language pictures reality, including the deep reality of the world that we do not normally see. His work on the relationship between meaning* and theoretical truth-claims shows that it is possible to hold that the Bible has the character of a propositional revelation from God. This is so even though most of the Bible is made up of historical narrative, with other sections of poetry, allegory, parable, and apocalyptic matter, and only a relatively small proportion of didactic material. Biblical history provides the meaning of the terms of the biblical propositions of the nature of God, sin, salvation, the Atonement, and the like. Biblical history, epitomized in the Gospels, combined the qualities of a good story with facticity (see: MYTH BECAME FACT). This kind of approach will bring more joy to evangelicals and other orthodox groups than to liberals.

C. S. Lewis's great dislike of liberal theology is expressed in an essay greatly admired by Austin Farrer:* "Fern Seeds and Elephants" (also called, "Modern Theology and Biblical Criticism"), first published in *Christian Reflections.** His orthodoxy was a traditional Anglican kind, and like Dorothy L. Sayers* and G. K. Chesterton,* he delighted in dogma.

See also: THEOLOGY OF ROMANCE.

Theology of romance Like his friends J. R. R. Tolkien* and Charles Williams,* C. S. Lewis worked in his fiction according to a theology of romanticism that owed much to the nineteenth-century writer who was Lewis's mentor, George MacDonald.* The term "romantic theologian," Lewis tells us, was invented by Charles Williams. What Lewis says about Williams in his introduction to *Essays Presented to Charles Williams** applies also to himself:

> A romantic theologian does not mean one who is romantic about theology but one who is theological about romance, one who considers the theological implications of those experiences which are called romantic. The belief that the most serious and ecstatic experiences either of human love or of imaginative literature have such theological implications and that they can be healthy and fruitful only if the implications are diligently thought out and severely lived, is the root principle of all his [Williams's] work.

"The imaginative man in me is older, more continuously operative, and in that sense more basic than either the religious writer or the critic," Lewis confessed in a letter written in 1954. His imagination had made him try to be a poet and after his conversion "to embody my religious belief in symbolical or mythopoeic forms." These forms included *The Screwtape Letters** and the science-fiction trilogy written for adults, and The Chronicles of Narnia,* which he wrote for children—not to give them what they wanted, "but because the fairy-tale was the genre best fitted for what I wanted to say."

Whereas a key preoccupation of Charles Williams was romantic love, C. S. Lewis was "theological" about romantic longing or joy,* and Tolkien reflected deeply on the theological implications of fairy tale and myth,* particularly the aspect of subcreation.*

In a doctoral thesis, *Romantic Religion in the Works of Owen Barfield, C. S. Lewis, Charles Williams, and J. R. R. Tolkien*, R. J. Reilly saw C. S. Lewis as an advocate of "romantic religion." This was the "attempt to reach religious truths by means and techniques traditionally called romantic, and . . . to defend and justify these techniques and attitudes of romanticism by holding that they have religious sanction." C. S. Lewis was not doing anything new in this. Rather, he was presenting in modern terms what seemed to be a normal attitude of mind a few centuries ago. The practice was perhaps beginning to be lost in the seventeenth century, when John Bunyan was forced to defend what now could be called "romantic religion" in his author's apology at the beginning of *The Pilgrim's Progress*. Bunyan's reasoning in that prologue follows lines similar to Lewis's defense of the imagination.*

In *Surprised by Joy*,* C. S. Lewis reported some of his sensations—responses to natural beauty, and literary and artistic responses—in the belief that others would recognize similar experiences of their own.

Several structural features of fairy tales and other stories that embodied myths fascinated J. R. R. Tolkien. These features are all related to a sense of imaginative decorum, a sense that imagining can, in itself, be good or bad, as rules or norms apply strictly in fantasy, as they do in thought. Meaning* can only be created by skill or art, and plays an essential part in human thought and language. As Tolkien said, "The incarnate mind, the tongue, and the tale are in our world coeval." As Barfield has shown in his introduction to the new edition of *Poetic Diction*,* the ideal in logical positivism and related types of modern linguistic philosophy is, strictly, absurd; it systematically eliminates meanings from the framing of truths, expecting thereby to guarantee their validity. In Tolkien's view, the opposite is the case. The richer the meanings involved in the framing of truths, the more certainty of their validity.

G. K. Chesterton* once wrote that we should sometimes take our tea in the top of a tree, as our perceptions tend to get dulled. One of the essential features of the fairy tale or mythopoeic fantasy is the sense of recovery*—the regaining of health or a clear view of things. Tolkien pointed out that we too often get caught in the specific corridor of daily, mundane life, and we lose a view of "things as we are (or were) meant to see them." Entry into an imaginary world "shocks us more fully awake than we are for most of our lives." C. S. Lewis said the latter of myth,* but it applies to this feature of recovery. Part of this recovery is a sense of imaginative unity, a survey of the depths of space and time. The essential patterns of reality are seen in a fresh way.

Charles Williams's "romantic religion," though concerned with romantic love, took the form of what he characteristically called the Way of the Affirmation of Images. In *The Allegory of Love*,* much admired by Williams, C. S. Lewis pointed out that there are basically two ways in which the mind may develop an essential equivalence between material and immaterial, natural and spiritual. When a person begins with immaterial fact—such as qualities like beauty or joy*—and invents *visibilia* to express them, he is allegorizing. It is possible, however, to reverse this process and to view the material world as itself a copy of the invisible world. When a person attempts to read something else through the sensible—to discover the idea or meaning in the copy—he is engaged in symbolism* or sacramentalism. "The allegorist," argues Lewis, "leaves the given—his passions—to talk of that which is confessedly less real, which is a fiction. The symbolist leaves the given to find that which is more real." Later C. S. Lewis was to write that allegory in its highest form approaches myth. The Neoplatonic idea of sacramentalism (see: PLATO) applies to Charles Williams, though when he leaves behind the given to find its meaning, he retains the importance of the given. It has a greater reality that can now be seen. Thus in romantic love (as when Dante saw Beatrice) the Beloved is both an image of Divine Beauty and important in himself or herself. To care for Divine Beauty is to care for the ordinary yet transfigured mortal before you. This is Philip's experience in Williams's novel *Shadows of Ecstasy*:

> Now, suddenly, he understood Rosamond's arm when she leant forward to pass a plate to her sister; somehow that arm always made him think of the Downs against the sky. There was a line, a curved beauty, a thing that spoke to both mind and heart; a thing that was there for ever. And Rosamond? Rosamond was like them, she was there for ever. It occurred to him that, if she was, then her occasional slowness when he was trying to explain something was there for ever. Well, after all, Rosamond was only human; she couldn't be absolutely perfect. And then as she stretched out her arm again he cried out that she was perfect, she was more than perfect; the movement of her arm was something frightfully important, and now it was gone.

This interplay between the reality of the image (here the image of perfection) and the reality pictured by the image is captured in Williams's distinctive doctrine of the twofold Way of the Affirmation and Rejection of Images. Here we say of any created person or thing in reference to the Creator: "This also is Thou; neither is this Thou." In his *The Descent of the Dove*, Williams described the principle like this:

> The one Way was to affirm all things orderly until the universe throbbed with vitality; the other to reject all things until there was nothing anywhere but He. The Way of Affirmation was to develop great art and romantic love and marriage and philosophy and social justice; the Way of Rejection was to break out continually in the profound mystical documents of the soul, the records of the great psychological masters of Christendom. All was involved in Christendom. . . .

The validity of both aspects of the twofold Way was connected in Williams's thinking with another key doctrine of Christianity—coinherence. This doctrine was captured for him, characteristically, in the beautiful Image of the City. This social image brings out, for Williams, the dependence of each of us upon others' labors and gifts and the necessity of bearing one another's burdens.

Lewis suggests that imaginative literature creates a symbolic perception of reality. He gave a very simple illustration of this kind of perception in his essay "On Stories," explaining the logic of the fairy story, which "is as strict as that of a realistic novel, though different." Referring to *The Wind in the Willows*, he asked:

> Does anyone believe that Kenneth Grahame made an arbitrary choice when he gave his principal character the form of a toad, or that a stag, a pigeon, a lion would have done as well. The choice is based on the fact that the real toad's face has a grotesque resemblance to a certain kind of human face—a rather apoplectic face with a fatuous grin on it. . . . Looking at the creature we thus see, isolated and fixed, an aspect of human vanity in its funniest and most pardonable form.

The Encyclopedia of Fantasy points out the subversive nature of fantasy in encouraging a perceptual shift: "It could be argued that, if fantasy (and debatably the literature of the fantastic as a whole) has a purpose other than to entertain, it is to show readers *how to perceive*; an extension of the argument is that fantasy may try to alter readers' perception of reality." This point is explained more, as follows: "The best fantasy introduces its readers into a playground of rethought perception, where there are no restrictions other than those of the human imagination. . . . Most full-fantasy texts have at their core the urge to *change* the reader; that is, full fantasy is by definition a subversive literary form."

Lewis is a key twentieth-century example of a writer of Christian fantasy, along with his friends J. R. R. Tolkien and Charles Williams. These writers stand in a rich tradition dating back to early stories of King Arthur. Such writers give a high place to the imagination* as an organ of meaning.*

In the light of a theological perspective on romance like Lewis's, the definition of fantasy in *The Encyclopedia of Fantasy* is helpful: "A fantasy text is a self-coherent narrative. When set in this world, it tells a story which is impossible in the world as we perceive it; when set in an otherworld, that otherworld will be impossible, though stories set there may be possible in its terms." This self-coherence requires belief in some kind of over-arching story. Thus the fantasy text might well differ from modernism and postmodernism in its use of the fantastic. Both modernism and postmodernism, according to the *Encyclopedia*, question the very nature of story in their different ways.

The imagination for C. S. Lewis is concerned with apprehending realities (even if they belong to the unseen world), rather than with grasping concepts. Imaginative invention is justifiable in its own right—it does not have the burden of carrying didactic truths.

This is why good works of imagination cannot be reduced to "morals" and lessons, although lessons can be derived from them, and the truer the work, the greater the lessons that can be drawn from it. In a review of Tolkien's *The Lord of the Rings,* Lewis noted that "What shows that we are reading myth, not allegory, is that there are no pointers to a specifically theological, or political, or psychological application. A myth points, for each reader, to the realm he lives in most. It is a master key; use it on what door you like." People may ask, "Why use fantasy to make a serious point?" Because, Lewis answered, the writer wants

> to say that the real life of men is of that mythical and heroic quality. One can see the principle at work in [Tolkien's] characterisation. Much that in a realistic work would be done by "character delineation" is here done simply by making the character an elf, a dwarf, or a hobbit. The imagined beings have their insides on the outside; they are visible souls. And Man as a whole, Man pitted against the universe, have we seen him at all till we see that he is like a hero in a fairy tale?

"The value of the myth is that it takes all the things we know and restores to them the rich significance which has been hidden by 'the veil of familiarity,'" he continued.

> The child enjoys his cold meat (otherwise dull to him) by pretending it is buffalo, just killed with his own bow and arrow. And the child is wise. The real meat comes back to him more savory for having been dipped in a story; you might say that only then is it the real meat. . . . By putting bread, gold, horse, apple, or the very roads into a myth, we do not retreat from reality: we rediscover it.

And similarly he wrote in "Sometimes Fairy Stories May Say Best What Needs to Be Said" that although this sort of writing works with some readers but not with others, when it works, fantasy can "generalize while remaining concrete" and "at its best it can do more: it can give us experiences we have never had and thus, instead of 'commenting on life,' can add to it." This has a special importance for Christian communicators because fantasy can "steal past" the religious associations and demands that destroy one's ability to feel the truth of the Christian revelation as one should. "[B]y casting all these things into an imaginary world, stripping them of their stained-glass and Sunday-school associations, one could make them for the first time appear in their potency." The writer could then "steal past those watchful dragons."

Out of this belief about the nature and necessity of the imagination, the features of Lewis's theology of romance emerge: a sense of otherness,* a recognition of the numinous,* a longing for joy, the understanding of art as subcreation,* and a yearning for recovery* and healing. Central to Lewis's theology of romance are several theological themes including God,* cosmic war,* myth became fact,* transposition,* and undeception and recognition.*

They Asked for a Paper (1962) A collection of literary and theological pieces, including several reprinted from *Transposition and Other Addresses.** The collection contains "*De Descriptione Temporum*,"* "The Literary Impact of the Authorized Version," "Hamlet: The Prince or the Poem?," "Kipling's World," "Sir Walter Scott," "Lilies That

Fester," "Psychoanalysis and Literary Criticism," "The Inner Ring,"* "Is Theology Poetry?," "Transposition,"* "On Obstinacy in Belief," and "The Weight of Glory."

They Stand Together (1979) Walter Hooper had the opportunity to assist C. S. Lewis with his correspondence near the end of his life and spent ten years editing Lewis's letters before publishing them in *They Stand Together*. In an interview Mr. Hooper told the author that this correspondence would easily run into many volumes. From this vast output he decided to select letters to one man, Arthur Greeves, a close friend of Lewis's over a period of almost fifty years—that is, from his atheistic mid-teens to literally days before Jack Lewis died. Walter Hooper's collection contains 296 letters that give rich insight into Lewis's life and the development of his Christian thought and imagination.*

As Mr. Hooper pointed out to the author, this selection makes up a more complete autobiography than *Surprised by Joy*,* where Lewis tells his life from a particular point of view—his awareness of joy,* the longing that no earthly philosophy or bodily pleasure could satisfy, and how only Christian theism made sense of it. Also that story finishes at C. S. Lewis's conversion.

A factor that fascinated Mr. Hooper in compiling the letters was the sheer detective work involved. He told the author, "I like detective work very much. I like details, and I like mysteries. I knew that I was up against something extremely difficult in dating these letters. But they do not make sense, perfect sense, unless they are in the right order." At the end of his life, Arthur Greeves had tried to put the correct dates on the letters from Lewis but was often confused. "Greeves notices, say, that Lewis had taken a holiday in Cornwall, so he assumes that a letter from Cornwall was written at the same time. There are really two visits, and the letters are years apart. When you put them together, you have to stretch the sense in them. Once you put them in their right place, the sense comes through—you get so much more out of them."

The biggest mystery was why there were originally so few letters toward the end of the correspondence. It was solved by accident. Walter Hooper says that in 1974, "I wrote on other business to the headmaster of Campbell College, Belfast, about one of Lewis's friends. He wrote back and told me that Greeves' cousin, Lisbeth Greeves, had had put in her keeping by Arthur a number of letters that dealt with his brother's alcoholism." As Major W. H. Lewis* was dead, and his alcoholism was now well known, Mr. Hooper felt that these letters, with their firsthand accounts, should be included. His brother's alcoholism "was a very great problem for C. S. Lewis," one of the many that he shared with Arthur Greeves in the letters. This is why in one place C. S. Lewis speaks of Arthur as "my father confessor." One letter vividly recounts his conversion to Christianity. We also learn much about the Ulsterman Arthur Greeves from these letters, though Lewis kept few of Arthur's side of the correspondence. The foundation of their friendship* was a common insight into the joy, with its longing, that was the main constant theme of Lewis's life and writings. See also: *LETTERS OF C. S. LEWIS.*

Thulcandra The name for planet Earth in the language of Old Solar* in *Out of the Silent Planet** and the other books in C. S. Lewis's science-fiction trilogy. See also: THE PLANETS.

Till We Have Faces (1956) At different times C. S. Lewis regarded *Till We Have Faces* or *Perelandra** as his best book. He retells an old classical myth, that of Cupid and Psyche,* in the realistic setting of a historical novel. The book is set several hundred years B.C. in the imaginary and barbaric country of Glome* somewhere to the north of the Greeklands. The story is told through the eyes of Queen Orual* of Glome. Having heard a legend in the nearby land of Essur* similar to the myth of Cupid and Psyche, she seeks to set the record straight. The gods, she claims, have distorted the story in certain key respects. She recognizes herself and her half-sister Psyche in the newly sprung-up legend.

The gods, she says, had called her deep love for Psyche jealousy. They had also said that she saw Psyche's palace,* whereas Orual had only seen shapes in a mist, a fantasy that momentarily resembled a palace. There had been no evidence that Psyche had married a god and dwelt in his palace. Orual therefore recounts her version of the story, being as truthful as possible. She had a reader in mind from the Greeklands, and she agreed with the Greek demand for truth and rational honesty. She has to tell her life story to do this properly.

Orual is a princess, the daughter of a barbarous and callous king, Trom,* and she has a sister, Redival.* Orual's mother died young, and Trom marries again. The stepmother dies giving birth to the beautiful Psyche. Psyche's outstanding beauty contrasts with Orual's ugliness (in later life she wore a veil). The king engages a Greek slave, named The Fox,* to teach his daughters. The Fox is able to pass on his Greek Stoicism and rationalism to Psyche and Orual, though the daughters never reject the paganism of their land.

In Glome the goddess Ungit,* a deformed version of Venus, is worshiped. After a drought and other disasters, a lot falls on the innocent Psyche to be sacrificed on the Gray Mountains to the Shadowbrute or West-wind,* the god of the mountain.

Sometime afterwards Orual, accompanied by a faithful member of the king's guard, Bardia,* seeks the bones of Psyche to bury her. Finding no trace of Psyche, Bardia and Orual explore farther and find the beautiful and sheltered valley of the god. Here Psyche is living, wearing rags but full of health. She claims to be married to the god of the mountain, whose face she has never seen. Orual, afraid that the "god" is a monster or outlaw, persuades Psyche, against her will, to shine a light on her husband's face while he is sleeping. As in the Greek myth, Psyche as a result is condemned to wander the earth, doing impossible tasks. In the terrible storm that disfigures the valley, Orual seems to see a beautiful god who tells her, "You also shall be Psyche."

Orual's account goes on to record the bitter years of her suffering and grief at the loss of Psyche, haunted by the fantasy that she can hear Psyche's weeping. Succeeding King Trom, she reforms the kingdom and does her best to rule justly, applying civilized principles learned via The Fox from the Greeks. She becomes a great queen and a renowned warrior. Late in life she decides to travel the wider world, and it is then she hears what she believes to be the warped story of Orual, Psyche, and the god, causing her to write her own account. Most of *Till We Have Faces* is made up of this narration.

The short second part of the novel—still in Orual's voice—continues a few days later. Orual has undergone a devastating undeception,* whereby in painful self-knowledge she discovers how her affection for Psyche had become poisoned by possessiveness. Her clinging and impossible love for Bardia had also blighted his life. In this discovery, which allowed the restoration of a true love for Psyche, was the consolation that she had also been Psyche, as the god had said. She had suffered on Psyche's behalf, in a substitutionary manner, bearing her burdens and thus easing her tasks. By what Charles Williams* called "the Way of Exchange," Orual had thus helped Psyche to be reunited with her divine husband. With the curing of her poisoned love, Orual in a vision sees that she herself has become beautiful. She has gained a face in becoming a full person. After this reconciliation, the aged Queen Orual dies, her narration ending with her.

This novel is unlike Lewis's other fiction and is consequently less easy to interpret. It repays several readings. One key to *Till We Have Faces* is the theme of love. It is helpful to see Lewis's study *The Four Loves** as parallel to it, in the way that *The Abolition of Man** is parallel to *That Hideous Strength*.* The loves of affection and eros are particularly explored. Another key to understanding the novel is the idea of substitution and atonement. Psyche is prepared to die for the sake of the people of Glome. Orual is a substitute for much of Psyche's suffering and pain.

Psyche herself represents a Christlikeness, though she is not intended as a figure of Christ. Lewis wrote in explanation to Clyde S. Kilby: "Psyche is an instance of the *anima naturaliter Christiana* making the best of the pagan religion she is brought up in and thus being guided (but always 'under the cloud,' always in terms of her own imagination or that of her people) toward the true God. She is in some ways like Christ, not because she is a symbol of Him, but because every good man or woman is like Christ."

This limitation of the imagination of paganism* comes out in the ugly figures of Ungit and the Shadowbrute, deformed images of the brighter Greek deities of Venus (Aphrodite) and Cupid. The truth that these poor images are trying to glimpse is even more beautiful, free of the vindictiveness of the Greek deities. Psyche is able to see a glimpse of the true God himself in all his beauty and in his legitimate demand for a perfect sacrifice.

A further key to this novel lies in the theme of the conflict of imagination* and reason, so important to Lewis himself throughout his life, and vividly portrayed in *Surprised by Joy*.* The final identification of the half-sisters Orual and Psyche in the story represents the harmony and satisfaction of both reason and imagination made fully possible, Lewis believed, only within Christianity. See also: *THE FOUR LOVES*.

Timeless at Heart See: UNDECEPTIONS.

Tirian, King In *The Last Battle*,* he is the final king of Narnia* who, along with his dear friend Jewel,* the unicorn, makes a heroic last stand against the Calormene* and other forces of darkness. Eustace Scrubb* and Jill Pole* come to help him in answer to his prayer to Aslan.* See also: NARNIA, HISTORY.

Tisroc The Calormene* sovereign.

Toadpipe Secretary to Screwtape* in *The Screwtape Letters*.*

Tolkien, J. R. R. (1892-1973) John Ronald Reuel Tolkien was one of C. S. Lewis's closest friends and, like Lewis, valued friendship* highly. Until the 1960s, Professor Tolkien was known mainly to a few learned scholars. Now in the post-hobbit era, he has been read by many millions of people. BBC radio successfully dramatized his *The Lord of the Rings* over thirteen hours. Since his death *The Silmarillion* and related material have been published. This book is set in an earlier age of the fictitious Middle-earth and related worlds than the adventures of the Bagginses.

Tolkien was born in South Africa in 1892, but his family soon moved to England. He attended King Edward VI Grammar School on the outskirts of Birmingham and was familiar with Worcestershire and the Vale of Evesham. It is said that the Malvern Hills helped to inspire the mountains of Gondor in Middle-earth. After graduating from Exeter College, Oxford, he saw bitter action in the First World War, losing all but one of his best friends.

It was during the Great War years that Tolkien began working on *The Silmarillion*, writing "The Fall of Gondolin" in 1917 while convalescent. In fact, in general plot and in several major episodes most of the legendary cycle of *The Silmarillion* was already constructed before 1930—before the writing and publication of *The Hobbit*, the forerunner of *The Lord of the Rings*. In the latter books there are numerous references to matters covered by *The Silmarillion*—ruins of once-great places, sites of long-ago battles, strange and beautiful names from the deep past, and elvish swords made in Gondolin, before its fall, for the Goblin Wars.

Tolkien's lifelong study and teaching of languages was the spring and nourishment of his imaginative creations. Just as science-fiction writers generally make use of plausible technological inventions and possibilities, Tolkien has used his deep and expert knowledge of language in his fantasies. He created in his youth two forms of the elvish tongue, starting a process that led to a history and geography to surround these languages and peoples to speak them (and other tongues). He explains: "I had to posit a basic and phonetic structure of Primitive Elvish, and then modify this by a series of changes (such as actually do occur in known languages) so that the two end results would have a consistent structure and character, but be quite different."

The imaginative possibilities of an invented language were also explored by his friend C. S. Lewis, under his influence. Lewis acknowledges a great debt, especially to Tolkien's idea of subcreation.* Lewis makes use of the possibilities of his own imagined language, Old Solar,* in *Out of the Silent Planet** and its sequels. The debt was mutual: It is unlikely that Tolkien would have completed *The Lord of the Rings* for publication without Lewis's fervent encouragement.

After the Great War, Tolkien began university teaching. After a few years he moved to Oxford to become Rawlingson and Bosworth Professor of Anglo-Saxon; this was in 1926. It was in this year that he met C. S. Lewis. Their long friendship was soon to begin. Lewis had then been an English don at Magdalen College for one year. They met at the English faculty meeting on May 11, 1926, and Lewis was not amused, recording in his diary: "He is a smooth, pale, fluent little chap. Can't read Spenser because of the forms—thinks language is the real thing in the English School—thinks all literature is written for the amusement of men between thirty and forty—we ought to vote ourselves out of existence if we are honest. . . . No harm in him: only needs a smack or two."

Any initial antipathy, however, was soon forgotten. Within a year or so they were meeting in each other's rooms and talking far into the night. These conversations proved crucial both for the two men's writings and for Lewis's conversion to Christianity. As the Ulsterman Lewis remarked in *Surprised by Joy**: "Friendship with . . . J. R. R. Tolkien . . . marked the breakdown of two old prejudices. At my first coming into the world I had been (implicitly) warned never to trust a Papist, and at my first coming into the English Faculty (explicitly) never to trust a philologist. Tolkien was both."

A typical note of the time occurs in a letter from C. S. Lewis to his Ulster friend Arthur Greeves* in December 1929: "Tolkien came back with me to college and sat discoursing of the gods and giants of Asgard for three hours."

Tolkien himself recalled sharing with Lewis his work on *The Silmarillion*, influencing Lewis's science-fiction trilogy. The pattern of their future lives, including the later Inklings,* was being formed. Tolkien remembered: "In the early days of our association Jack used to come to my house and I read aloud to him *The Silmarillion* so far as it had then gone, including a very long poem: 'Beren and Luthien.'"

The gist of one of the long conversations between Lewis and Tolkien was fortunately recorded by Lewis in another letter to Arthur Greeves in October 1931. It was a crucial factor in his conversion, as he moved from mere theism to Christianity. Tolkien argued that human stories tend to fall into certain patterns and can embody myth. In the Christian Gospels there are all the best elements of good stories, including fairy stories, with the astounding additional factor that everything is also true in the actual, primary world. The Bible combines mythic and historical, factual truth, with no divorce between the two. C. S. Lewis's conversion deepened the friendship. (See: MYTH BECAME FACT.)

Tolkien's academic writings were sparing and rare. In 1937 he published an article entitled "Beowulf: the Monsters and the Critics," which, according to Donald K. Fry, "completely altered the course of Beowulf studies." It was a defense of the artistic unity of that Old English tale. In 1938 Tolkien gave his Andrew Lang Lecture at St. Andrews university, "On Fairy Stories," which was later published in *Essays Presented to Charles Williams**—the Inklings' tribute to the writer who had a great deal in common with Tolkien and Lewis. The address sets outs Tolkien's basic ideas concerning imagination,* fantasy, and subcreation.

The professor's famous children's story, *The Hobbit,* came out in 1937. He continued with its adult sequel, *The Lord of the Rings*, more and more leaving aside his first love, *The Silmarillion*. Writing the sequel was a long, painstaking task, undertaken in the converted garage of his Oxford home (he had four children). At one point, he did not touch the manuscript for a whole year. He wrote on it in the evenings, for he was fully engaged in his university work. During the Second World War years and afterwards, he read portions to the Inklings or simply to Lewis alone. He attended almost all the Inklings meetings, even though he was very busy. In 1945 Tolkien was honored by a new chair at Oxford, Merton Professor of English Language and Literature, reflecting his by-now wider interests. He was not now so cool to the idea of teaching literature at the university as he had been previously. Tolkien retained the chair until his retirement in 1959.

With C. S. Lewis's marriage to Joy Davidman* the relationship between the two friends was not sustained so deeply, and Tolkien grieved over the change. The scholarly storyteller's retirement years were spent revising the Ring trilogy, brushing up and publishing some shorter pieces of story and poetry, and working on various drafts of *The*

Silmarillion. Tolkien also spent much time dodging reporters and youthful Americans as the 1960s marked the exploding popularity of his fantasies when his readership went from thousands to millions. An interviewer at the time, Daphne Castell, tried to capture his personal manner: "He talks very quickly, striding up and down the converted garage which serves as his study, waving his pipe, making little jabs with it to mark important points; and now and then jamming it back in, and talking round it. . . . He has the habits of speech of the true storyteller. . . . Every sentence is important, and lively, and striking."

FURTHER READING

Humphrey Carpenter, *J. R. R. Tolkien: A Biography* (1977); *The Inklings: C. S. Lewis, J. R. R. Tolkien, Charles Williams and Their Friends* (1978); Editor of *The Letters of J. R. R. Tolkien* (1981).

Daphne Castell, "The Realms of Tolkien," in *New Worlds SF*, Vol. 50, No. 168, 1966.

Colin Duriez, *The Tolkien and Middle-earth Handbook* (1992).

Tombs of the ancient kings In the tale of *The Horse and His Boy.*,* tombs north of the great city of Tashbaan,* capital of Calormen.* Reputed to be haunted, they looked like giant beehives. Shasta (Cor*) spent the night there. He had agreed to rendezvous at the tombs with Aravis* and the two Narnian* talking horses, Bree* and Hwin.*

Transposition C. S. Lewis's name for a concept he explained in one of the most important addresses he ever gave, published in *Transposition and Other Addresses.** The talk was preached originally as a sermon on Whitsunday in Mansfield College, Oxford,* May 28, 1944.

C. S. Lewis's theory of transposition has affinities with the ideas of another Oxford Christian thinker, Michael Polanyi (1891-1976). Transposition, says Lewis, is an "adaptation of a richer to a poorer medium." No denigration of the poorer medium is implied, only an assessment of its necessary limits. In a Christian universe, as understood by C. S. Lewis, all parts have value in themselves.

To explain the idea of transposition, C. S. Lewis begins his address considering the phenomenon of speaking in tongues at Pentecost. Looking from below, in a purely naturalist way, one would say that the phenomenon was "merely" or "nothing but" an affair of the nerves and sensations, resulting in gibberish. Seen from above, however, both the fact and the meaning are clear—this event is a supernatural act of the Holy Spirit. The spiritual is transposed into physical language.

In a similar way, in our emotional life we can reduce emotion to mere sensation if we refuse to see its meaning on a higher level. An identical sensation can stand for a variety of emotions, as the emotions are a richer medium translating into a poorer one.

This point about the danger of reduction came home vividly to Lewis during his conversion to Christianity. In his quest for joy* he suddenly realized that he had made the basic mistake of identifying the quality of joy, or inconsolable longing, with the sensation that it aroused. When his attention focused on the sensation, joy itself vanished, leaving only its traces. He had to focus outside of himself on the object of the joy. This dramatically changed the nature of his quest, which helped to lead him eventually to God himself.

Lewis illustrated the principle of transposition in language and music. He points out: "If you are to translate from a language which has a large vocabulary into a language which has a small vocabulary, then you must be allowed to use several words in more than one sense. If you are to write a language with twenty-two vowel sounds in an alphabet with only five vowel characters then you must be allowed to give each of those five characters more than one value. If you are making a piano version of a piece originally scored for an orchestra, then the same piano notes which represent flutes in one passage must also represent violins in another."

Lewis found the concept of transposition very helpful in understanding the incarnation of Christ. The insight of one of the creeds is that the Incarnation worked "not by conversion of the Godhead into flesh, but by taking of the Manhood into God." The idea of humanity being veritably drawn into deity seemed to C. S. Lewis a kind of transposition. It was like what happens, for example, "when a sensation (not in itself a pleasure) is drawn into the joy it accompanies."

The idea of transposition also helped him understand the bodily resurrection and underpins his discussion of nature and supernature in *Miracles*.* He didn't conceive of the natural and spiritual or think of the mind and the body in a kind of Platonic hierarchy, where the natural and the bodily is less real than the spiritual and the mental. Rather, he saw the relationship as transpositional, with the spiritual and natural worlds as equally parts of God's creation. In a fine passage, C. S. Lewis speculates that there may be many natures in a transpositional relationship with each other. "There cannot, from the nature of the case, be evidence that God never created and never will create more than one system. Each system would be at least extra-natural in relation to all the others; and if any one of them is more concrete, more permanent, more excellent, and richer than another, it will be to that other supernatural. Nor will a partial contact between any two obliterate their distinctiveness. In that way there might be natures piled upon natures to any height God pleased, each supernatural to that below it and subnatural to that which surpassed it. But the tenor of Christian teaching is that we are actually living in a situation even more complex than that. A new nature is being not merely made out of an old one. We live amid all the anomalies, inconveniences, hopes, and excitements of a house that is being rebuilt. Something is being pulled down, and something is going up in its place" (*Miracles*, chapter XVI).

Michael Polanyi develops ideas rather similar to Lewis's transposition into a theory of how we know and what we know. His theory has the value of avoiding subjectivism (as in existentialist thinking) and objectivism (as in positivism). We know, and grow in knowledge, by indwelling and being committed to what we know, not by artificially trying to stand outside our knowledge and to neutrally observe it. It is from a vantage point that we see truth. If our attention becomes focused on our vantage point, we are no longer attending to the truth. Our point of vantage provides clues that can never be fully expressed, and we have skills that we have to rely on. For Polanyi, the meaning of the particulars of a lower level resides in a higher level. We could say that the higher level has been transposed into the lower level. If we take the genetic code, the meaning of biological life cannot be reduced to the physics and chemistry of that code. It would be like saying that the meaning of a tape recording of Beethoven's *Fifth Symphony* could be reduced to a description of the magnetic patterns on the tape.

C. S. Lewis's notion of transposition has led some to see his theology as sacramental. Lewis does write: "The word symbolism is not adequate in all cases to cover the relation between the higher medium and its transposition in a lower. . . . If I had to name the relation I should call it not symbolical but sacramental." However, the term *sacramental* doesn't seem entirely adequate either to Lewis, at least as it is understood by Roman Catholic, Lutheran, or Orthodox theologians, all of whom use it in different senses. Lewis regarded transposition as most like incarnation, rather than as most like transubstantiation or consubstantiation. In his theory of transposition C. S. Lewis is making a metaphysical case that (as the thought of Polanyi seems to show) has important consequences for theories of knowledge. He is not, I think, making a theological point about the means of grace and salvation. The Incarnation in itself is not the means of grace, rather Christ's death on the cross.

That C. S. Lewis was aware of the consequences of his view of transposition for knowledge is clear from his ideas on meaning and imagination.* Like his friend Owen Barfield,* he believed that mankind has moved away from a unitary consciousness into a division of subject and object. Theoretical reasoning abstracts from real things, real emotions, real events. In his theory of transposition Lewis is revealing his tangible vision of how all things—especially the natural and the supernatural—cohere. He saw this desirable unity, for example, in the gospel story, where the quality of myth* is not lost in the historical facticity of the events. There is no separation of story and history (see: MYTH BECAME FACT).

> There is . . . in the history of thought, as elsewhere, a pattern of death and rebirth. The old, richly imaginative thought which still survives in Plato has to submit to the deathlike, but indispensable, process of log-

> ical analysis: nature and spirit, matter and mind, fact and myth, the literal and metaphorical, have to be more and more sharply separated, till at last a purely mathematical universe and a purely subjective mind confront one another across an unbridgeable chasm. But from this descent, also, if thought itself is to survive, there must be re-ascent and the Christian conception provides for this. Those who attain the glorious resurrection will see the dry bones clothed again with flesh, the fact and the myth remarried, the literal and the metaphorical rushing together. (*Miracles*, chapter XVI)

Transposition and Other Addresses (1949) A selection of addresses given by C. S. Lewis during the war years and immediately afterwards, including a famous sermon, one of the outstanding of such documents in the history of Christianity. The contents are "Transposition,"* "Learning in War-Time,"* "Membership," "The Inner Ring,"* and the sermon "The Weight of Glory."

Trom In *Till We Have Faces*,* the bullying and insensitive king of Glome,* father of Orual,* Redival,* and Psyche.* His savage temper led him on impulse to beat his daughters (usually Orual, whose ugly face he despised), send a faithful servant to certain death in the silver mines, and castrate Tarin,* a young officer who had flirted with Redival. When the lot fell on Psyche to be the atoning sacrifice, his feeling was of relief that he was spared, rather than sorrow for his daughter. Later his conscience troubled him as he lay dying, and he mistook the veiled Orual for Psyche, come back to haunt him.

Trufflehunter In the story of *Prince Caspian*,* a badger and loyal Old Narnian who helps Caspian* against the tyrant King Miraz.* See also: TALKING ANIMALS.

Trumpkin the dwarf In *Prince Caspian*,* Trumpkin is the dwarf rescued by the Pevensie* children from some of the men of King Miraz.* Trumpkin is a loyal Old Narnian, and he leads them to the hideout of Prince Caspian* in Aslan's How.* The dwarf is referred to as the D.L.F. (the Dear Little Friend). By the time of the events recorded in *The Voyage of the "Dawn Treader,"** he is Caspian's* regent, and later, in *The Silver Chair,** he is an aged lord chancellor.

Trunia In *Till We Have Faces*,* a prince of Phars,* a country neighboring Glome.* He was at war with his surly brother Argan* and the old king, their father. After Orual* kills Argan in single combat, Trunia is proclaimed king of Phars and marries Redival.* Their son Daaran* is pronounced heir to Glome's throne by the virgin Queen Orual.

Mr. Tumnus A faun first encountered by Lucy Pevensie* as she stepped through the wardrobe into the land of Narnia,* as told in *The Lion, the Witch and the Wardrobe*.* For not handing Lucy over to the White Witch,* Tumnus is punished by being turned to stone. He is later restored by Aslan,* the great lion. In the tale of *The Horse and His Boy*,* set in the same period, Mr. Tumnus is with the visiting Narnian party in Tashbaan,* the capital of Calormen.*

C. S. Lewis tells us that the story of *The Lion, the Witch and the Wardrobe*, and thus the idea for the entire Chronicles of Narnia,* began with Mr. Tumnus. "The Lion all began with a picture of a Faun carrying an umbrella and parcels in a snowy wood. This picture had been in my mind since I was about sixteen. Then one day, when I was about forty, I said to myself: 'Let's try to make a story about it.'"

Tynan, Kenneth (1927-1980) Drama critic Kenneth Tynan was one of C. S. Lewis's most famous pupils at Magdalen College, Oxford.* Tynan was there from 1945-1949. In an interview given shortly before he died, he confessed: "Lewis was undoubtedly the most powerful and formative influence of my whole life up to that point. I found him the most impressive mind I had ever seen in action." Like others, Tynan compared Lewis to Dr. Samuel Johnson: "He had the breadth and clarity of mind . . . he had the same swiftness to grasp the heart of a problem and the same sort of pouncing intelligence to follow it through to its conclusion. I found him immensely invigorating, stimulating and inspiring."

As a teacher Tynan found Lewis "incomparable." Lewis's study *English Literature in the Sixteenth Century** was regarded by Tynan as "the most brilliant book of any literary criticism to have been published in my adult lifetime." Most of the opinions in it he heard expressed when Lewis was his tutor. Lewis's greatest quality was his ability as a teacher to "take you into the mind of a medieval poet and make the man seem a living being." Tynan felt that he had been in Chaucer's mind after talking to C. S. Lewis. For this student, no other teacher could do that.

U

Ulster novel, C. S. Lewis's See: "EASLEY FRAGMENT, THE."

Ulvilas In *Prince Caspian,** a lord of Caspian* the Ninth whom the usurper Miraz* had shot with arrows during a hunting party.

Undeception and recognition Undeception was a favorite theme of C. S. Lewis, for whom a characteristic of the human condition is the state of being deceived by others, by sin, or by oneself. He refers to the concept of undeception in his essay "A Note on Jane Austen" in *Selected Literary Essays*. He finds the theme in her novels, which were favorite reading for him. Many of Lewis's fictional characters experience undeception, usually associated with salvation. Such characters include Mark Studdock* in *That Hideous Strength,** Prince Rilian* in *The Silver Chair,** and Queen Orual* in *Till We Have Faces.** In *The Pilgrim's Regress** John* undergoes many undeceptions about the nature of joy* (as Lewis himself did, as recounted in *Surprised by Joy**). John, for instance, confuses a desire for The Island* with sexual lust. "Regress," in fact, in the book's title, is its dynamic term for the state of being deceived. Lewis regarded the purpose of his fiction as helping to undeceive modern people, who are separated from the past, with its knowledge of perennial human values, and from an acquaintance with even basic Christian teaching about the realities of sin, redemption, immortality, divine judgment, and grace.

Undeception is an instance of the category of recognition in Lewis's fiction—a quality that has theological implications. According to the *Encyclopedia of Fantasy*, recognition affirms a story-shaped world. For Aristotle, "Recognition marks a fundamental shift in the process of a story from increasing ignorance to knowledge." Protagonists, in a sense, recognize that they are in a story—a narrative structure precedes the event they are in and will reach a conclusion subsequent to that event. In C. S. Lewis's fiction, recognition is perhaps best illustrated by the moment in *The Last Battle** when the children and others realize that they are in a new Narnia,* a Narnia that is also linked to England transfigured, the beginning of a new chapter in the great story.

This sense of story, of beginnings and endings, and new beginnings, is also evident in Lewis's science fiction. In the second volume of his space trilogy, the king of Perelandra* is explaining future events to Dr. Elwin Ransom,* the unlikely visitor from Earth:

> "Then it is Maleldil's purpose to make us free of Deep Heaven. Our bodies will be changed, but not all changed. We shall be as the eldila, but not all as the eldila. And so will all our sons and daughters be changed in the time of their ripeness, until the number is made up which Maleldil read in His Father's mind before times flowed."
>
> "And that," said Ransom, "will be the end?"
>
> Tor the King stared at him.
>
> "The end?" he said. "Who spoke of an end?"
>
> "The end of your world, I mean," said Ransom.
>
> "Splendor of Heaven!" said Tor. "Your thoughts are unlike ours. About that time we shall be not far from the beginning of all things. . . ." (*Perelandra*, p. 179)

For Lewis, and also for Tolkien, a key moment of recognition in the Gospels is Christ's resurrection—the sudden turn that denies final defeat. Lewis memorably captures this turn in the restoration of Aslan* after his cruel death on the Stone Table.*

Undeceptions: Essays on Theology and Ethics (1971) Published in the United States under the title *God in the Dock*, this is a large collection of C. S. Lewis's pieces written over a period of many years. Subsequently, much of the contents of *Undeceptions* has been republished in two small paperback collections, *God in the Dock* (1979) and *Timeless at Heart* (1987).

Undeceptions includes a number of articles of interest, including Lewis's account of the founding of the Oxford University Socratic Club,* "Vivisection," "Cross-Examination" (an interview for *Decision* magazine), and "The Humanitarian Theory of Punishment."

Underland In *The Silver Chair*,* the realm of the Green Witch* where she kept Prince Rilian* in enchanted imprisonment. Underland was known by the even deeper world of Bism* as the Shallow Lands. Gnomes under the Green Witch's rule had been forced to dig tunnels to be used in an invasion of Narnia.* Eustace Scrubb* and Jill Pole,* with the lugubrious help of Puddleglum,* the marshwiggle,* enter Underland and rescue Prince Rilian after his undeception.* With the death of the Green Witch, Underland is destroyed, but not before the party escape and the gnomes joyfully return to Bism.

Ungit In *Till We Have Faces*,* the deity worshiped in Glome.* A paganized form of Aphrodite or Venus, she is the mother of the god of the Gray Mountains* (or Cupid in Greek myth).

Un-man See: WESTON, EDWARD ROLLES.

V

Valley of the god In *Till We Have Faces,** the secret and beautiful valley beyond the Gray Mountains where Psyche* dwelt in the palace of the god. See also: PSYCHE'S PALACE; GOD OF THE GRAY MOUNTAINS.

Vanauken, Sheldon (1914-1996) See: *A SEVERE MERCY.*

Virgil See: *THE AENEID.*

The Voyage of the "Dawn Treader" (1952) The sequel to *Prince Caspian,** this is the story of a double quest, for seven lords* of Narnia* who disappeared during the reign of the wicked King Miraz,* and for Aslan's Country* at the End of the World over the Eastern Ocean.* Reepicheep,* the mouse, is particularly seeking Aslan's Country, and his quest embodies Lewis's characteristic theme of joy.* During the sea journey of the *Dawn Treader,* various islands are encountered, each with its own kind of adventure. Of the original Pevensie* children, only Edmund and Lucy return to Narnia* in this story. Their spoiled cousin, a "modern boy" named Eustace Scrubb,* is also drawn into Narnia. At one stage he turns into a dragon,* and he is sorry for his behavior. Only Aslan,* the great lion, is able to peel off his dragon skin and restore him.

The children join the ship on its journey between Narnia and the Lone Islands.* Here they fall into the hands of slave traders. Beyond the Lone Islands they encounter a great storm, and the bedraggled *Dawn Treader* limps into the haven of Dragon Island,* where Eustace becomes a better boy. Pursuing their quest eastward, and beyond Burnt Island,* they are endangered by a great Sea Serpent. Nearby at Deathwater Island,* they find a missing lord turned to gold and narrowly miss the same fate. Yet farther east they come across the mysterious Island of Voices,* where Lucy reads a great magician's book of magic, in one of the most delightful episodes in The Chronicles of Narnia.* Farther on, after the nightmare adventure at Dark Island,* they find refreshment at World's End Island.* Here they meet Ramandu* and his beautiful daughter. She later becomes Caspian's* queen. After sailing across the final Silver Sea,* they reach Aslan's Country, the end of Reepicheep's quest.

Voyage to Venus (1943) See: *PERELANDRA.*

W

Wain, John (1925-1994) A famous pupil of C. S. Lewis's and for a time member of the Inklings.* His autobiographical *Sprightly Running* records his experiences of wartime Oxford*: "Once a week, I trod the broad, shallow stairs up to C. S. Lewis's study in the 'new building' at Magdalen. And there, with the deer-haunted grove on one side of us, and the tower and bridge on the other, we talked about English literature as armies grappled and bombs exploded." In 1947 John Wain became Lecturer in English at Reading University, staying there until 1955. His novel *Hurry on Down* (1953) was followed by further novels, as well as by books of criticism and poetry. From 1973 to 1978 he was Professor of Poetry at Oxford.

War See: COSMIC WAR.

Water rat In *The Last Battle*,* Tirian* and Jewel* come across a water rat on a raft on the river carrying logs destined for Calormen.* Thus Tirian learns that something is gravely wrong in Narnia.*

Western Wild A region of high hills and broken mountain ranges to the far west of Narnia.* In the story of *The Magician's Nephew*,* Digory Kirke* and Polly Plummer* travel there on the back of Fledge,* the flying horse, in their quest for the magic apple. See also: NARNIA, GEOGRAPHY.

Weston, Edward Rolles (1896-1942) In *Out of the Silent Planet** and *Perelandra*,* a scientist who represents all that C. S. Lewis dislikes about the modern world. Weston embodies the destruction of universal human values as set out in Lewis's book *The Abolition of Man*.* Weston represented scientism,* the idolatry of science, as opposed to true science, which Lewis approved. With Weston, science becomes totalitarian as a means of guaranteeing the survival of mankind.

In the first story, Weston has invented a spacecraft capable of reaching Mars (Malacandra*). He and Devine* kidnap Dr. Elwin Ransom.* In the later story, Ransom again encounters him, this time on the planet Venus (Perelandra*). Weston is increasingly demonized as he allows a satanic possession of his faculties, and he eventually becomes an Un-man.

West-wind See: GOD OF THE GRAY MOUNTAINS.

White Witch Another name for Jadis,* the destroyer of the exhausted world of Charn,* visited by Digory Kirke* and Polly Plummer* in the story of *The Magician's Nephew.** Through foolish curiosity, and despite Polly's reservations, Digory rings a bell that awakens the witch. Jadis is drawn with them first back to Edwardian London and then to Narnia* just as it is being created. As the Narnian ages flow on, she grows in power and puts the land under a curse of perpetual winter but never Christmas. Finally, as told in *The Lion, the Witch and the Wardrobe,** she is slain by Aslan.* Jadis is the progenitor of a line of witches, including the Green Witch,* who tries to dominate Narnia during the time of King Caspian* the Tenth, as recounted in the tale of *The Silver Chair.**

Charles Williams (1886-1945) Equally enigmatic as an author and a person, Charles Williams became a firm friend of C. S. Lewis's in the 1930s after Lewis read his novel *The Place of the Lion* (1931). This coincided with Williams's delighted reading of the proofs of Lewis's *The Allegory of Love** for Oxford University Press. Lewis wrote to Williams on March 11, 1936:

> A book sometimes crosses one's path which is so like the sound of one's native language in a strange country that it feels almost uncivil not to wave some kind of flag in answer. I have just read your *Place of the Lion* and it is to me one of the major literary events of my life—comparable to my first discovery of George MacDonald, G. K. Chesterton, or Wm. Morris. [Original copy by W. H. Lewis in The Marion Wade Center, Wheaton, Illinois.]

Williams was admitted into the literary circle surrounding Lewis, the Inklings,* and exerted a deep and lasting influence on Lewis. J. R. R. Tolkien* describes Lewis as being under Williams's "spell" and did not entirely approve, feeling that Lewis was too impressionable a man.

Charles Williams's writings—encompassing fiction, poetry, drama, theology, church history, biography, and literary criticism—become more accessible in the light of the writings of C. S. Lewis, who was influenced by him. There are many elements consciously drawn from Williams in Lewis's *That Hideous Strength,** *The Great Divorce,** *Till We Have Faces,** and *The Four Loves.** Lewis was particularly influenced by Williams's novel *The Place of the Lion*, his Arthurian cycle of poetry (including *Taliessin Through Logres*), and his theological understanding of romanticism,* especially the experience of falling in love*—romantic love.

Anne Ridler captured the essence of Charles Williams when she wrote, "In Williams's universe there is a clear logic, a sense of terrible justice which is not our justice and yet is not divorced from love." George MacDonald* similarly spoke of God's "inexorable love." For Anne Ridler "the whole man . . . was greater even than the sum of his works." Similarly T. S. Eliot—who greatly admired Charles

Williams—said in a broadcast talk: "It is the whole work, not any one or several masterpieces, that we have to take into account in estimating the importance of the man. I think he was a man of unusual genius, and I regard his work as important. But it has an importance of a kind not easy to explain."

Like C. S. Lewis and J. R. R. Tolkien, Williams's thought and writings centered around the three themes of reason, romanticism, and Christianity. Like Lewis, he was an Anglican, but much more high church, an Anglo-Catholic. His interest in romanticism comes out in a literary way in his interest in and use of symbols—or "Images," as he preferred to call them. In the business of living, he was interested in the experience of romantic and other forms of love and the theological implications of human love. As regards reason, he rejected the equation of rational abstraction with reality and helped to introduce the writings of Søren Kierkegaard to English readers. Yet he felt passionately that the whole human personality must be ordered by reason to have integrity and spiritual health. His least satisfactory novel, *Shadows of Ecstasy* (1933), concerns a conflict between the over-intellectualized European races and the deeply emotional, intuitive approach to life of the Africans. Charles Williams constantly sought the balance between the abstract and the "feeling" mind, between intellect and emotion, between reason and imagination.*

Charles Williams was in his early forties when his first novel, *War in Heaven*, was published in 1930. Prior to this he had brought out five minor books, four of verse and one a play. His important work begins with the novels; it is after 1930 that his noteworthy works appear, packed into the last fifteen years of his life. During these final years twenty-eight books were published (an average of almost two a year) as well as numerous articles and reviews. The last third of these years of maturity as a thinker and writer were spent in Oxford. They involved Williams's normal editorial duties with Oxford University Press, lecturing and tutorials for the university, constant meetings with C. S. Lewis and the Inklings, and frequent weekends in his London home. His wife stayed behind to look after the flat when Williams was evacuated to Oxford with Oxford University Press.

Islington, London, was the birthplace of Charles Williams on September 20, 1886. His father was a foreign correspondence clerk in French and German for a firm of importers until his failing eyesight forced the family to move out of London to the countryside at St. Albans. There they set up a shop selling artists' material, and his father contributed short stories to various periodicals. He guided his son's reading, and they went on long walks together. Charles Williams dedicated his third book of poems to "My father and my other teachers." The talented boy gained a county council scholarship to St. Albans Grammar school. Here he formed a friendship that lasted many years with a George Robinson, who shared his tastes, pursuits, and literary inventions. With Williams and his sister Edith, the friend sometimes acted plays for the family circle. The two friends gained places at University College, London, beginning their studies at the age of fifteen. The family unfortunately were not able to keep up paying the fees, and Charles Williams managed to get a job in a Methodist bookshop.

His fortunes changed through meeting an editor from the London office of the Oxford University Press who was looking for someone to help him with the proofs of the complete edition of Thackeray which in 1908 was going through the press. Williams stayed on the staff until his death, creating a distinctive atmosphere affectionately remembered by those who worked with him, particularly by women. He married, was considered medically unfit for the wartime army, and lost two of his closest friends in the Great War. In 1922 his only son, Michael, was born.

In the autumn of that year Charles Williams began what was to become a habitual event—giving adult evening classes in literature for the London County Council to supplement the modest family income. He wrote his series of seven supernatural thrillers, including *The Place of the Lion*, for the same reason.

When Williams was evacuated to Oxford, he brought his distinctive atmosphere there, vividly captured in John Wain's* autobiography, *Sprightly Running*. Wain comments, "He gave himself as unreservedly to Oxford as Oxford gave itself to him."

Oxford University recognized Charles Williams in 1943 with an honorary M.A. In his *Preface to Paradise Lost*,* C. S. Lewis publicly acknowledged his debt to Williams's interpretation of Milton. T. S. Eliot praised Williams's work on Dante, as did Dorothy L. Sayers* (who made a vivid translation of *The Divine Comedy*). After Williams's unexpected death, Lewis published a commentary on his unfinished cycle of Arthurian poetry, *Arthurian Torso*.* This poetry has continued to be an influence today in Stephen Lawhead's Pendragon cycle of stories. Several of the Inklings—including Lewis, Tolkien, Owen Barfield,* and W. H. "Warnie" Lewis*—contributed to a posthumous tribute, *Essays Presented to Charles Williams*.* See also: THEOLOGY OF ROMANCE.

FURTHER READING

Alice Hadfield, *Charles Williams: An Exploration of His Life and Work* (1983).

Humphrey Carpenter, *The Inklings: C. S. Lewis, J. R. R. Tolkien, Charles Williams and Their Friends* (1978).

Glen Cavaliero, *Charles Williams: Poet of Theology* (1983).

John Wain, *Sprightly Running: Part of an Autobiography* (1962, 1965).

Wimbleweather A giant, one of the loyal Old Narnians in the tale of *Prince Caspian*.* He is a marshal in the combat between Peter Pevensie* and the usurper King Miraz.* Like most giants he is not at all clever, at one stage muffing a strategic battle move. His tears of misery after that occasion soaked some sleeping talking mice in the hideout of *Prince Caspian** in Aslan's How.*

Wisdom An allegorical figure in *The Pilgrim's Regress** from whom John* learns the shortcomings of ideologies he had hitherto held dear, such as Idealism* in philosophy, Hegelianism, and naturalism.*

World's End Island An island encountered by the travelers in the story of *The Voyage of the "Dawn Treader."** It is so far to the east of Narnia,* across the Eastern Ocean,* that it is close to Aslan's Country.* The island is carpeted with a fine, springy turf, sprinkled with a plant something like heather. On the island is a roofless wide space paved with smooth stones and surrounded by gray pillars. A long table stands on this space, known as Aslan's Table, as he placed it there. The table is covered with a crimson cloth and stocked with food each day by flocks of great white birds. As they swoop toward the island, the birds sing an unknown human language. Three of the missing seven lords* lie asleep at Aslan's Table.

Ramandu,* an elderly star, and his beautiful daughter live on this island.

Wormwood An incompetent junior tempter and nephew of the eminent Screwtape,* high in hell's bureaucracy, in *The Screwtape Letters.** Wormwood is a recent graduate of the Tempters' Training College,* and he fails to make the grade on his first assignment, despite guidance by letter from Screwtape and the frequent progress reports demanded by him. Wormwood's charge successfully stays in the clutches of the Enemy.

Wynyard School See: BELSEN.

"Wyvern" See: MALVERN COLLEGE.

BIBLIOGRAPHY OF C. S. LEWIS

Major Writings of C. S. Lewis in Order of First Publication

Spirits in Bondage: A Cycle of Lyrics. London: William Heinemann, 1919.

Dymer. London: J. M. Dent, 1926.

The Pilgrim's Regress: An Allegorical Apology for Christianity, Reason and Romanticism. London: J. M. Dent, 1933.

The Allegory of Love: A Study in Medieval Tradition. Oxford: Clarendon Press, 1936.

Out of the Silent Planet. London: John Lane, 1938.

Rehabilitations and Other Essays. London: Oxford University Press, 1938.

The Personal Heresy: A Controversy (with E. M. W. Tillyard). London: Oxford University Press, 1939.

The Problem of Pain. London: Geoffrey Bles, Centenary Press, 1940.

Broadcast Talks. London: Geoffrey Bles, 1942.

A Preface to Paradise Lost. London: Oxford University Press, 1942.

The Screwtape Letters. London: Geoffrey Bles, 1942. Reprinted with an additional letter as *The Screwtape Letters and Screwtape Proposes a Toast.* London: Geoffrey Bles, 1961. Further new material in *The Screwtape Letters with Screwtape Proposes a Toast.* New York: Macmillan, 1982.

The Weight of Glory. London: S.P.C.K., Little Books on Religion No. 189, 1942.

Christian Behavior: A Further Series of Broadcast Talks. London: Geoffrey Bles, 1943.

Perelandra. London: John Lane, 1943. Reprinted in paperback as *Voyage to Venus.* London: Pan Books, 1953.

The Abolition of Man: Reflections on Education with Special Reference to the Teaching of English in the Upper Forms of Schools. Riddell Memorial Lectures, fifteenth series. London: Oxford University Press, 1943.

Beyond Personality: The Christian Idea of God. London: Geoffrey Bles, Centenary Press, 1944.

That Hideous Strength: A Modern Fairy Tale for Grown Ups. London: John Lane, 1945. A version abridged by the author was published as *The Tortured Planet* (New York: Avon Books, 1946) and as *That Hideous Strength* (London: Pan Books, 1955).

The Great Divorce: A Dream. London: Geoffrey Bles, Centenary Press, 1946. Originally published as a series in *The Guardian.* Bles inaccurately dated the book as 1945.

George MacDonald: Anthology. Compiled by, and with an introduction by, C. S. Lewis. London: Geoffrey Bles, 1946.

Essays Presented to Charles Williams. Edited by, and with an introduction by, C. S. Lewis. London: Oxford University Press, 1947.

Miracles: A Preliminary Study. London: Geoffrey Bles, 1947. Reprinted with an expanded version of chapter 3. London: Collins Fontana Books, 1960.

Arthurian Torso: Containing the Posthumous Fragment of the Figure of Arthur by Charles Williams and a Commentary on the Arthurian Poems of Charles Williams by C. S. Lewis. London: Oxford University Press, 1948.

Transposition and Other Addresses. London: Geoffrey Bles, 1949. Published in the United States as *The Weight of Glory and Other Addresses.* New York: Macmillan, 1949.

The Lion, the Witch and the Wardrobe. London: Geoffrey Bles, 1950.

Prince Caspian: The Return to Narnia. London: Geoffrey Bles, 1951.

Mere Christianity. London: Geoffrey Bles, 1952. A revised and expanded version of *Broadcast Talks, Christian Behavior,* and *Beyond Personality.*

The Voyage of the "Dawn Treader." London: Geoffrey Bles, 1952.

The Silver Chair. London: Geoffrey Bles, 1953.

The Horse and His Boy.. London: Geoffrey Bles, 1954.

English Literature in the Sixteenth Century Excluding Drama. Volume III of *The Oxford History of English Literature.* Oxford: Clarendon Press, 1954. In 1990 the series was renumbered, and Lewis's volume was reissued as Volume IV, *Poetry and Prose in the Sixteenth Century.*

The Magician's Nephew. London: Bodley Head, 1955.

Surprised by Joy: The Shape of My Early Life. London: Geoffrey Bles, 1955.

The Last Battle. London: Bodley Head, 1956.

Till We Have Faces: A Myth Retold. London: Geoffrey Bles, 1956.

Reflections on the Psalms. London: Geoffrey Bles, 1958.

The Four Loves. London: Geoffrey Bles, 1960.

Studies in Words. Cambridge: Cambridge University Press, 1960.

The World's Last Night and Other Essays. New York: Harcourt, Brace & Co., 1960.

A Grief Observed (published under the pseudonym "N. W. Clerk"). London: Faber & Faber, 1961.

An Experiment in Criticism. Cambridge: Cambridge University Press, 1961.

They Asked for a Paper: Papers and Addresses. London: Geoffrey Bles, 1962.

Posthumous Writings and Collections

Letters to Malcolm: Chiefly on Prayer. London: Geoffrey Bles, 1964.

The Discarded Image: An Introduction to Medieval and Renaissance Literature. Cambridge: Cambridge University Press, 1964.

Poems. Walter Hooper, ed. London: Geoffrey Bles, 1964.

Studies in Medieval and Renaissance Literature. Walter Hooper, ed. Cambridge: Cambridge University Press, 1966.

Letters of C. S. Lewis. Edited, with a memoir, by W. H. Lewis. London: Geoffrey Bles, 1966. Revised edition edited by Walter Hooper, 1988.

Of Other Worlds: Essays and Stories. Walter Hooper, ed. London: Geoffrey Bles, 1966.

Christian Reflections. Walter Hooper, ed. London: Geoffrey Bles, 1967.

Spenser's Images of Life. Alistair Fowler, ed. Cambridge: Cambridge University Press, 1967.

Letters to an American Lady. Clyde S. Kilby, ed. Grand Rapids, Mich.: Eerdmans, 1967; London: Hodder and Stoughton, 1969.

A Mind Awake: An Anthology of C. S. Lewis. Clyde S. Kilby, ed. London: Geoffrey Bles, 1968.

Narrative Poems. Edited, with a preface, by Walter Hooper. London: Geoffrey Bles, 1969.

Selected Literary Essays. Edited, with a preface, by Walter Hooper. Cambridge: Cambridge University Press, 1969.

God in the Dock: Essays on Theology and Ethics. Edited, with a preface, by Walter Hooper. Grand Rapids, Mich.: Eerdmans, 1970. In the UK published as *Undeceptions: Essays on Theology and Ethics* (London: Geoffrey Bles, 1971). A paperback edition of part of the book was published as *God in the Dock: Essays on Theology* (London: Collins Fontana Books, 1979).

Fern Seeds and Elephants and Other Essays on Christianity. Edited, with a preface, by Walter Hooper. London: Collins Fontana Books, 1975.

The Dark Tower and Other Stories. Edited, with a preface, by Walter Hooper. London: Collins, 1977.

The Joyful Christian: Readings from C. S. Lewis. William Griffin, ed. New York: Macmillan, 1977.

They Stand Together: The Letters of C. S. Lewis to Arthur Greeves (1914-1963). Walter Hooper, ed. London: Collins, 1979.

Of This and Other Worlds. Walter Hooper, ed. London: Collins Fount, 1982.

The Business of Heaven. Daily Readings from C. S. Lewis. Walter Hooper, ed. London: Collins Fount, 1984.

Boxen: The Imaginary World of the Young C. S. Lewis. Walter Hooper, ed. London: Collins, 1985.

Letters to Children. Lyle W. Dorsett and Marjorie Lamp Mead, eds. New York, London: Collins, 1985.

First and Second Things: Essays on Theology and Ethics. Edited, with a preface, by Walter Hooper. Glasgow: Collins Fount, 1985.

Present Concerns. Walter Hooper, ed. London: Collins Fount, 1986.

Timeless at Heart. Walter Hooper, ed. London: Collins Fount, 1987.

Letters: C. S. Lewis and Don Giovanni Calabria: A Study in Friendship. Edited, with an introduction, by Martin Moynihan. Glasgow: Collins, 1988. Includes Latin text. First issued as *The Latin Letters of C. S. Lewis,* paperback edition (Wheaton, Ill.: Crossway Books, 1987), without Latin text.

All My Road Before Me: The Diary of C. S. Lewis 1922-27. Walter Hooper, ed. London: HarperCollins, 1991.

The Collected Poems of C. S. Lewis. Walter Hooper, ed. London: HarperCollins, 1994.

C. S. Lewis: Collected Letters, Family Letters 1905-1931, Vol. 1. Walter Hooper, ed. London: HarperCollins, 2000.

Selected Writings About C. S. Lewis

Adey, Lionel. *C. S. Lewis's "Great War" with Owen Barfield.* Canada: University of Victoria, 1978.

_____. *C. S. Lewis: Writer, Dreamer and Mentor.* Grand Rapids, Mich. and Cambridge: Eerdmans, 1998.

Aeschliman, Michael D. *The Restitution of Man: C. S. Lewis and the Case Against Scientism.* Grand Rapids, Mich.: Eerdmans, 1983.

Arnott, Anne. *The Secret Country of C. S. Lewis.* London: Hodder, 1974.

Beversluis, John. *C. S. Lewis and the Search for Rational Religion.* Exeter: The Paternoster Press, 1985.

Blount, Margaret. *Animal Land: The Creatures of Children's Fiction.* London: Hutchinson, 1974; New York: William Morrow, 1975.

Burson, Scott and Jerry Walls. *C. S. Lewis and Francis Schaeffer.* Downers Grove, Ill.: InterVarsity Press, 1998.

Carnell, Corbin S. *Bright Shadows of Reality.* Grand Rapids, Mich.: Eerdmans, 1974.

Carpenter, Humphrey. *J. R. R. Tolkien: A Biography.* London: George Allen and Unwin, 1977; Boston: Houghton Mifflin, 1977.

_____. *The Inklings: C. S. Lewis, J. R. R. Tolkien, Charles Williams and Their Friends.* London: George Allen and Unwin, 1978; Boston: Houghton Mifflin, 1979.

Christensen, Michael J. *C. S. Lewis on Scripture.* London: Hodder, 1980.

Christopher, Joe R. and Joan K. Ostling. *C. S. Lewis: An Annotated Check List of Writings About Him and His Works.* Ohio: Kent State University Press, 1974.

Christopher, Joe R. *C. S. Lewis.* Boston: Hall and Co., 1987.

Clute, John and John Grant. *The Encyclopedia of Fantasy.* London: Orbit, 1997.

Como, James T., ed. *C. S. Lewis at the Breakfast Table and Other Reminiscences.* New York: Macmillan, 1979.

Como, James T. *Branches to Heaven: The Geniuses of C. S. Lewis.* Dallas: Spence Publishing, 1998.

Cunningham, Richard B. *C. S. Lewis, Defender of the Faith.* Philadelphia: The Westminster Press, 1967.

Dorsett, Lyle. *Joy and C. S. Lewis.* London: HarperCollins, 1988, 1994.

Downing, David. *Planets in Peril: A Critical Study of C. S. Lewis's Ransom Trilogy.* Amherst: University of Massachusetts Press, 1992.

Duriez, Colin. *The C. S. Lewis Handbook.* Eastbourne: Monarch, 1992; Grand Rapids, Mich.: Baker Book House, 1992.

_____. *The Tolkien and Middle-earth Handbook.* Eastbourne: Monarch, 1992; Pymble, NSW: Angus and Robertson, 1992. *The J. R. R. Tolkien Handbook.* Grand Rapids, Mich.: Baker Book House, 1992.

_____. "Subcreation and Tolkien's Theology of Story" in *Scholarship and Fantasy.* Turku, Finland: University of Turku, 1994.

_____. "Tolkien and the Other Inklings," in Reynolds, Patricia and Glen H. GoodKnight. *Proceedings of the J. R. R. Tolkien Centenary Conference: Keble College, Oxford, 1992.* Altadena, Calif.: The Tolkien Society, Milton Keynes and The Mythopoeic Press, 1995.

_____. "J. R. R. Tolkien" in *British Children's Authors 1914-1960*, a volume of the *Dictionary of Literary Biography.* Columbia, S.C.: Bruccoli Clark Layman, 1996.

_____. "The Theology of Fantasy in C. S. Lewis and J. R. R. Tolkien," in *Themelios*, Vol. 23, No. 2, February, 1998.

_____. "C. S. Lewis's Theology of Fantasy," in *The Pilgrim's Guide*. David Mills, ed. Grand Rapids, Mich.: Eerdmans, 1998.

_____. "'Art has been verified . . . ' The Friendship of C. S. Lewis and J. R. R. Tolkien," in Armstrong, Helen. *Digging Potatoes, Growing Trees: 25 Years of Speeches at the Tolkien Society's Annual Dinners*. Vol. 2. The Tolkien Society, 1998.

_____. "Tolkien and the Old West" in Armstrong, Helen. *Digging Potatoes, Growing Trees: 25 Years of Speeches at the Tolkien Society's Annual Dinners*. Vol. 2. The Tolkien Society, 1998.

_____. "In the Library: Composition and Context," in *Reading Literature with C. S. Lewis*. Thomas Martin, ed. Grand Rapids, Mich.: Baker Book House (forthcoming).

Edwards, Bruce L. *A Rhetoric of Reading: C. S. Lewis's Defense of Western Literacy.* Provo, Utah: Brigham Young University, 1986.

_____, ed. *The Taste of the Pineapple: Essays on C. S. Lewis as Reader, Critic, and Imaginative Writer.* Bowling Green, Ohio: Bowling Green State University Popular Press, 1988.

Elgin, Don D. *The Comedy of the Fantastic: Ecological Perspectives on the Fantasy Novel.* Westpoint, Conn.: Greenwood, 1985.

Filmer, Kath. *The Fiction of C. S. Lewis: Mask and Mirror.* New York: Macmillan, 1993.

Ford, Paul F. *Companion to Narnia.* San Francisco: Harper and Row, 1980.

Fuller, Edmund. *Books with Men Behind Them.* New York: Random House, 1962.

Gardner, Helen. "Clive Staples Lewis 1898-1963." *Proc. British Academy,* vol. 51 (1965), 417-428.

Gibb, Jocelyn, ed. *Light on C. S. Lewis.* London: Geoffrey Bles, 1965.

Gibson, Evan. *C. S. Lewis: Spinner of Tales.* Washington D.C.: Christian University Press, 1980.

Glaspey, Terry. *Not a Tame Lion: The Spirit and Legacy of C. S. Lewis.* Elkton, Md.: Highland Books, 1996.

Glover, Donald E. *C. S. Lewis: The Art of Enchantment.* Athens, Ohio: Ohio University Press, 1981.

Goffar, Janine. *The C. S. Lewis Index.* Riverside, Calif.: La Sierra Press, 1995; Wheaton, Ill.: Crossway Books, 1998.

Green, R. L. and Walter Hooper. *C. S. Lewis: a Biography.* London: Collins, 1974.

Gresham, Douglas. *Lenten Lands: My Childhood with Joy Davidman and C. S. Lewis.* London: Collins, 1989.

Griffin, William. *Clive Staples Lewis: A Dramatic Life.* San Francisco: Harper and Row, 1986. *C. S. Lewis: The Authentic Voice.* Tring: Lion, 1988.

Hannay, Margaret. *C. S. Lewis.* New York: Ungar, 1981.

Harris, Richard. *C. S. Lewis: The Man and His God.* London: Collins Fount, 1987.

Hart, Dabney A. *Through the Open Door: A New Look at C. S. Lewis.* Tuscaloosa, Ala.: University of Alabama Press, 1984.

Hillegas, Mark R., ed. *Shadows of Imagination: The Fantasies of C. S. Lewis, J. R. R. Tolkien and Charles Williams.* Carbondale, Ill.: Southern Illinois University Press, 1969, new edition 1979.

Holbrook, David. *The Skeleton in the Wardrobe: C. S. Lewis's Fiction, A Phenomenonological Study.* Cranbury, N.J., London: Bucknell University and Associated University Presses, 1991.

Holmer, Paul L. *C. S. Lewis: The Shape of His Faith and Thought.* New York: Harper and Row, 1976; London: Sheldon Press, 1977.

Hooper, Walter. *C. S. Lewis: A Companion and Guide.* London: HarperCollins, 1996.

_____. *Past Watchful Dragons.* London: Collins Fount, 1979.

Howard, Thomas. *The Achievement of C. S. Lewis: A Reading of His Fiction.* Wheaton, Ill.: Harold Shaw, 1980.

Huttar, Charles A., ed. *Imagination and the Spirit: Essays in Literature and the Christian Faith.* Grand Rapids, Mich.: Eerdmans, 1971.

Karkainen, Paul A. *Narnia Explored.* Old Tappan, N.J.: Revell, 1979.

Keefe, Carolyn, ed. *C. S. Lewis: Speaker and Teacher.* London: Hodder, 1974.

Kilby, Clyde S. *The Christian World of C. S. Lewis.* Grand Rapids, Mich.: Eerdmans, 1965, 1996.

_____. *Images of Salvation in the Fiction of C. S. Lewis.* Wheaton, Ill.: Harold Shaw, 1978.

Kilby, Clyde S. and Douglas Gilbert. *C. S. Lewis: Images of His World.* Grand Rapids, Mich.: Eerdmans, 1973.

Kilby, Clyde S. and Marjorie Lamp Mead, eds. *Brothers and Friends: The Diaries of Major Warren Hamilton Lewis.* San Francisco: Harper and Row, 1982.

Knight, Gareth. *The Magical World of the Inklings.* Longmead, Dorsett: Elements Books, 1990.

Kranz, Gilbert. *C. S. Lewis: Studien zu Leben und Werk.* Bonn: Bouvier, 1974.

Kreeft, Peter. *C. S. Lewis.* Grand Rapids, Mich.: Eerdmans, 1969.

_____. *C. S. Lewis for the Third Millennium: Six Essays on* The Abolition of Man. San Francisco: Ignatius, 1994.

Lawlor, John. *C. S. Lewis: Memories and Reflections.* Dallas: Spence Publishing, 1998.

Lawlor, John, ed. *Patterns of Love and Courtesy: Essays in Memory of C. S. Lewis.* London: Edward Arnold, 1966.

Lindskoog, Kathryn. *The C. S. Lewis Hoax.* Portland, Ore.: Multnomah Press, 1988.

_____. *C. S. Lewis: Mere Christian.* Glendale, Calif.: Gospel Light, 1973.

_____. *The Lion of Judah in NeverNeverLand: God, Man and Nature in C. S. Lewis's Narnia Tales.* Grand Rapids, Mich.: Eerdmans, 1973.

Lochhead, Marion. *Renaissance of Wonder: The Fantasy Worlds of C. S. Lewis, J. R. R. Tolkien, George MacDonald, E. Nesbit and Others.* Edinburgh: Canongate, 1973; San Francisco: Harper and Row, 1977.

Lowenberg, Susan. *C. S. Lewis: A Reference Guide, 1972-1988.* New York: Maxwell Macmillan International, 1993.

Manlove, C. N. *Modern Fantasy.* Cambridge: Cambridge University Press, 1975.

_____. *C. S. Lewis: His Literary Achievement.* New York: St. Martin's Press, 1987.

_____. *Christian Fantasy: From 1200 to the Present.* Basingstoke and London: The Macmillian Press, 1992.

Meilaender, Gilbert. *The Taste for the Other: The Social and Ethical Thought of C. S. Lewis.* Grand Rapids, Mich.: Eerdmans, 1978.

Menuge, Angus, ed. *Lightbearer in the Shadowlands: The Evangelistic Vision of C. S. Lewis.* Wheaton, Ill.: Crossway Books, 1997.

Mills, David, ed. *The Pilgrim's Guide: C. S. Lewis and the Art of Witness.* Grand Rapids, Mich.: Eerdmans, 1998.

Montgomery, John Warwick, ed. *Myth, Allegory and Gospel: An Interpretation of J. R. R. Tolkien, C. S. Lewis, G. K. Chesterton and Charles Williams.* Minneapolis: Bethany Fellowship, 1974.

Moorman, Charles. *Arthurian Triptych: Mythic Materials in Charles Williams, C. S. Lewis and T. S. Eliot.* Berkeley: University of California Press, 1960.

_____. *The Precincts of Felicity: The Augustinian City of the Oxford Christians.* Gainesville: University of Florida Press, 1966.

Myers, Doris. *C. S. Lewis in Context.* Kent, Ohio: Kent State University Press, 1994.

Patrick, James. *The Magdalen Metaphysicals: Idealism and Orthodoxy at Oxford 1901-1945.* Macon, Ga.: Mercer University Press, 1985.

Payne, Leanne. *Real Presence: The Holy Spirit in the Works of C. S. Lewis.* Eastbourne: Monarch Publications, 1989.

Peters, John. *C. S. Lewis: The Man and His Achievement.* Exeter: The Paternoster Press, 1985.

Purtill, Richard L. *J. R. R. Tolkien: Myth, Morality and Religion.* San Francisco: Harper and Row, 1985.

_____. *Lord of the Elves and Eldils: Fantasy and Philosophy in C. S. Lewis and J. R. R. Tolkien.* Grand Rapids, Mich.: Zondervan, 1974.

_____. *C. S. Lewis's Case for the Christian Faith.* New York: Harper and Row: 1982.

Reilly, Robert J. *Romantic Religion: A Study of Barfield, Lewis, Williams and Tolkien.* Athens, Ga.: University of Georgia Press, 1971.

Reynolds, Patricia and Glen H. GoodKnight. *Proceedings of the J. R. R. Tolkien Centenary Conference: Keble College, Oxford, 1992.* Altadena, Calif.: The Tolkien Society, Milton Keynes and The Mythopoeic Press, 1995.

Rossi, Lee D. *The Politics of Fantasy.* Epping: UMI Research, 1984.

Sammons, Martha C. *A Guide Through Narnia.* London: Hodder, 1979.

_____. *A Guide Through C. S. Lewis's Space Trilogy.* Westchester, Ill.: Cornerstone Books, 1980.

Sayer, George. *Jack: A Life of C. S. Lewis.* Wheaton, Ill.: Crossway Books, 1994.

Schakel, Peter J., ed. *The Longing for a Form: Essays on the Fiction of C. S. Lewis.* Kent, Ohio: Kent State University Press, 1977.

_____. *Reading with the Heart: The Way into Narnia.* Grand Rapids, Mich.: Eerdmans, 1979.

_____. *Reason and Imagination in C. S. Lewis: A Study of "Till We Have Faces."* Exeter: Paternoster Press, 1984.

Schakel, Peter J. and Charles A. Huttar, eds. *Word and Story in C. S. Lewis.* Columbia, Mo.: University of Missouri Press, 1991.

Schofield, Stephen, ed. *In Search of C. S. Lewis.* Los Angeles: Bridge Publications, 1984.

Schultz, Jeffrey D. and John G. West Jr., eds. *The C. S. Lewis Readers' Encyclopedia.* Grand Rapids, Mich.: Zondervan, 1998.

Sibley, Brian. *Shadowlands.* London: Hodder, 1985.

_____. *The Land of Narnia.* London: Collins Lions, 1989.

Smith, Robert H. *Patches of Godlight: The Pattern of Thought of C. S. Lewis.* Athens, Ga.: University of Georgia Press, 1981.

Starr, Nathan Comfort. *C. S. Lewis "Till We Have Faces" Introduction and Commentary.* New York: Seabury Press, 1968.

Urang, Gunnar. *Shadows of Heaven: Religion and Fantasy in the Writing of C. S. Lewis, Charles Williams and J. R. R. Tolkien.* London: SCM Press, 1970; Philadelphia: United Church Press, 1971.

Vanauken, Sheldon. *A Severe Mercy.* London: Hodder, 1977; New York: Harper and Row, 1979.

Wain, John. *Sprightly Running.* London: Macmillan, 1962.

Walker, Andrew and Patrick, James, eds. *A Christian for All Christians: Essays in Honor of C. S. Lewis.* London: Hodder, 1990.

Walsh, Chad. *C. S. Lewis: Apostle to the Skeptics.* New York: Macmillan, 1949.

_____. *The Literary Legacy of C. S. Lewis.* New York: Harcourt Brace Jovanovich, 1979.

Watson, George, ed. *Critical Thought 1: Critical Essays on C. S. Lewis.* Aldershot: Scolar Press, 1992.

White, William L. *The Image of Man in C. S. Lewis.* London: Hodder, 1970.

Willis, John. *Pleasures for Evermore: The Theology of C. S. Lewis.* Chicago: Angel Press/Loyola University Press, 1989.

Wilson, A. N. *C. S. Lewis: A Biography.* London: Collins, 1990.

Zipes, Jack. *Breaking the Magic Spell: Radical Theories of Folk and Fairy Tales.* Austin, Tex.: University of Texas Press, 1979.

Reference Guide

This guide provides a handy reference by grouping together the titles of some of the related articles in *The C. S. Lewis Encyclopedia*. The sections are as follows:

1. Life of C. S. Lewis
2. Works of C. S. Lewis
3. The Literary Criticism of C. S. Lewis
4. The Themes of C. S. Lewis
5. The Thought and Context of C. S. Lewis
6. Science Fiction
7. *The Screwtape Letters*
8. *Till We Have Faces*
9. *The Pilgrim's Regress*
10. *The Great Divorce*
11. The Chronicles of Narnia

(a) Who's Who in Narnia
(b) What's What in Narnia

1. Life of C. S. Lewis

Aldwinckle, Estelle "Stella" (1907-1990)
Alexander, Samuel (1859-1938)
All My Road Before Me: The Diary of C. S. Lewis 1922-1927 (1991)
Annie, Aunt
Anscombe, G. E. M. (1919-)
Anthroposophy
Anya (1940)
Arthurian Torso (1948)
Askins, John Hawkins (1877-1923)
Baker, Leo Kingsley (1898-1986)
Balder
Balfour, Arthur James (1848-1930)
Barfield, Owen (1898-1997)
Baynes, Pauline Diana (1922-)
BBC (British Broadcasting Organization)
"Belsen"
Bennett, J. A. W. (1911-1981)
Bernagh
Betjeman, Sir John (1906-1984)
Bide, The Reverend Peter (1912-)
Bird and Baby
Blamires, Harry (1916-)
Bodleian Library, Oxford
Boxen
Brothers and Friends: The Diaries of Major Warren Hamilton Lewis (1982)
Calabria, Giovanni (1873-1954)
Campbell College
Cancer
"Chartres"
Chesterton, Gilbert Keith (1874-1936)
"Christina Dreams"
Chronological snobbery

2. Works of C. S. Lewis

Arthurian Torso (1948)
Baynes, Pauline Diana (1922-)
BBC (British Broadcasting Organization)
Bible
Boxen
Calabria, Giovanni (1873-1954)
Christian Reflections (1967)
"Christianity and Literature" (1939)
Collected Poems of C. S. Lewis, The (1994)
Dark Tower and Other Stories, The (1977)
"*De Descriptione Temporum*" (1954)
Discarded Image: An Introduction to Medieval and Renaissance Literature, The (1964)
Dymer (1926; new edition, 1950)
"Easley Fragment"
English Literature in the Sixteenth Century (Excluding Drama) (1954)
Essays Presented to Charles Williams (1947)
Experiment in Criticism, An (1961)
Four Loves, The (1960)
God in the Dock
Great Divorce, The (1945)
Grief Observed, A (1961)
Hooper, Walter (1931-)
Horse and His Boy, The (1954)
"Inner ring"
Last Battle, The (1956)
"Learning in War-Time"
Letters of C. S. Lewis
Letters to Malcolm: Chiefly on Prayer (1964)
Lewis Family Papers
Lion, the Witch and the Wardrobe, The (1950)
Magician's Nephew, The (1955)
Mere Christianity (1952)
Miracles: A Preliminary Study (1947; revised new edition, 1960)
Narnia, The Chronicles of
Narrative Poems (1969)
Of Other Worlds (1966)
Out of the Silent Planet (1938)
Perelandra (Voyage to Venus), (1943)
Personal Heresy: A Controversy, The (1939)
Pilgrim's Regress: An Allegorical Apology for Christianity, Reason and Romanticism, The (1933; new edition, 1943)
Poems (1964)
Preface to Paradise Lost, A (1942)
Problem of Pain, The (1940)
Reading of C. S. Lewis
Reflections on the Psalms (1958)
Rehabilitations and Other Essays (1939)
Screwtape Letters, The (1942)
Screwtape Proposes a Toast (1965)
Silver Chair, The (1953)
Spenser's Images of Life (1967)
Spirits in Bondage: A Cycle of Lyrics (1919)
Studies in Words (1960; 1967)
Surprised by Joy: The Shape of My Early Life (1955)
That Hideous Strength (1945; abridged paperback version 1955)
They Asked for a Paper (1962).
They Stand Together
Till We Have Faces (1956)
Transposition and Other Addresses (1949)
Undeceptions: Essays on Theology and Ethics (1971)
Voyage *of the "Dawn Treader," The* (1952)

3. The Literary Criticism of C. S. Lewis

Allegory of Love, The (1936)
Arthurian Torso (1948)
Bible
"Christianity and Literature" (1939)
"*De Descriptione Temporum*" (1954)
Discarded Image: An Introduction to Medieval and Renaissance Literature, The (1964)
English Literature in the Sixteenth Century (Excluding Drama) (1954)

4. The Themes of C. S. Lewis

5. The Thought and Context of C. S. Lewis

Everlasting Man, The, G. K. Chesterton
Experiment in Criticism, An (1961)
Farrer, Austin (1904-1968)
Final Honor School
Friendship of J. R. R. Tolkien and C. S. Lewis
God
Golden Ass, The, Apuleus
"Greats"
"Great Knock"
"Great war" (between C. S. Lewis and Owen Barfield)
Heaven
Historicism
Idea of the Holy, The (1917), Rudolf Otto
Idealism, C. S. Lewis and
The imagination (imaginative fantasy)
Inklings
"Inner ring"
Joy
Kirkpatrick, William T. (1848-1921)
"Learning in War-Time"
Lewis, Helen Joy Davidman (1915-1960)
Life of Samuel Johnson, James Boswell (1791)
Literary critic, C. S. Lewis as a
MacDonald, George
Mappa Mundi
Meaning and imagination
"Mere Christianity"
Mere Christianity (1952)
Miracles: A Preliminary Study (1947; revised new edition, 1960)
Myth
Myth Became Fact
Naturalism and supernaturalism
Nature
New psychology
Numinous
Old West
Otherness
Oxford
Oxford University Socratic Club (1941-1972)
Paganism and mysticism in Lewis
Personal Heresy: A Controversy, The (1939)
Phantastes, George MacDonald
Pilgrim's Regress: An Allegorical Apology for Christianity, Reason and Romanticism, The (1933; new edition, 1943)
Plato
Platonism
Poetic Diction, Owen Barfield (1928)
Prelude, The, William Wordsworth (1850)
Problem of Pain, The (1940)
Reading of C. S. Lewis
Recovery
Romanticism
Sayers, Dorothy Leigh (1893-1957)
Scientism
Tale of Squirrel Nutkin, The, Beatrix Potter (1903)
Subcreation
Surprised by Joy: The Shape of My Early Life (1955)
Symbolism
Tao, The
Temple, Sacred Poems and Private Ejaculations, The, George Herbert (1633)
Theism and Humanism, Arthur James Balfour, 1915
Theology, C. S. Lewis and
Theology of romance
Tolkien, J. R. R. (1892-1973)
Transposition
Undeception and recognition
Williams, Charles (1886-1945)

6. **Science Fiction** (*Out of the Silent Planet, Perelandra, That Hideous Strength, The Dark Tower*)

Alcasan, Francois
Angels
Aphallin
Arthurian Torso (1948)
Atlantis
Augray
Belbury
Bracton College
Bragdon Wood
Cure Hardy

Dark Tower and Other Stories, The (1977)
Denniston, Arthur and Camilla
Devine, Dick (Lord Feverstone)
Dimble, Dr. Cecil
Dimble, "Mother" Margaret ("Margery")
Edgestow
Eldila
Green Lady
Handramit
Harandra
Hardcastle, Major "Fairy"
Hrossa
Hyoi
Malacandra
Maleldil the Young
Meldilorn
Merlin
N.I.C.E.
Numinor
Old Solar
Out of the Silent Planet (1938)
Oyarsa
Perelandra (Voyage to Venus) (1943)
Pfifltriggi
Ransom, Dr. Elwin (1898?-)
St. Anne's
Sterk
Studdock, Jane
Studdock, Mark Gainsby
*That Hideous Strength (*1945; abridged paperback version 1955)
Thulcandra
Un-man
Weston, Edward Rolles (1896-1942)

7. *The Screwtape Letters*

Angels
House of Correction for Incompetent Tempters
Intelligence Department
Macgowan, John
Screwtape
Screwtape Letters, The (1942)
Screwtape Proposes a Toast (1965)
Slubgob
Slumtrimpet
Tempters' Training College
Toadpipe
Wormwood

8. *Till We Have Faces*

Adonis
Ansit, Lady
Arnom
Batta
Essur
Fox, The
Glome
God of the Gray Mountains
Golden Ass, The, Apuleus
Istra
Orual
Phars
Psyche
Psyche's palace
Redival
Shadowbrute
Talapal
Tarin
Till We Have Faces (1956)
Trom
Trunia
Ungit
Valley of the god
West-wind

9. *The Pilgrim's Regress*

Aesthetica
Anthroposophia
Behmenheim
Canyon, The
Cruelsland
Dialectica
Eastern Mountains
Mr. Enlightenment
Glamaria
Golnesshire
Hegeliana
Mr. Humanist
Island, the
John
Landlord, The
Main Road
Mappa Mundi
Mother Kirk
North
Pagus

Pilgrim's Regress: An Allegorical Apology for Christianity, Reason and Romanticism, The (1933; new edition, 1943)
Puritania
Mr. Sensible
South
Spirit of the Age
Wisdom

10. *The Great Divorce*

Angels
Bright people
Dick
Dwarf, The
Frank
Heaven
MacDonald, George
Smith, Sarah
Solid People

11. The Chronicles of Narnia

Baynes, Pauline Diana (1922-)
Chronicles of Narnia, The
Evacuees
Horse and His Boy, The (1954)
Last Battle, The (1956)
Lion, the Witch and the Wardrobe, The (1950)
Magician's Nephew, The (1955)
Narnia, The Chronicles of
Narnia—geography
Narnia—history
Prince Caspian (1951)
Silver Chair, The (1953)
Voyage of the "Dawn Treader," The (1952)

(a) Who's Who in Narnia

Ahoshta
Alimash
Andrew, Uncle
Anradin
Aravis
Argoz
Arlian
Arsheesh
Aslan
Axartha Tarkaan
Bar
Mr. and Mrs. Beaver
Bern
Bowman, Master
Bree
Bricklethumb
Bulgy Bears
Cabby
Caspian
Centaur
Chervy the Stag
Chief Voice
Chlamash
Christmas, Father
Clipsie
Cloudbirth
Coalblack
Colin
Cor
Coriakin
Cornelius, Doctor
Destrier
Dragon
Drinian
Dufflepuds
Dumnus
Earthmen
Edmund, King
Emeth the Calormene
Emperor-over-sea
Erimon
Farsight
Father Time
Fenris Ulf
Fledge
Frank the Cabby
Gale
Giant
Ginger the Cat
Girbius
Glenstorm
Glimfeather
Glozelle
Gnomes
Golg
Green Witch
Griffle
Gumpas
Hag
Hermit of Southern March
Hwin
Ilgamuth

(b) What's What in Narnia

Dawn Treader
Deathwater Island
Doorn
Dragon Island
Eastern Ocean
Ettinsmoor
Experiment House
Felinda
Galma
Glasswater Creek
Great River
Harfang
Hyaline Splendor
Ilkeen
Island of the star
Island of Voices
Lantern Waste
Lone Islands
Mount Pire
Muil
Narnia—geography
Narrowhaven
Rush River
Seven Isles
Shadow Lands
Shallow Lands
Shribble River
Silver Sea
Sorlois
Spear-head
Stable Hill
Stone knife
Stone Table
Sunless Sea
Tashbaan
Telmar, Land of
Terebinthia
Tombs of the ancient kings
Underland
Western Wild
World's End Island